T0356022

The Complete Engineering Manager

Build High-Performing Engineering Teams for Your Organization

Ananth Ramachandran

Apress®

The Complete Engineering Manager: Build High-Performing Engineering Teams for Your Organization

Ananth Ramachandran
Berlin, Germany

ISBN-13 (pbk): 979-8-8688-0266-9 ISBN-13 (electronic): 979-8-8688-0267-6
https://doi.org/10.1007/979-8-8688-0267-6

Managing Director, Apress Media LLC: Welmoed Spahr
Acquisitions Editor: Shivangi Ramachandran
Development Editor: James Markham
Coordinating Editor: Jessica Vakili

Cover designed by eStudioCalamar

Distributed to the book trade worldwide by Apress Media, LLC, 1 New York Plaza, New York, NY 10004, U.S.A. Phone 1-800-SPRINGER, fax (201) 348-4505, e-mail orders-ny@springer-sbm.com, or visit www.springeronline.com. Apress Media, LLC is a California LLC and the sole member (owner) is Springer Science + Business Media Finance Inc (SSBM Finance Inc). SSBM Finance Inc is a **Delaware** corporation.

For information on translations, please e-mail booktranslations@springernature.com; for reprint, paperback, or audio rights, please e-mail bookpermissions@springernature.com.

Apress titles may be purchased in bulk for academic, corporate, or promotional use. eBook versions and licenses are also available for most titles. For more information, reference our Print and eBook Bulk Sales web page at http://www.apress.com/bulk-sales.

Any source code or other supplementary material referenced by the author in this book is available to readers on GitHub (https://github.com/Apress). For more detailed information, please visit https://www.apress.com/gp/services/source-code.

If disposing of this product, please recycle the paper

To my parents, wife, and son

Table of Contents

About the Author

Ananth Ramachandran is a seasoned engineering leader who has experience building happy, productive, and high-performing engineering teams. He has worked as a developer, lead engineer, and manager in varied domains ranging from healthcare to traditional and modern banking systems to shipping business. He started his career in a Fortune 500 company and later found his passion in startups and building engineering teams from the ground up. He's passionate about scaling up people, products, and technology strategies ultimately contributing to an organization's success.

A team architect, who orchestrated multiple team re-organizations and transformations to achieve organization goals and objectives, Ananth runs a newsletter for engineering managers (techmanagerguide.substack.com), where he writes about day-to-day experiences, challenges, and modern engineering management practices and techniques. He also speaks on podcasts and at meetups and mentors and trains software professionals and aspiring leaders.

Acknowledgments

Thank you, Oksana Vynokurova, for your clear and thoughtful illustrations. Your work has greatly enhanced the value of my book.

Introduction

I wouldn't have believed it if someone had told me in 2010 that I'd be writing a book and one on management even. Back then I was practicing Java to clear a coding interview to get a job at a Fortune 500 company. I was turning pages of the book *Java: The Complete Reference* by Herbert Schildt, a comprehensive tome spanning 1,312 pages. Yes, you read it right: 1,312 pages! And that wasn't the only resource I had access to. There were lots of books on programming and every technical topic.

Fast-forward to years later, when I became an engineering manager and I was left with little to no learning resources. I had to learn the hard way: by doing the management wrong. *Do it wrong, learn, do better, repeat.* And I realized, when I screw up something, the impact was not only on me. It was on my whole team. But there were also times that I had immense joy and success when I helped an under-performer see through the tough phase and move toward improvement through continuous feedback and enablement.

Have you ever rebooted your system when upgrading software? I did when I transitioned from an individual contributor to a manager. A complete reboot.

Just as a computer system initializes its hardware and software during a reset, transitioning to a manager involves initializing a new set of skills and perspectives. You start by laying the groundwork for your new role, understanding your responsibilities, and aligning with your team's and organization's goals. Upon restart, a computer loads its operating system and essential programs. Similarly, as a new manager, you begin to load the essential "programs" or skills needed for management, such as leadership, communication, delegation, and strategic thinking.

These are critical for performing effectively in your new role. Many systems perform diagnostic checks to ensure everything is functioning correctly. As you transition into management, it's a time for self-reflection and assessment. You might identify areas for personal development or team improvement, just as diagnostics identify system issues that need addressing. Ultimately, the goal of restarting a system is to improve its performance. As a new manager, your goal is to enhance both your performance and that of your team. By effectively managing resources, motivating your team, and aligning efforts with organizational objectives, you contribute to improved overall performance.

This book does exactly that for you: help you to reboot your management journey and become an effective engineering manager on a daily basis.

It's not Management vs. Leadership

If there's one word that has triggered more debate and critique in recent years, it has to be the term *management*—it is not inherently controversial, but its application and execution has raised many eyebrows. It has gained a bad rap in the industry due to the experience that people have with their managers, which significantly affects their performance, their morale, and ultimately their career. Managers are seen as someone who sits on an ivory tower, runs meeting after meeting, and turns up only to deliver bad news or when your engineering systems go haywire.

Management practices cannot keep up with the pace at which technology is evolving and organizations are innovating. In fact, they haven't evolved considerably over the years at all. We're still hearing stories about managers who are micromanaging, absentee managers, managers who employ fear-based leadership, managers who are inefficient, and managers who are not adaptable to the team or environment and who instead stick to their own needs and beliefs.

As Eric Ries writes, "Entrepreneurship is management" in his book *The Lean Startup*, it's true in every sense. We're living in the age of extreme uncertainty. Business priorities are changing in the matter of days, teams are being transformed and restructured, new technology is being introduced and adopted as we speak, and engineering processes are being refined for agility and speed in delivery. Managers should adopt modern practices in leading engineering teams and how they build software. Old management approaches sadly don't fit the bill. This book has got you covered in adopting modern delivery practices, effectively bringing change as a leader, managing chaos and change in priorities, and—last but not the least—building a champion engineering team in the midst of all.

Throughout this book, I have used the terms *leader* and *manager* interchangeably, not by mistake but by intention. Leadership and management are one and the same. In organizations where it starts to diverge, it creates a void. A big void.

Who Are You? Who Do You Want to Be?

These are the two most important questions to answer before you continue reading the book: Who are you? Who do you want to be?

If you are a software engineer transitioning into management, this book will help you to become an engineering manager that every team needs, step-by-step. One chapter at a time. Even if you haven't given a thought to becoming a manager, this book will give you a better idea of what it means to be one and equip you to be a leader when the time comes.

If you're already an engineering manager, you will find modern and pragmatic approaches to challenges that you face in your teams on a day-to-day basis and the recipes to build a high-performing engineering team.

Or if you love reading about management, personal development, organizational leadership, and dynamics to gain a fresh perspective? This book is for you!

What's in the Book?

In the first part of the book, you have all the time in the world to get settled into your new role as an engineering manager and get yourself oriented. You'll identify your core values, leadership style, and what makes you a successful and complete engineering manager, wrapped inside the "Engineering Manager's Starter Kit," also containing guidance on writing your "Manual of Me" and drafting your first six-month plan to get a head start into your engineering management career.

Then you'll get to the most important part of the book, "Managing People." Starting from managing yourself, you'll move on to building trust with the people around you in order to build world-class engineers. Am I leaving out your manager? Certainly not. You should know better how to work with your manager and peek into their world of successes and worries, see what they care the most (and least) about, and learn to manage conflicts and differences.

In the third part, you will learn how to identify what's working and not working for your engineering team and to evolve your team's development, delivery, and technical processes to improve their efficiency and throughput.

In the fourth part, you'll get to (de)prioritize actively between product and technical initiatives, build a compelling roadmap partnering with the product manager (your partner in crime), and set strategy, direction, and goals to deliver the most important value.

If you think the previous parts covered a lot of ground, the remaining parts of the book will leave you in awe. In the fifth part, you'll master iteratively delivering value and impact for your organization through close collaboration of cross-functional stakeholders. Fine-tune your team's delivery metrics, resolving blockers and challenges, and report progress to senior leadership.

Finally, you'll learn how to build a happy, productive, and high-performing engineering team and go on to become an organizational leader.

This book is organized in a way that you can hop into any chapter you want, as they are written with less to no interconnections so you can be up to speed in no time.

Finally...

I strongly believe every book you read should transform you into something else that you hadn't imagined otherwise. I hope this book will help you to become a complete and pragmatic engineering manager that every team and organization needs.

I don't want to keep you waiting for too long.

Happy reading, and I wish you all the best in your engineering leadership journey!

PART I

Congratulations, You're an Engineering Manager

My memory hasn't faded yet.

It was a cold winter day. I was sitting in one corner of the office and looking at an error screen that said "Your deployment failed...." I was trying to redeploy the application and stumbling over StackOverflow for the zillionth time in my decade-long software engineering career. A Slack message came from my manager's manager that read, "Hey, I would like to talk to you really quick for 15 minutes." I know I did either something terribly wrong to put my job at stake or something extraordinary, which I'm sure was not the case.

"Ralph is leaving in a month's time as we decided to part ways" (Ralph was my manager). I nodded in disbelief. He continued, "Would you like to be the engineering manager?" I was taken aback as I wasn't ready for that question and was completely clueless. I asked him, "Are you sure? I may need more time to think about it as I never had plans to get into management." He replied, "I'm sure you can do justice to this role as I can see good leadership values in you and you can grow in our organization. Take your time, think about it, and let me know."

That's where it all started. After a series of self-confrontation and self-doubt, I decided to give it a shot. Years down the line, I was in deep dark woods of engineering management.

For the first few months, it was harsh to transform into a management role from an individual contributor (IC). Gone are the days when I used to sit on my couch for hours and happily code all day long alone. I didn't mean I wasn't happy after becoming a manager. It's safe to say that my happiness has been redefined. I have found my new happiness in making people, teams, and organizations successful.

As a manager, you have bigger problems to tackle than writing code, in the form of prioritization, evolving processes, motivating and caring for your people, and ultimately being responsible for delivering value to your organization through your team's work.

You're in good company with other readers of this book who are either curious about how to start their engineering management career on a high note or the experienced ones who are rolling up their sleeves to learn new tricks to becoming a complete, successful, and pragmatic engineering manager.

Do You Want to Become an EM?

The most important question to answer is, do you want to become an EM, and is it worth it?

Are you a fairly experienced engineer who wants to get into management? Does management come naturally to you, and have you always dreamt of becoming one? Or is it just happening like it happened to me?

Engineering manager is a high-stakes role as you can make or break a team. You're responsible for driving your team autonomously in the right direction and course-correcting whenever needed. People look up to you for guidance and direction, and you need to be a mentor for their careers.

An EM is not some superpower where you can do everything on your own, however. You have limited time and energy. Your calendar will be a living proof of that. You should focus on the top priorities and don't be shy about delegating or saying no to unimportant ones. It's hard at first, but you have to get better at it and you will.

Decision-making will become part of your day-to-day work. You have to make well-informed, unbiased, and tough decisions for your team's cause. You should hold yourself accountable and own the consequences as your decisions will be questioned and challenged.

Your role is quite significant, especially in rapidly growing organizations where you have to adopt and evolve your team's processes and keep them motivated and engaged in the midst of frequently changing priorities. You have to work closely with different expertise and job functions like product managers, designers, data, and business teams to collaborate and build what's most important for your organization.

Take a sticky note; write "Building a happy, productive, and high-performing engineering team that delivers" in bold; and stick it in front of your desk as your "EM's

Mantra." Everything that you do revolves around this central idea; it's so deep that I ended up writing a whole book based on this one line.

Well, that's my honest shot at describing what EM will do. If you're looking for challenges on a larger scale and maximize your impact, this book is for you. I bet you will not regret it.

The Complete Engineering Manager

An engineering manager's responsibilities vary from organization to organization. I was doing engineering management even before assuming a title. Yes, there are engineers who are doing the job of an engineering manager without a title based on the size and need of an organization.

Once I formally started being an engineering manager, I experienced different needs and responsibilities in different organizations. In my first engineering management job, it was more tech oriented and less responsibility on the people's side; I was mainly looking into project delivery, prioritization between product/tech initiatives, and technical decisions. Later, focus shifted toward people management, bringing up performance of the team as a whole and contributing more toward creating impact at the organization level by working closely with cross-functional stakeholders as one team.

In an ideal world, what does the engineering manager job entail? How does the responsibility get split between different areas? See Figure 1.

- *People management*: You manage yourself and the people around you to get better.

- *Project and delivery*: You deliver impactful projects with good quality and in a timely manner by fine-tuning the delivery practices and metrics of your engineering team.

- *Wider organization*: You work with the wider organization and align your team's priorities to deliver business impact.

- *Processes*: You identify the processes that are working or not working for your engineering team, and you evolve the development, delivery, and technical processes to improve their efficiency and throughput.

- *Technical*: You are technical enough to take part in tech discussions, decisions, code reviews, and sometimes hands-on coding.

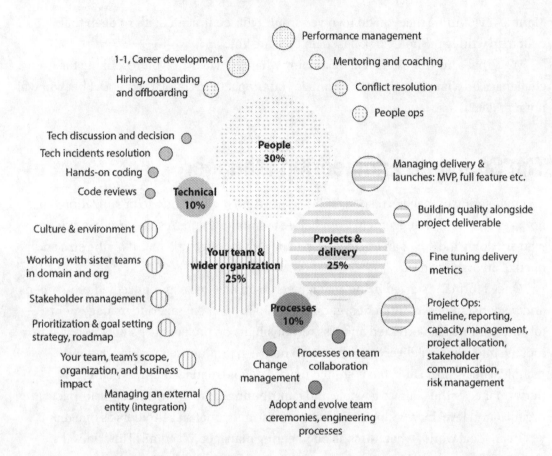

Figure 1. *The complete engineering manager*

Typically, people management will make up the largest portion (around 30%) of your job, followed by project delivery and contributions to the wider organization (each around 25%). Processes and technical skills generally make up smaller portions, around 10% each.

These percentages are approximate and will vary based on the organization and team. For instance, if your team expects you to be hands-on with coding or if you're working on a highly technical product, your technical contribution may increase beyond 10%, but that would naturally reduce the time spent in other areas—it's all a balancing act.

If your engineering team is still being formed, more of your time will need to go into setting up processes and team practices, increasing that share. In smaller startups with fewer people to manage, your focus on people management and organizational responsibilities will shrink, allowing for more technical involvement. On the other hand, if you're managing a larger team, with staff in the double digits, people management will take up proportionally more of your time.

In today's rapidly changing landscape, being adaptable is crucial. Building skills across all of these areas will help you become the complete engineering manager that every team needs.

CHAPTER 1

Engineering Manager's Starter Kit

I wish someone had offered me a starter kit to get started in the world of engineering management. Here's my present to you—the "Engineering Manager's Starter Kit." Let's unwrap it and see what's inside:

- *Your core values*: Identifying core values that you strongly believe in and that match with your personality.

- *Your leadership style*: Defining a leadership style that aligns to your core values so you can be more adaptable rather than following a rigid style.

- *Your success*: What does success mean for you? How do you know that you're succeeding? How do you yield quick wins?

- *Your "Manual of Me"*: A written document detailing who you are, the values you believe in, your management style, and ways of working together with others.

- *Your first six months*: Detailed and actionable month-by-month plan of your first six months in the engineering manager role.

This starter kit will help you to get up to speed and set you up for long-term success in your engineering management career.

© Ananth Ramachandran 2024
A. Ramachandran, *The Complete Engineering Manager*, https://doi.org/10.1007/979-8-8688-0267-6_1

Your Core Values

You're an EM now and wondering where to start with. There might be an ocean of responsibilities waiting for you and people are eager to meet you. Before anything, you have to associate yourself with a set of core values that you believe in. These values are the ones fundamental to how you work, behave, communicate, and lead.

Prior to me becoming an EM, my manager's manager said, "I'm sure you can do justice to this role as I can see good leadership values in you." It left me wondering what the values were that he meant. I went into self-discovery mode and came up with my top three core values: adaptability, accountability, and transparency. I still live with these fundamentals from that day on.

You carry your own self to work—you're not someone else when you log into work life. Without realizing, you'll expose your personal identity and that's completely normal. But is it as simple as that? Especially when you become a leader of a team, there are some values that align with leadership.

How can you align your authentic self with the values essential to leadership, especially in an engineering management role? Start by understanding your personal values.

Your Personal Values

Start with understanding who you are as a person and what values you believe in. Do you like to be authentic? Are you hard-working? Are you humorous? Find out your top three values. Here are some common personal values, but it's not an exhaustive list:

Authenticity	Empathy	Humorous
Equality	Hard work	Adventurous
Open-minded	Integrity	Loyal

When you were an individual contributor, your space was confined to the work that you were doing individually, and your work values would reflect that. Here are some values that you probably related to:

Technical excellence	Problem solving	Autonomy
Healthy work-life balance	Ownership	Continuous learning

An individual contributor's core values tend to be pretty hands-on. They generally value excellence in their technical solutions, love to solve problems, and are autonomous in the work they do. Continuous learning is at the core of what they do in the middle of an ever-changing technological landscape.

Identify Leadership Values

The core values of a leader tend to be broad and related to the nature of their work where they need to be good at managing people, focusing on the bigger picture, communicating clearly, managing crisis and risks in project delivery, and so on and so forth.

Clear vision	Problem defining (strategic)	Accountability
Empathy	Decisiveness	Mentor
Communication	Collaboration	Ownership

As you can observe, you gradually move toward team and organizational aspects and your newly found core values such as *empathy, collaboration*, and *clear vision are proof of that.*

Transform and Live

As you transform into a leader, you have to revisit your core values that you assumed when you were an individual contributor and assess them as per the values expected from a leader. The most important part is to live your values by your behaviors and actions.

Let's take a few leadership core values and see what behaviors and actions you can adopt (Table 1-1).

Table 1-1. *Leadership Core Values*

Core Value	Behaviors	Actions
Clear Vision	Communicating a compelling vision for the future, setting clear goals and objectives for the team or organization	Regularly sharing the long-term vision, mission, and goals with the team, providing a sense of direction and purpose
Problem Definition (Why Part)	Actively seeking to understand the root causes of challenges, conducting thorough analyses before attempting to solve problems	Prioritizing the identification of underlying issues, asking probing questions to clarify the "why" behind problems, and encouraging team members to do the same
Accountability	Taking responsibility for one's actions and decisions, holding oneself and others accountable for meeting expectations and achieving goals	Acknowledging mistakes, addressing challenges head-on, and ensuring that the team is collectively accountable for project outcomes
Empathy	Demonstrating understanding and consideration of others' perspectives and feelings, fostering a supportive and inclusive work environment	Actively listening to team members, recognizing and addressing their concerns, and showing genuine care for their growth and well-being
Decisiveness	Making timely and informed decisions, even in the face of uncertainty, and taking responsibility for the outcomes	Weighing available information, consulting relevant stakeholders, and making decisions confidently while considering the best interests of the team and organization
Mentorship	Providing guidance, support, and developmental opportunities to team members, actively contributing to their professional growth	Engaging in regular one-on-one meetings, offering constructive feedback, and facilitating skill development and career advancement for team members

On becoming an engineering manager, you will observe changes in perspectives and values that you can closely relate with:

- *Problem-solving to problem-defining (strategic)*: You start to define problems and provide more context around why and what's the impact rather than solving problems yourself.

- *Technical excellence to clear vision and prioritization*: Importance shifted to having clear vision and prioritization over technical excellence as you believe in balancing speed and quality. In fact, you're realizing that speed is getting more important.

- *Self-orientation to team-orientation*: You've become more team oriented as you have to be. It's not about you now, but rather it's them—it's your team.

Values like *ownership* and *empathy* apply for both individual contributors and engineering managers as well.

Remember that transitioning into an engineering manager is a learning process, and your values will continue to evolve as you gain experience in your new role. Remaining open to growth, feedback, and continuous improvement is key.

Now, it's your turn. What are the top three leadership values would you like to live? List them in Table 1-2 with specific behaviors and actions.

Table 1-2. *Your Leadership Core Values*

Core Value	Behaviors	Actions

Now you're all set with core values that form the basis for you as an engineering manager. Up next, we'll define your leadership style.

Your Leadership Style

During my time as an individual contributor, I was led by six different managers, and everyone had a different leadership style. Some are direct. Some are micromanagers. Some are laissez-faire. Some are visionary. The style of my managers influenced how I worked, and my experience in a team can easily be summed up by my manager's leadership style. When I became a manager, that was the first thing running through my mind. What type of manager should I be? What does my team think about me? How does it influence my team? By the end of this section, you'll be able to relate your personality to a certain leadership style.

Common Leadership Style

Before defining a leadership style for yourself, let's take a look at common leadership styles in the industry (Table 1-3).

Table 1-3. *Common Leadership Styles*

Style	Mindset	Behavior
Adaptive	How can we adjust?	Encourages flexibility in complexity. Useful in changing environments. Example: Adjust and adapt to changes in priorities and the scope of your team.
Autocratic	Follow this plan!	Makes quick, firm decisions. Useful in crises or when quick decisions are crucial. Example: Handling an emergency situation like resolving technical incidents.
Coaching	Have you tried this?	Develops people's skills for the future. Good for personal growth. Example: Mentoring a team member.
Democratic	What do you think?	Values everyone's input. Best for collaborative environments. Example: Deciding on a team project direction and effort estimations.

(*continued*)

Table 1-3. (*continued*)

Style	Mindset	Behavior
Inspirational	Let's aim higher!	Motivates with vision and passion. Great for uniting teams. Example: Rallying a team around company vision.
Laissez-Faire	You've got this!	Gives team independence. Ideal for skilled, self-driven teams that prefer autonomy over control. Example: Managing a group of experienced engineers.
Servant	How can I support you?	Puts the team's needs first. Great for creating supportive cultures. Tends to listen a lot more than you speak. Example: Focusing on team well-being.
Strategic	Here's my vision.	Aligns actions with long-term goals. Ideal for guiding through growth. Example: Developing a yearly team strategy.
Transactional	Meet these goals.	Rewards or penalizes based on performance. Effective for goal-oriented tasks. Example: Meeting quarterly goals and targets. Managing the performance of an individual or your team as a whole.
Transformational	Let's change the game.	Use when leading a team through innovative projects or significant changes. Example: Restructuring a team or introducing a new approach in how they build and deliver software.

That should give you a glimpse into what different leadership styles are and the mindset and behavior that you could adopt. Nice, let's put it to practice.

In Action

Now it's your turn. Provided the situation, what leadership style will you adopt and what actions that you will take? Fill in Table 1-4.

Table 1-4. *What Leadership Style Will You Adopt?*

Situation	Leadership Style	What Action Will You Take?
Your team is facing challenging times and having high stress. They need your support addressing their concerns, and ensuring a positive work environment.		
Your team has seasoned engineers who are experts at what they do. They are feeling less autonomous and restricted by the team dynamics and heavy processes.		
A new quarter starts and you as a manager need to give direction to your team so that they have the context and contribute to success.		
Your team misses delivery project after project and loses its credibility. How do you get them back on track achieving goals?		

As you can see in the previous exercise, you can't adopt the same leadership style for different situations. You need to understand the situation, what people expect from you, and what works best for the team.

Keep in mind:

- *Align with your core values*: Let your core values guide your leadership style. Instead of letting your style dictate your values, ensure that your actions are rooted in your deeply held beliefs. Tailor your approach based on your values and the specific circumstances.

- *Easy to work with*: Cultivate approachability. Be open to feedback and actively listen to your team's perspectives on how your leadership style influences their work. Building a collaborative and positive work environment doesn't have to be challenging. The most effective engineering managers are those who are both skilled and approachable.

- *Influence, don't impress*: Strive for authenticity. Rather than trying to impress others with unrealistic commitments or undue niceness, focus on authentic influence. Be genuine in your interactions, and let your leadership style emerge naturally from your authentic self. Influence, when grounded in authenticity, is more lasting and impactful than mere attempts to impress.

- *Reflect and adapt*: Regularly reflect on your leadership style. Seek feedback from your team and your manager to stay adaptable. Being aware of how your style resonates with different personalities and situations within your team enables you to make necessary adjustments for continued growth and effectiveness.

Remember, effective leadership is an ongoing journey of self-awareness, adaptability, and genuine connection with your team.

Your Success

What is success for you as an engineering manager? It is delivering value in a timely manner and impacting what matters the most for your business, while keeping your engineering team happy, productive, and high performing. Yes, it's like walking a tightrope. You might fall, but you have to get up and retry the balancing act. The more you do it, the better you will get at it.

Will a business owner ever say, "We've achieved our target, and I've earned money for my lifetime. Now let's shut down the company"? Nope. Success isn't an end state. A business doesn't settle if they achieve success. Rather, they look to continuously thrive by setting new targets. You play a crucial role in your organization's success by evolving your team, processes, and technology to enable them to re-assess and achieve their targets to ultimately embrace the inevitable—the change. Your organization's success is your success.

Maybe I got a bit carried away associating it only to your organization. You can't succeed yourself as an engineering manager. That's why you're given a team to succeed. An entire team. Let's reframe by bringing your team into the equation: **delivering success to your organization through your team**. Much better, isn't it?

In the process of making your organization successful, you can't leave out your people's success. With millions of jobs available in the market, why did they choose to join your organization? They believe that they can learn, contribute, grow, and succeed in their own career at your organization. As a manager, it's your job to set them up for success and show them how they can contribute better to your team and organization. **Your people's success is your success.**

Your success = success to your business delivered through your team + the success of your people.

It will take time to taste success as a first time EM. Define what success means for you with your manager and be clear about success metrics.

Listen to your team's current challenges and understand what matters the most for your team at that moment. Those are your quick wins to gain the trust and confidence of your team and of your manager. Here are some quick wins that you can go for:

- Look into a delivery concern that your team is struggling with.

- Boost your team's motivation and engagement, especially for who is feeling hopeless and disinterested after the last reorganization happened.

- Address unproductive situations that your team is suffering from.

- Listen to and help an underperforming engineer in your team with a clear plan on areas of improvement, actionable feedback, and get them the right projects to prove their mettle.

Table 1-5 presents some of the important success criteria for engineering managers.

Table 1-5. *Engineering Manager's Success Criteria*

Area of Responsibility	Success Metric
Project Delivery: Successfully leading the team and collaborating with cross-functional teams to deliver projects according to the defined schedule and budget demonstrates effective planning, execution, and resource management	On-time and within-budget delivery of projects
Team Performance: Monitoring and improving team performance metrics, such as velocity, sprint success rates, and overall project completion, reflects the manager's ability to lead and motivate the team	Team productivity, efficiency, and overall performance
Quality of Work: Ensuring that the team delivers high-quality software with minimal defects and meets or exceeds customer expectations indicates effective leadership	Software quality, bug rates, and customer satisfaction
Employee Satisfaction and Retention: A satisfied and engaged team is more likely to be productive and stay with the organization, reflecting positively on the manager's ability to create a positive work environment	Employee engagement, satisfaction surveys, and retention rates
Individual Development: Supporting and facilitating the growth of individual team members by providing learning opportunities and career paths demonstrates effective leadership and mentorship	Professional development, skill acquisition, and career progression of team members
Customer Impact: Successful delivery of products or features that enhance the customer experience and meet their needs is a key measure of success	Positive impact on end users or customers
Risk Management: Proactive identification and management of risks demonstrate foresight and strategic thinking in engineering management	Effectiveness in identifying and mitigating risks
Adaptability and Change Management: The ability to lead the team through changes, whether in technology, project scope, or organizational structure, demonstrates resilience and adaptability	Successful adaptation to change, flexibility in handling unexpected challenges
Strategic Contribution: Ensuring that the team's efforts contribute to the overall strategic goals of the organization demonstrates a manager's understanding of the broader business context	Alignment of team goals with organizational objectives

It's essential for you to align these success criteria with the goals and values of the organization. Regular self-assessment, feedback from team members, and collaboration with other leaders can help you continuously improve and demonstrate success in their role.

Your Manual: "Manual of Me"

You have to express yourself and set the expectations early so that you can avoid any misunderstandings, conflicts, or miscommunication. You should have documented a lot when you used to be a software engineer; have you documented about yourself? That's the "Manual of Me."

The "Manual of Me" is a written document about you detailing who you are, the values you believe in, your management style, and ways of working together with others. Through the writing process, you'll find answers about yourself. Being open about qualities that you possess or lack will show that you're vulnerable and will let your team be transparent about it as well. Especially if you're a new EM, it's a powerful tool to introduce yourself and start building that relationship with your team from the ground up.

Let's take a look at what can be part of this document:

- *Who am I?*: There's nothing better than introducing yourself short and sweet. Start with your title, a word or two about your family, where you are from, and where you are living now.

- *Values I believe in*: Describe the top three values that you believe in and what defines you. This will act as a guiding light for whatever you do and you have to keep yourself collected and consistent around these values irrespective of the situation.

- *My leadership style*: Describe your leadership style with clear intent, without getting too philosophical.

- *What is success for me?*: Be clear about what success meant for you as an EM. This will enable your teammates to align their success to yours and contribute if they are mutually inclusive (if you ask me, it should be).

- *What do I expect from my team?*: Be clear on the expectations that you have for your team so that you can agree right from the start.

- *What can my team expect from me?*: This includes what your team can expect from you. Be clear on what you can commit without overpromising.

- *How do I make decisions?*: This includes how you make decisions and how that could impact the team.

- *How technical am I?*: Be deliberate about your technical prowess and your involvement in technical discussions and decisions.

- *Do I like meetings?*: There's a misconception that managers like meetings. It's time to break the shackles. Explain your view on meetings and how you conduct them.

- *What do I love and hate at work?*: Be transparent about what you love and hate at work.

- *How do I see feedback?*: Explain how you share and expect feedback.

- *Working hours and focus time*: Explain your preferred working hours and how people can find about your availability at a given time. Express your flexibility here to accommodate the team's needs.

- *What do I do outside work?*: Last but not the least, it's time for some fun. Express what you do outside your work. Who knows? You might find a like-minded person in your team with similar interests as you.

Great, It's time to share your "Manual of Me" with your team, your manager, and your closest stakeholders so that they can run through before your first one-on-one. You can do this as an exercise with your team as well in your one-on-one where they write their "Manual of Me"—it will be fun and a great opportunity to get to know each other better.

Writing is one part; execution is the rest. Review then and there how you lived up to the expectation and the qualities you defined for yourself.

Your First Six Months

Over the days and weeks, you will gradually start to have a feeling this role is for you. You also attend onboarding sessions on how the company came into existence, about the presence of your domain and team, as well as completing mandatory training one after the other.

Pretty relaxed, huh?

When you feel like you have all the time in the world, there's a Slack message coming in rushing, "Hey, can your team look at this issue that leads to a failure of 10,000+ bookings as it's causing a massive impact to the business and a bad reputation with our customers?" You might be thinking "Where have all those meet-and-greet words gone and there's a person here who got straight to the point?"—Welcome aboard. Now, now, you've officially started your first day as an engineering manager!

As a new EM, people will be keen to know about you and how you will be leading the team. It's a defining moment for your direct reports as you'll have a major role to play in their career and help them to do their best job. Your manager will be hoping that you can build a champion team. Your stakeholders will be expecting you to prioritize delivery by cutting corners even though it means compromising on the technical front. You should look to getting off to a good start in the first six months. In fact, a flying start.

Whether you get promoted in the same organization to an EM or join a new organization, your first six months are crucial on how you perform as you seek a good start in your new role. What will be going through your mind? Excited? Anxious? Curious? I would assume butterflies will be fluttering through your stomach.

Month 1: The Larger Context and the People

The first month is all about getting yourself oriented. Get to know a bit of everything about people, organization, product, processes, your domain and the business, ultimately understanding what role you play in the mix.

- ☑ Book your first one-on-one with your manager, direct reports, your product counterpart, and cross-functional stakeholders as you'll work closely with them and with your peer EMs, your manager's boss, and your peers of your manager—even though you may not work closely with them every day, it's good to build that rapport from the beginning. Explore each other's strengths, weaknesses, and aspirations, as well as core values that you believe in and wrap up with understanding ways of working together. Woah, that's a lot of people to meet. It's overwhelming but rewarding at the end. Schedule weekly one-on-ones with people that you will work closely with your manager, your direct reports, and your product counterpart in your team.

☑ Write your "Manual of Me" and share with all the people you will work closely with. Do a deep dive one-on-one with your direct reports to discuss commonalities and differences, expectations, and decide how you can work together better.

☑ Complete onboarding sessions about your organization and how everything works together. It's a good chance to connect with executives and senior leaders in your organization and interact with them about the journey so far and the general direction of the organization.

☑ Define your three-month and six-month goals with your manager and create regular check-ins to reflect on how you're progressing toward your goals. It's quite important to align on expectations at the earliest to avoid any differences in opinions that may arise later.

☑ Understand your team's scope, current goals, and roadmap and how that connects to the organization's strategy, vision, and mission. Clarify how your team does the prioritization and makes decisions. It will greatly help you in aligning your thoughts.

☑ Take part in processes on how your team collaborates, builds, and delivers software to get a feeling for yourself. In addition to making notes of your impression on the team's processes, ask explicitly what's working well and not, their pain points and gather ideas for improvements. Probably you need to revisit in subsequent months to assist the team by reviewing and refining processes.

☑ Understand the top three immediate priorities where your team needs you the most as an engineering manager. Are they struggling with prioritization? Do they need someone to push back on product decisions? Do they need someone to guide in their career and fast track achieving their goals? Find it out.

You'll end your first month with a better understanding of what this role means to you, who are the people you'll be working with, and the significance to the larger context. It's fair to say that the first month will be full of first impressions on everything that you will come across and leave you wanting to know more and eager to contribute.

On the other end of the spectrum, people would have known about you, getting the feeling of who you are as a person, but not yet on the hard skills as an engineering manager and eager to witness how you perform this role on a day-to-day basis and handle challenging situations.

Month 2: A Level Deeper

With the head start that you gained in the first month, you should look to strengthen relationships with people around you and deep dive into your team's product and technical scope, ongoing projects, pressing problems, and priorities. Don't leave observing your team's performance too late. This is the month to understand where they stand in terms of deliverables, challenges they face, and where they need to improve.

- Observe your team's communication pattern and style within and outside your team, as well as the jargon used, and identify gaps. Recommend training and development programs for individuals who could improve their communication, once you build rapport with your direct reports.

- Review each of your report's goals, progress, and challenges in the past months and understand areas where they need managerial support.

- Pair with an engineer and get onboarded on internal tools, technologies, and technical integration. Fancy setting up technical projects locally? Go for it.

- Look into your team's performance metrics to understand how your team has been performing, as well as challenges and areas to improve. Take a specific project case or situation when team performance suffered and what followed after.

- Understand expectations of each career level and how the performance review and evaluation process is carried out in your organization. Read previous performance reviews of your reports to get an understanding of the conversation that happened, promises and misses.

- Deep dive into ongoing projects, milestones, and its status. Understand how project updates are reported to management and the role you play.

- Listen to your stakeholders to understand their pain points, expectations from your team and make a note of their impressions about your team working in a project or deliverable.

- Book a bi-weekly one-on-one with your peer engineering manager to build connections and discuss how your teams can work together. None can explain better than them on how the engineering management function works in your organization.

Month 3: Taking Ownership

By now, you've spent a good amount of time understanding people, processes, problems, and technical side of things and are able to summarize your team's performance. Your team can see your active participation in the second month and can see you gradually getting into the groove. The only thing you haven't done yet is, to take ownership.

You might still have questions and doubts on the scope that your team owns, but that shouldn't stop you from taking ownership so that you can exhibit your managerial abilities sooner than later. This is the month where you will get to collaborate closely with your team in day-to-day work and understand their challenges and concerns.

- Own your team's roadmap and delivery, communicating progress and potential delays in key projects to stakeholders and to the leadership team.

- Prioritize and plan short-term goals (sprints), negotiate, and set realistic expectations.

- Take a project from start to finish and work closely with your teammates to resolve a blocker and help them move forward as that will grow your confidence.

- Lead team ceremonies and observe your team's interaction and engagement from the moderator's point of view. Share your feedback in one-on-ones on how you see an individual's interaction, understand their perspective, and suggest improvements.

- Take ownership of the stability of your technical systems and define an incident prioritization and management process. Interface with your stakeholders and other business teams on the resolution as your team will be busy fixing it.

- Consider adopting a definition of ready (DoR) and a definition of done (DoD) to ensure completeness and quality of your team's delivery.

- On nearing the end of your third month, ask for feedback from your teammates on how you handle situations from the time you took ownership and what could have been better.

- Do a quarterly review with your manager on how you are progressing toward your goals and general feedback on what you are doing well and should continue. What could you have done better? What you haven't done yet that you should have done or something that you need to look into sooner?

Month 4: Drive Change and Foster Collaboration

By this month, you're slowly feeling at home. With earned trust and rapport, you can look to drive change that your team dearly needs. A change that takes your team forward. A change that they were thinking about for quite some time but couldn't pull it off by themselves. You're a change agent in a way, isn't it?

- Assess and evolve your team's current processes to improve efficiency and effectiveness in how they collaborate, build and deliver software.

- Encourage knowledge sharing and nurture a collaborative learning environment among team members to foster continuous learning and personal growth.

- Lead a workshop in defining the team's current performance level, where you want to be in a few months' time and how will you reach there?

- Openly discuss failures and perform post mortems that ensure a fail safe environment in your team and be pragmatic about it.

- Encourage your direct reports to do a skip level one-on-ones to share feedback and exchange perspectives with your manager on a regular basis. Facilitating regular connection between your direct reports and your manager is a healthy way of collaboration that sets up 360° feedback.

- Leverage team retrospective and bring action items to life by taking lead and driving them. Give kudos to deserving people by recognizing wins and learnings.

- Review and refine your team meetings that have a purpose and produce tangible outcomes.

Month 5: Strategic Planning

Taking ownership and driving change should have given you enough confidence to start strategic planning around people, roadmaps, and the long-term goals of your team. This month, you'll spend time on long-term goals as the vision has become less blurry than the previous months. As you're taking more ownership, your manager will lean on your expertise and seek out your plans, your needs, and your team's priorities and be less concerned about it themself—it's a moment where you feel autonomy is given to you without being asked. That's all the earned trust can do for someone.

- Plan your team's mid-to-long term goals and roadmap with your product manager and discuss with your team based on the direction and vision that the leadership team set.

- Prioritize initiatives taking reach, impact, confidence, and effort into account. Through the process, you've said "no" to low-priority requests and communicated to stakeholders accordingly.

- Advocate investing in tech initiatives that contribute to technology strategy which will bring long term benefits alongside product initiatives.

- Build a tech radar for technologies that your team will adopt, try, and assess and let your team make decisions autonomously.

- Regulate hiring needs for your team at least for the next one year based on the growth opportunity.

- Start doing performance reviews of your direct reports, drafting growth plans for a high performing engineer, performance improvement plan for a low performing engineer, and decisive future plans for each engineer in your team.

- Delegate to leverage individual team members' strength and areas that they would like to learn and grow.

Month 6: Reflection and Looking Ahead

By this month, everyone around you should have already witnessed the impact that you bring to your people, team, business, and environment in general. Reflect on your journey so far and your plans ahead. You're no longer a new manager after having nearly six months under your belt and becoming a familiar face in the organization.

- Plans for the next big thing for you and your team. Tailor the learning and training needs for you and your team to be prepared.

- Your reputation and credibility are established beyond your manager, and higher management is able to recognize your performance as an engineering manager.

- Challenge yourself to get out of your comfort zone and do what you haven't done yet. It could be involved in product discovery for a week, attending customer calls, shadowing your stakeholders, debugging a production incident with your engineer—I assure you it will be a lot of fun and totally worth it.

- Challenge and push back on decisions from other teams and were able to negotiate scope and priorities.

- Your team slowly starts to become autonomous and you can see them taking more ownership on deliverables and driving continuous improvements.

- Share your first six months of experience as an engineering manager through writing on a platform internal to your organization or a blog.

- Do a six-month review with your manager on how you have progressed toward your goals and general feedback on what you have you done well and should continue. What could you have done better? What you haven't done yet that you should have done or something that you need to look into sooner?

By the end of six months, your goal should be to establish yourself as a trusted and capable engineering manager. Some elements will remain constant throughout this period: ongoing learning, regularly checking progress toward your goals, seeking and integrating feedback, making necessary adjustments, and collaborating closely with your team.

Depending on your team's unique circumstances, you may need to prioritize certain aspects sooner and potentially shorten the timeline to three months. For example, if you're managing a team struggling with performance, your primary focus should be on driving improvements in delivery and fostering collaboration right from the start. If you're taking over a team with high attrition and low morale, your top priority would be to motivate the team, rebuild from the ground up, and create a sense of purpose. Alternatively, if the team is performing well but overworked and burnt out, you'll need to step in as a gatekeeper, pushing back to protect the team's well-being.

The key is adaptability. Adjust the six-month plan to suit your team's specific needs.

Summary

Congratulations! You've made a strong start, covering a lot of ground and getting a glimpse into the world of engineering management. Who says management can't take a practical approach? Throughout this chapter, you've been involved in hands-on exercises and gained practical insights. But get ready, we're just getting started.

By now, you should be able to:

- Understand what it takes to be an engineering manager and navigate the transition from an individual contributor to decide for yourself.

- Recite the EM mantra: "Building a happy, productive and high performing engineering team that delivers."

- Explain what it takes to be a complete engineering manager and responsibilities split up among people management, delivering impactful projects, working with wider organization and leadership team, evolving team's development, delivery and technical processes, and staying hands-on.

- Define your leadership core values that suit your personality.

- Comprehend different leadership styles and be able to adapt your behavior and actions according to situations.

- Acknowledge what success means for engineering managers and associated success criteria.

- Write your "Manual of Me" to realize yourself about you and to get introduced to your closest associates.

- Plan your first six months for smoother onboarding and to get off to a flying start.

You're probably wondering what's next. If this chapter has given you the launchpad into engineering management, the next chapter will elevate you even further—it's about managing people. You'll learn how to manage yourself, your team, and your manager.

PART II

Managing People

Managing people is like flying a plane.

I haven't flown a plane myself, but when reading the book, *3 Feet to the Left* by Captain Korry Franke on his life as a flight captain, I felt it.

I feel you, engineering managers, are the captain piloting the plane—which is your team. People will be all around the axis: your manager, your stakeholders, your peer EMs, and, last but not the least, your crew (in other words, your teammates).

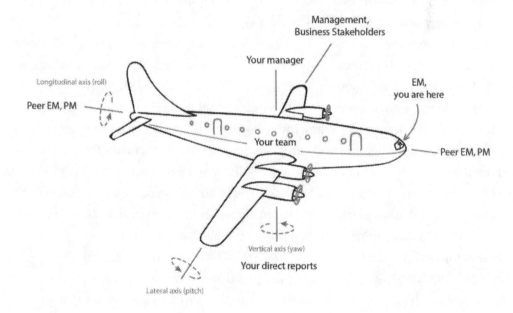

You should manage and balance all the axes to fly your plane smoothly to set it in the right direction and reach your destination safely and on time. This equates to reaching your team's goals within the runway available. *Runway*, a term that doesn't need an introduction in the aviation industry, has become significant in tech startup circles as well. In this context, it means the amount of time until your startup runs out of money. Needless to say, time, money, and people have become scarce resources in recent years, so we need to manage all three efficiently.

You may be in the driver seat, but you can't drive alone without others' help. People around you influence how you steer your team toward goals. If you're not listening to them and can't establish trust and rapport, driving your team will be a daunting task. As a new engineering manager, your first and foremost goal is to gain credibility and trust from people who you'll work closely with.

Talk about self-management. You have to keep yourself calm and composed in challenging situations that test your ability as a leader. You need to observe how you handle situations and what you could have done better. Pilots handle situations with changing weather conditions, air traffic, and technical issues.

Decision-making and adaptability to various situations are key. You have to make crucial and timely decisions navigating through challenges in projects, team dynamics, and organizational goals and communicate to people around you clearly so that they understand and can be part of it, much like a pilot who has to communicate their decisions clearly to air traffic control, crew members, and passengers.

Regulating your own emotions, continuous learning, and maintaining your focus will set you up for long-term success. You need to be smart enough to know where to focus and what can be delegated to your people. This will make you an energy-efficient engineering manager who knows where to focus, what to delegate, and when to say no.

To build a high-performing team, investing in your people is your best bet. You need to understand their motivation and career aspirations to connect with the purpose of your team's existence and organization's goals. They see a mentor in you to guide them through difficult situations at work and want you to share regular feedback on how they are performing and areas of improvement. After all, a career without a clear goal and direction is like flying a plane without a proper navigation system.

Managing performance in engineering teams is a hard nut to crack but not impossible. Adopting the right mindset and practices for managing an individual's performance and being transparent about it with them will enable them to become a better engineer. But when their performance doesn't show signs of improvement over an extended period and actively collaborating with them to drive improvements yields no positive outcomes, you have to make tough decisions.

Did you know that pilots do pre-flight briefings and engage in ongoing communication during the flight and post-flight briefings to discuss performance? Yes, pilots make sure there's a continuous feedback loop, emphasizing communication and effective collaboration among the people involved.

In this part, you'll get to learn about the tools and frameworks you can use to manage yourself to building trust and rapport with your people from day 1 so you can go on to build a champion team.

- *Self-management*: A framework called "SELF" to manage yourself and be mindful of how you handle situations, your own emotions, learning and focus.

- *Building trust and rapport*: Pragmatic approach to build trust and rapport from the ground up, knowing when trust breaks and how to rebuild.

- *Conducting mindful 1-1s*: Conduct mindful 1-1s with your direct reports more effectively by showing "care" and one meeting that both of you really care about.

- *Managing people's performance*: Understanding factors affecting people's performance, team dynamics, setting goals and expectations, performance criteria and calibration, writing a performance review and mastering performance conversations.

- *Managing your manager*: What it takes to manage your manager and how you can enhance the relationship with your manager.

Are you all set to learn how to fly a plane? I mean, to manage your people? Buckle up, you're in for a ride!

CHAPTER 2

Self-Management

You were told that you have to manage people well. That advice is spot-on. But in your role, people are everywhere: your direct reports, manager, peer engineering managers, executives, and stakeholders. So, who should you manage well first?

The answer is simple: start with yourself. Before you can effectively manage others, you need to master self-management. To bring out the best in others, you must first bring out the best in yourself. Neglecting self-management doesn't just affect you—it impacts your team and the entire environment you influence. Your position carries significant weight, and your ability to manage yourself is crucial to your success and theirs.

So, how do you manage yourself? The answer lies within "yourSELF":

- *Situation*: How do you navigate diverse, challenging, new, and unexpected situations?

- *Emotion*: How do you regulate your emotions, and what impact does this have on your team and environment?

- *Learning*: What are you currently learning? How, when, and where are you expanding your knowledge?

- *Focus and Energy*: How do you maintain focus amidst competing priorities? Are you mindful of your energy levels and efficiency?

These are the foundations of self-management, and mastering them is your first step toward effective leadership.

Situation

Think about your morning: that heated discussion with your product counterpart over competing priorities, followed by a mindful one-on-one with a team member. Or recall the intense moment when your team was scrambling to resolve a system downtime while you managed communications with stakeholders. For an engineering manager,

© Ananth Ramachandran 2024
A. Ramachandran, *The Complete Engineering Manager*, https://doi.org/10.1007/979-8-8688-0267-6_2

navigating diverse situations is just another day at the office. You'll move through different scenarios constantly, and having situational awareness, along with clarity on your role, is crucial. How you perceive and handle these situations defines you, as your temperament plays a significant role.

Types of Situations

The mood and tone of each situation may not be the same. Let's take a look at a few of those situations and get you prepared.

Mood: Happy and Accomplished

Scenario: Celebrating a release of a major feature, promotion of a team member, completion of a challenging project that brings value, successful cross-team collaboration.

What can you do? Well, live the moment. Celebrate with your team. Volunteer or encourage others in your team to organize and celebrate the win that you recently had. Call out the individuals who contributed to the team's success and give credit that they deserve.

Mood: Challenging and Stressful

Scenario: Discussing a poor performance of your direct report, addressing technical challenges that's impacting the business, not delivering projects after projects on the committed time.

What can you do? More often than not, you'll find yourself in these types of situations. Nevertheless you have to face it. Managing a structured approach for managing an individual's performance, clear communication and collaboration when not delivering projects on a committed time among people involved will ease down the tension around.

Mood: Hopeful and Optimistic

Scenario: Starting a new quarter with a new set of goals and priorities, onboarding a new engineer to your team, even joining a new team as an engineering manager.

What can you do? You should look forward to maintaining a positive outlook in these situations irrespective of the past challenges and setbacks you and your team had. Balance optimism with pragmatism so that you're not overly optimistic but be mindful in your commitments, promises, and goals.

Mood: Overwhelmed and Burned Out

Scenario: Overworked to finish projects, yearend performance reviews for umpteen direct reports, being in too many meetings.

What can you do? Take a walk right in the middle of the day to get some fresh air, say no to unimportant tasks and meetings, manage your commitment by setting the right expectations and delegating effectively.

Mood: Reflective and Thoughtful

Scenario: Retrospective with your team, reflect on your personal path over the past year as an engineering manager, focus time to get things done, reflecting on mistakes that you committed last time.

What can you do? Very rarely do engineering managers spend time for themselves. Have some time to make self-love and reflect on what went well and what didn't.

Great, that should give you some idea about situations that you'll come across and how you can keep yourself composed. How can you be more proactive and have situational awareness right from the start? *Anticipate, Assess, Immerse, and Reflect.*

Anticipate

Begin your day by considering the various situations you'll likely encounter. Create a mental or written "situation timeline" that outlines the key events and interactions on your agenda. This practice helps you to mentally prepare and prioritize your approach to each situation.

However, it's important to recognize that it's impossible—and even inadvisable—to be fully prepared for every scenario. Over-preparation can make you appear scripted or insincere, which can undermine your effectiveness. Instead, aim to be "half prepared." This approach ensures that you have a basic understanding of what to expect, without being so rigid that you can't adapt to the natural flow of the situation.

Whether it's a meeting where you have limited context, a regular one-on-one with a team member, or a progress report to senior leadership, anticipating the likely mood and expectations in the room will equip you to engage confidently and respond with a pragmatic mindset.

Keep in mind that unexpected situations will inevitably arise—ones you couldn't have anticipated. When this happens, don't panic. It's perfectly normal. Focus on staying calm and composed, assess the situation quickly, and concentrate on what's most important at that moment. The more you practice this approach, the more adept you'll become at handling a wide range of scenarios with poise and effectiveness.

Assess

The moment you enter a situation, take a step back to evaluate the mood and context of those involved. Pay close attention to the emotional undercurrents and the motivations driving the people in the room. Are they tense or relaxed? Is there a sense of urgency or calm? Understanding the emotional landscape will give you critical insights into how best to navigate the situation.

Next, consider the broader context: What are the underlying goals and expectations? What does success look like for this particular interaction? Clarifying the expected outcomes will help you align your approach with the needs of the moment, allowing you to contribute more effectively and steer the situation toward a positive resolution.

By quickly assessing both the emotional tone and the strategic goals, you'll be better equipped to adapt your communication style, anticipate potential challenges, and make informed decisions that keep the situation on track.

Immerse

To truly immerse yourself in a situation means being fully present, both mentally and emotionally. However, there will be times when you find your focus wavering. Perhaps you're still dwelling on a difficult conversation you had earlier with your manager, stressing over a prioritization that didn't go as planned, or preoccupied with an upcoming task that remains incomplete. When your mind is divided, your ability to engage and contribute is significantly diminished, leaving you as little more than a passive observer.

So, how can you ensure you're fully immersed in the moment?

- *Clear Your Mind of Unrelated Thoughts*: Before entering any situation, take a moment to transition mentally. Set aside lingering concerns from previous events and focus on the context of the upcoming interaction.

- *Listen with Undivided Attention*: Engage fully by listening intently. Clarify any questions and strive to understand the goals, challenges, and dynamics at play.

- *Contribute Meaningfully*: Understand your role and participate actively, whether by offering ideas, making decisions, or collaborating with others. Avoid being a passive observer.

- *Commit to the Situation's Purpose*: Focus on shared goals and empathize with others' perspectives to stay aligned with the group's objectives.

By fully immersing yourself in each situation, you not only enhance your own effectiveness but also positively influence the outcome for everyone involved. This level of engagement fosters better communication, stronger relationships, and more successful results.

Reflect

As you navigate various situations throughout your day, it often takes a moment to process what just transpired. You may realize that you've overreacted, under-reacted, or missed the opportunity to respond when it was needed. Without taking the time to reflect, it's difficult to fully understand the dynamics of each situation, your role in it, and the impact it had on both you and your team.

Reflection is a critical step in self-management and growth. It allows you to gain insights into how you handle different scenarios, identify patterns in your behavior, and make adjustments where necessary. By reflecting, you develop a deeper awareness of how your actions align with your intentions and how they affect others.

Now, it's your turn: Create a rough timeline of the situations you anticipate encountering over the course of a day as an engineering manager. Select two diverse scenarios, and describe the mood in each, as well as how you plan to approach them. Afterward, reflect on how well you anticipated the events, assessed the context, and immersed yourself in the situations. Consider what you did well and what you could improve for next time.

Emotion

When I was an individual contributor, I didn't pay much attention to the emotions I or those around me were experiencing. My focus was on my technical skills, contributions to the team, and delivering quality solutions on time. I valued intelligence quotient (IQ) more than emotional quotient (EQ).

Was this focus due to the nature of my work, where I spent much of my day in front of a screen with occasional interactions? Or was it because performance evaluations emphasized hard skills? Perhaps it was the environment or my personality? Reflecting on it, I realize it was a mix of all these factors.

Over the years, expectations have shifted. Individual contributors are now expected to be emotionally aware and regulate their behavior, as collaboration and teamwork are increasingly important. For engineering managers, emotional intelligence is even more crucial. You need to manage your emotions to coach teams effectively, handle stress, resolve conflicts, deliver feedback, and make important decisions.

Your Emotions

As an engineering manager, you'll face a range of emotionally charged situations, from missed deadlines and team conflicts to celebrating successes and navigating sudden changes. The emotions you might experience such as stress, empathy, defensiveness, happiness, concern can shift rapidly, making your workday an emotional rollercoaster (Figure 2-1).

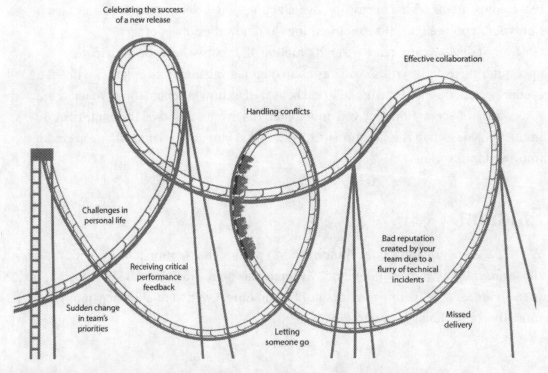

Figure 2-1. *Emotional roller coaster of an engineering manager*

You have to understand what emotions are, the adrenaline rush that you go through and how to regulate them.

What Are Emotions?

Emotions are a psychological state that includes a subjective experience, physiological response, and behavioral expression. They are messages from us to us. It tries to convey to you how you are feeling about something.

Mondays are the perfect example to understand the range of emotions you might experience. Depending on what's coming up, emotions start setting in right from Sunday evening.

Sunday evening: As you're enjoying barbeque with your family and friends, you find yourself momentarily zooming out from the lively chatter and laughter. As the aroma of sizzling meats and vegetables fills the air and the warmth of the sun embraces you, you may begin to mentally transition to the week ahead. Was it about the missed deadline of a project and stressing out how your team will be achieving it? or concerned over lack of strategic planning for the upcoming quarter? or the recent team reorganization that impacted your team's morale?.

You feel as if you're behind even before the week has begun. Strange feeling, isn't it?

Monday morning: As the work week kicks off, you find yourself immersed in the hustle and bustle of the day. Sitting at your desk, you're greeted by a flurry of emails and meeting reminders, each one a reminder of the challenges that lie ahead. The missed project deadline weighs heavily on your mind, overshadowing the start of the week with a sense of urgency and pressure.

In the midst of tackling the immediate tasks at hand, you're confronted with the broader issues plaguing your team. Lack of strategic planning for the upcoming quarter looms large, casting doubt on the path forward and adding an additional layer of complexity to your already packed schedule. As you prepare for meetings with both your team and senior management, you grapple with the daunting task of charting a course forward amidst uncertainty.

Despite the challenges and uncertainties that lie ahead, you remain steadfast in your commitment to leading your team through the storm. Drawing upon your experience and resilience, you approach each task with determination and resolve. Whether it's addressing project deadlines, navigating strategic decisions, or rebuilding team morale, you tackle each challenge head-on.

The Adrenaline Rush

As an engineering manager, you're no stranger to the adrenaline rush that accompanies high-stakes situations and intense workdays, where the surge of adrenaline can be both exhilarating and overwhelming.

Have you heard about the 90-second rule of managing emotions? It's when an adrenaline rush is triggered in the brain, it typically takes about 90 seconds for it to fully surge and then dissipate, provided it is allowed to run its natural course without being fueled by additional thoughts or reactions.

Let's say you receive an urgent message about a major technical issue that threatens to derail an important project. Your heart rate spikes, your palms may sweat, and your mind races as you consider the potential impact and the actions needed to address the situation. In this moment, you're experiencing a surge of adrenaline: an automatic physiological response designed to prepare your body for action in the face of perceived threat or danger.

However, instead of immediately reacting to the adrenaline rush with frantic problem-solving or impulsive decision-making, you consciously choose to pause and allow the 90-second rule to unfold. You take a few deep breaths, acknowledging the rush of adrenaline without judgment or resistance. As you do so, you notice the intensity of the adrenaline gradually subsiding, replaced by a sense of calm and clarity. 90-second is an example, you choose how long you want to take before responding. Even a day or two to process your emotions and thoughts? Completely fine.

What do you do in live situations?

Ninety seconds works like a charm in async communication. What if you had an adrenaline rush in the middle of a large meeting where everyone is looking at you waiting for your response? Clock is ticking. 1. 2. 3.... Now, you don't have the luxury to craft a well-thought-out response. What will you do? Why the adrenaline rush? - Feeling defensive? Overwhelmed? or What was it?. You need a strategy to keep adrenaline rush in check in live situations.

- *Stay calm and take deep breaths*: As an engineering manager, it's crucial to stay composed when the pressure is on. When you feel that adrenaline rush in a big meeting, start by taking a few deep breaths to help center yourself. This technique will help reduce anxiety, steady your nerves, and enhance your focus. Deep breathing sends a signal to your brain that you're in control, mitigating the fight-or-flight response triggered by adrenaline.

- *Ask clarifying questions*: If you're feeling overwhelmed or unsure how to respond, don't hesitate to ask clarifying questions. This not only buys you a little more time to think but also ensures you fully understand the issue at hand. Phrasing questions like, "Can you please elaborate on that point?" or "Could you clarify what you mean by...?" helps you gather more information, allowing you to provide a more accurate and thoughtful response.

- *Be assertive and pragmatic*: In high-pressure situations, being assertive and pragmatic is key. Speak clearly and confidently, even if you feel uncertain inside. Focus on providing practical and actionable responses that address the core issues. It's acceptable to admit if you need a moment to gather your thoughts or to suggest revisiting a complex topic later when you've had more time to consider it. Being straightforward and solution-oriented demonstrates your leadership and composure, even under pressure.

By harnessing the power of mindfulness and self-awareness, you can navigate the adrenaline rush with grace and resilience, ultimately leading your team to success.

Regulating Your Emotions

To be an effective engineering manager, you need to regulate your emotions. Emotional attachment to your ideas can lead to bias and resistance to change.

Our minds often see small conversations as battles to win, but practicing humility and openness can foster collaboration. For instance, if a team member disagrees with your solution, listen actively and let them try their approach. Even if their method isn't perfect, it offers a learning opportunity. Similarly, in discussions about priorities, consider and validate other viewpoints. Knowing when to let go of your stance and when to hold firm is crucial.

- *Label Your Emotions*: Recognize and name your emotions, such as frustration or excitement. Keep a journal to track these feelings, especially during high-stress situations, to become aware of your emotional patterns and their impact on decision-making.

- *Question Your Emotions and Triggers*: Reflect on why you feel a certain way. Determine the triggers, whether it's stress over deadlines or concerns about perceptions.

- *Show Up*: Be present and engaged in team activities. Demonstrate emotional stability and actively participate in meetings and interactions.

- *Seek Feedback*: Regularly ask for feedback from your team, peers, and supervisors on your emotional regulation and leadership style. Use this input to improve and adjust your approach.

Ah, the Imposter Syndrome

Stepping into the role of an engineering manager often comes with the harsh reality of feeling unqualified for many aspects of the job. It's a common experience to find yourself grappling with tasks like resolving team conflicts, managing underperformance, prioritizing crucial deliverables, and negotiating project terms, all of which may be outside your initial training and comfort zone. This uncharted territory can stir up a blend of anxiety, self-doubt, and imposter syndrome.

It's natural to feel overwhelmed by the weight of your new responsibilities, fearing that any misstep could negatively impact team morale or project success. The pressure to perform and prove yourself can lead to significant stress and frustration. Yet, amid these challenging emotions, there are also opportunities for growth. As you face these hurdles, you will encounter moments of pride and satisfaction, gradually building your confidence and skills through hands-on experience.

Acknowledging and managing these emotions is essential for your development and effectiveness as a manager. By embracing the learning curve and understanding that feeling like an imposter is part of the process, you can better navigate your role and grow into a more capable and confident leader.

- *Develop a Support System*: Establish a network of support by connecting with fellow managers, mentors, and peers. Share experiences, seek advice, and gain insights to navigate challenges effectively. Building strong relationships within your team also fosters a collaborative environment where everyone feels valued and supported.

- *Accept and Learn*: Recognize that you can't know every detail and focus on the broader picture. Trust your team to handle specifics and adopt a mindset of continuous learning. Seek opportunities to expand your knowledge and skills, allowing you to lead effectively without needing all the answers.

- *Set Realistic Goals and Priorities*: Manage your workload by setting achievable goals and breaking large projects into manageable tasks. Prioritize based on importance and deadlines to avoid feeling overwhelmed. Delegate responsibilities to your team, empowering them and utilizing their strengths to achieve collective objectives.

Others' Emotions

You might wonder, "How can I truly understand the emotions of others? Is it even possible?" This is a valid question, and it's important to acknowledge that it's not always straightforward. As engineering managers, we're not equipped with telepathic abilities.

However, there are practical and effective techniques you can use to gain insight into others' emotions:

- *Observe Body Language and Expressions*: Pay attention to nonverbal cues like engagement levels, eye contact, and changes in voice tone. These signs can indicate whether someone is struggling or disinterested, signaling the need for a one-on-one discussion.

- *Ask, Don't Assume*: Instead of guessing how someone feels about a project or recent changes, directly ask them. Inquire about their feelings regarding specific situations and how you can offer support.

- *Listen Actively*: Focus on understanding, not just responding. Ask follow-up questions to clarify their perspective and emotions, especially if their performance is below expectations. Use active listening to gauge how you can assist them better.

- *Empathize*: Put yourself in their situation. Reflect on your own experiences of stress or uncertainty and consider how you would have liked to be supported. For example, if a team member is anxious about a deadline, recall similar experiences and use those insights to provide effective support, such as adjusting deadlines or offering additional resources.

Learning

As you settle into your role as an engineering manager, you may find yourself operating smoothly, like a stream flowing along its path. However, this ease can sometimes lead to drifting off course. Reflecting on your career and personal learning aspirations might not be at the forefront of your mind, but it's crucial to periodically reassess these aspects. It's common for managers to neglect their own development, as their focus shifts predominantly to team management and organizational priorities.

Recall the time when you were an individual contributor; learning was a daily ritual. But as a manager, the concept of learning can change. The nature of what constitutes "learning" evolves, and it's easy to overlook personal growth amid the demands of leadership.

Take a moment to ponder how you can integrate ongoing personal development into your managerial duties. Effective leadership requires not only managing your team but also committing to your own growth. Balancing these aspects is key to maintaining both your effectiveness as a leader and your professional satisfaction.

Comfort Circle

Let's engage in a brief exercise to help you evaluate your comfort zone as a manager. Draw a circle on a piece of paper (Figure 2-2). Inside the circle, list the engineering manager responsibilities you feel confident handling. Outside the circle, note the areas where you feel less comfortable or face challenges. This simple exercise can help you identify areas for improvement and focus your efforts on developing skills and knowledge that will enhance your overall effectiveness as a leader.

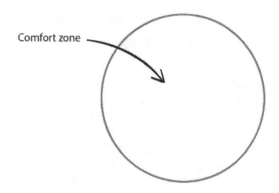

Comfort zone

Figure 2-2. *Your comfort zone*

Table 2-1 is a sample list of responsibilities/skills for you to mark it in the comfort circle.

Table 2-1. *Sample List of EM Responsibilities*

Prioritization	People Management	Project delivery
Evolving team processes	Conflict Management	Performance Management
Tech Strategy	Team Engagement	Product and Business Context
Technical skills	Presentation skills	Cross-functional collaboration

Your time starts now.

...

...

Beeeep, time is up.

Now that you've plotted your comfort circle, take a moment to review the skills and responsibilities you feel comfortable with versus those that are outside your comfort zone. At the end of this section, I'll share what my comfort circle looked like to provide further context and insights.

What to Learn?

As an engineering manager, you have a wealth of learning opportunities at your fingertips. From mastering people management and prioritization to refining processes, honing negotiation skills, and conducting fair performance reviews, the possibilities are vast. But with so many areas to explore, how do you decide what to focus on?

- *Assess Team Needs*: Start by understanding where your team needs the most support. If they're struggling with frequent interruptions, consider learning how to define and implement processes that streamline requests and improve workflow. If team productivity and impact have been lacking, you might need to enhance your skills in prioritizing work and collaborating with product managers and stakeholders to focus on high-impact projects. If career guidance is a need, investing in mentorship techniques and goal-setting strategies could be beneficial.

- *Seek Feedback from Your Manager*: Your manager can provide valuable insights into areas where your development could make the most difference. Discuss with them the organization's current priorities and where your learning could align with strategic needs. Gaining a broader understanding of business perspectives and strategic decision-making can also guide your growth.

- *Identify Personal Interests*: Reflect on what excites you and where you want to grow next. If public speaking interests you, seek out opportunities to develop this skill. By aligning your learning with your interests and passions, you'll be more motivated and engaged in your professional development.

By focusing on these areas, you can tailor your learning journey to meet both your team's needs and your personal growth goals, ensuring that you evolve into a more effective and well-rounded engineering manager.

How to Learn?

Consider the following:

- *Real-World Experience*: The best way to learn is through the day-to-day challenges of your role. Every difficult conversation, project presentation, and team interaction is an opportunity to grow. Embrace these situations as practical learning experiences where you refine your skills by actively engaging with real problems.

- *Books and Magazines*: In addition to the book you're currently reading, further your knowledge with essential reads for engineering managers such as *Become an Effective Software Engineering Manager* by James Stanier and *The Manager's Path* by Camille Fournier. To stay up-to-date with management trends, subscribe to reputable magazines like *Harvard Business Review* and *MIT Technology Review*.

- *Learn from Peers*: Connect with other engineering managers to share experiences and strategies. Learning from peers can provide valuable insights and shortcuts to handling similar challenges.

- *Build Your Network*: Attend industry meetups, conferences, and engage with professionals on platforms like LinkedIn and Twitter. A strong network provides diverse perspectives and ongoing learning opportunities.

- *Newsletters and Online Content*: Subscribe to newsletters on platforms like Medium and Substack for insights from experienced professionals. Consider following writers like James Stanier (`https://theengineeringmanager.substack.com`), Lucca Rossi (`https://refactoring.fm`) and my own newsletter (`https://techmanagerguide.substack.com`) for practical insights into industry and management trends.

I promised to share my own comfort circle from when I began my engineering management career. Comparing my initial comfort circle with one from a few years into the role reveals significant growth (Figure 2-3).

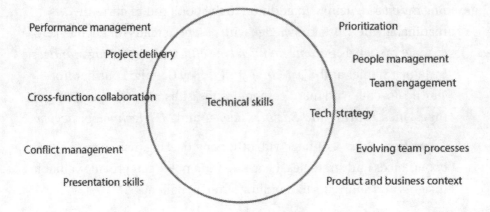

When I started as an engineering manager

After few years as an engineering manager

Figure 2-3. *My comfort circle when I started and after few years as an
engineering manager*

However, this growth doesn't imply mastery of all skills or that I see myself as an
expert. Instead, it underscores the importance of continuous learning and adaptation.
The process of enhancing existing skills, acquiring new leadership capabilities, and
adjusting to evolving team dynamics is ongoing. Embracing this mindset of perpetual
learning is crucial for thriving as an engineering manager.

The journey of learning and development never truly ends. Throughout my career,
I've continually faced challenges that required me to learn and grow through practical
experience and various learning resources. This ongoing process involves not only

strengthening my existing skills but also acquiring new ones and adapting to different contexts and organizational needs. By recognizing that learning is a continuous journey, you can remain adaptable and effective in your role as an engineering manager.

Focus and Energy

Here's a question for you: What are your current focal points as an engineering manager? Can you clearly identify and list your top three priorities with confidence? Take a brief pause and reflect on this: take a few moments to center your thoughts and then revisit the question.

Were you able to recall your top priorities? If so, congratulations; you're among the exceptional engineering managers who have a clear sense of focus. However, if you found it challenging to pinpoint your top three priorities amid a fog of competing demands, you're not alone. As an engineering manager, it can often feel like everything is urgent and essential. This overwhelming sense of priority can lead to a paradox where trying to address everything means addressing nothing effectively.

In such situations, it's vital to recalibrate and manage your focus. Prioritizing is key to directing your energy and efforts effectively. Both personal and team priorities need to be clearly defined and addressed to ensure that you're not only managing but also leading with purpose and clarity.

Focus on Terms

As an engineering manager, you have to focus on different terms ranging from the present day until a quarter or even beyond that if you are planning a yearly roadmap or strategically aligning with other teams in your domain. How you split your focus among terms matters a lot.

Work you do every day can be split into focus based on different terms.

- *Daily focus*: Tasks and responsibilities that you carry out on a day-to-day basis

- *Short-term focus*: Focusing on your work that ranges from a week or two

- *Mid-term focus*: Focusing on monthly goals and initiatives

- *Long-term focus*: Focusing on quarterly goals and beyond

Table 2-2 are some examples of your work that get split into multiple terms.

Table 2-2. *Daily, Short-Term, Mid-Term, and Long-Term Focus for an Engineering Manager*

Daily focus	• Be part of daily stand-up meetings with the team and understand where you can help them. Maybe to get them unblocked or connect them with the right stakeholder.
	• Addressing urgent technical issues and interfacing stakeholders while your team is busy into the details
	• Reviewing and responding to messages in Slack: Large part of your day will be spent responding to and acknowledging messages in slack resolving day-to-day questions or concerns
Short term focus	• One-on-ones with your direct reports
	• Planning and executing a sprint for the development team
	• Conducting a short-term retrospective and implementing improvements
	• Pairing with one of your engineers to technically design your system
	• Regular coordination with cross-functional teams to meet discuss about progress, problems and plans
	• Resolving conflicts or bottlenecks hindering short-term project goals
Midterm focus	• Setting and reviewing monthly team goals
	• Evolving team's processes to let your team collaborate, build and deliver software efficiently
	• Planning and coordinating team workshops and training sessions
	• Balancing product development and technical initiatives
	• Reporting progress, impact delivered, hits and misses to senior leadership
Long term focus	• Building a high-performing engineering team over a course of time
	• Developing a quarterly team roadmap
	• Conducting performance reviews and providing feedback
	• Aligning team goals with the organization's long-term objectives
	• Strategic planning for team growth and skills development
	• Initiating discussions and collaborations for long-term projects or partnerships

What does the split between focus on terms could look like?

Let's take extreme cases to understand why splitting your focus based on terms is quite important:

- *Excessive Focus on Daily Tasks*: If you spend 70–90% of your time on daily operational tasks, you may be neglecting long-term planning and strategic goals. This excessive focus might also indicate that you're micro-managing, getting bogged down in details instead of guiding your team effectively.

- *Excessive Focus on Long-Term Goals*: Conversely, if you allocate most of your time to long-term strategic planning and remain disconnected from daily operations, your team may struggle with immediate challenges. This detachment can hinder their ability to meet short-term goals and lead to a sense of neglect or frustration among team members.

It's normal for some days to be skewed towards either daily tasks or long-term planning due to specific demands, such as an influx of urgent requests or a full-day workshop for future initiatives. However, such fluctuations should not become your routine.

If the daily focus split feels too granular, you might consider a weekly perspective. For a typical 40-hour work week, your time might break down to about 16 hours (40%) on daily tasks, 10 hours (25%) on short-term objectives, 8 hours (20%) on mid-term goals, and 6 hours (15%) on long-term planning. Adjusting this split according to your schedule and priorities is essential.

The key takeaway is to manage and balance your focus effectively. Spending too much time on daily tasks can prevent you from setting strategic direction and preparing for future goals, while an excessive focus on long-term planning can leave your team struggling with immediate issues and short-term objectives. Regularly reassess and adjust your focus based on team dynamics, needs, and organizational context.

Now, it's your turn. Reflect on your current focus distribution. What does your typical split look like? Use your experience to estimate how much time you dedicate to daily, short-term, mid-term, and long-term tasks. Consider how you might shift your focus to align more closely with your ideal balance.

Check-In and Check-Out

How you start and end your day matters the most and can even change the perspective and outcome of your day. Personally I have found great benefit in deciding my focus area by having a check-in at the start of my workday and reviewing how it went with a check-out at day's end.

What can be done at the check-in?

As you switch from your personal life to work mode, take a moment to center yourself and plan your day. Here's what you might include in your morning check-in:

- *Wrap Up Previous Tasks*: Address any lingering items from the previous day, such as unanswered messages or pending approvals. Tackle quick, high-priority tasks to clear your plate and start fresh.

- *Sanity Check*: Review project updates, system metrics, and your calendar to ensure you're aware of current statuses and deadlines.

- *Set Top Priorities*: Identify and outline your top three priorities for the day. Determine if these tasks are immediate or if they require longer-term planning.

What can be done at the check-out?

After a long day at work with ups and down in your focus and energy, it's time to wind up! Reflect on how the day went, how whether you made progress on your priorities, and what's on your mind when you close your day.

The following can be the agenda of the check-out:

- *Has the day gone as per the plan?* Review how your day went, what went well, and what didn't.

- *How was your progress on priorities?* Have you made progress on your top three priorities, or is it another day that got filled up with last-minute meetings or a whole day in Slack? Make a note of behaviors that you could change to improve your productivity and to reclaim focus.

- *What's on your mind?* What's that one thing on your mind that you need to clear right at the start of tomorrow? I used to have at least one or two such thoughts occupying my mind and that won't allow me to get into my personal life. I have learned to pause until tomorrow so that it won't bug me in other parts of my life.

Winding up helps you close your day and give you a sense of calmness to go into your life mode. After all, we have a life, isn't it?

When can you check-in and check-out?

The timing of your check-ins and check-outs depends on your personal schedule and daily demands. For example, I typically allocate 25 minutes for my check-in around 9 a.m. and another 25 minutes for my check-out around 5:15 p.m. Flexibility is key, as unforeseen meetings or urgent issues may shift these times. Find a routine that suits your workflow and allows you to effectively plan and reflect on your day.

Managing Your Energy

Your energy levels (Figure 2-4) play a crucial role in determining how effectively you can focus and enhance productivity as an engineering manager. The demanding nature of the role (constant context switching, navigating complex challenges, attending numerous meetings, and steering your team through turbulent periods) can deplete your energy more rapidly than you might realize.

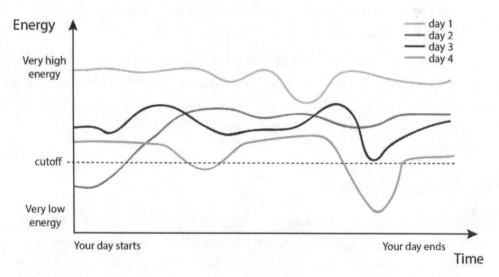

Figure 2-4. Your fluctuating energy levels

If you're not mindful of how you manage your energy, it will not only affect your performance but also impact your team. Your energy, whether positive or negative, influences those around you, consciously or unconsciously.

To be an energy efficient engineering manager:

- *Delegate Details*: Avoid getting bogged down in every technical detail. Trust your team to handle these tasks, allowing you to focus on higher-level responsibilities.

- *Promote Self-Management*: Empower your team to manage their own work wherever possible. This reduces your need to be involved in every decision and helps conserve your energy.

- *Prioritize and Say No*: Be selective about the commitments you take on. Saying no to less critical tasks will help you preserve your energy for what truly matters.

- *Channel Energy Effectively*: Direct your energy toward activities that align with your key objectives and priorities. This ensures that your efforts have a meaningful impact.

- *Identify Peak Energy Times*: Recognize when you are most energetic and focused during the day. Use these peak times for tackling your top priorities and most challenging tasks.

Avoid adopting a "go-go-go" mentality or falling into the trap of micro-management. This approach is not only energy-draining but can lead to burnout and diminish team morale. Instead, adopting a strategic approach to energy management will help you lead more effectively and sustain both your well-being and that of your team.

SELF Love Journal

With the SELF framework in mind for managing your role as an engineering manager, how can you track your progress and ensure continual improvement? The answer lies in dedicating regular time for self-reflection and personal development. I call this practice the "SELF Love Journal." To make this effective, schedule a regular slot in your calendar—whether weekly or bi-weekly—that suits your routine. Use this time to review and reflect on your experiences and growth.

Here's a suggested agenda for your SELF Love Journal sessions:

- *Situation Reflection*: Analyze how you handled specific situations. Choose one positive and one challenging scenario from the past period and reflect on your reactions and decisions. Consider what you did well and what could be improved in similar future situations.

- *Anticipation and Immersion*: Evaluate your ability to anticipate, assess, and engage with different situations. Identify areas for improvement and strategies for handling future situations better.

- *Emotional Regulation*: Reflect on how you managed your own emotions and understood those of others in various scenarios. Assess your emotional intelligence and consider ways to enhance it.

- *Comfort Circle and Learning*: Review your comfort circle and the skills you're currently developing. Determine what new skills you want to acquire next and outline a plan for achieving them.

- *Focus on Priorities*: Analyze how effectively you focused on your priorities. Examine how you divide your attention between daily tasks, short-term goals, mid-term objectives, and long-term aspirations. Assess whether your focus distribution aligns with your goals.

- *Energy Levels*: Reflect on your energy levels over the past period. Consider what actions you could take to manage your energy more efficiently and avoid burnout.

During these reflection sessions, choose a few specific cases to discuss with your direct reports and manager to gather their feedback. Use the insights gained to plan actionable improvements and set goals for your ongoing development. By investing in this process, you'll foster continuous personal and professional growth, ultimately enhancing your effectiveness as an engineering manager.

Summary

In this chapter, you got to know how to organize and manage yourself better using the SELF framework, setting yourself up for success but not disregarding your challenges, failures and importance of continuous learning.

By now, you should be able to:

- *Self-Management*: Recognize its role as the foundation of effective leadership, enabling you to handle both routine and complex challenges.

- *Situational Awareness*: Use techniques to adeptly navigate various scenarios, from celebrating successes to addressing urgent issues, with the right mix of emotional and practical intelligence.

- *Emotional Intelligence (EQ)*: Understand and enhance your EQ to transition smoothly from an individual contributor to a manager who can effectively manage both personal and team emotions.

- *Continuous Learning*: Engage in ongoing development to align with role demands and foster a culture of improvement within your team.

- *Focus and Energy Management*: Balance daily tasks, short-term objectives, and long-term goals to optimize productivity and leadership effectiveness.

- *SELF Love Journal*: Regularly reflect on your management experiences, emotional responses, and growth areas to aid in personal and leadership development.

Next up, we're on to managing others around you, starting from building trust and rapport from the ground up.

CHAPTER 3

It's All About Trust

I trust you.

When someone says "I trust you," they really mean it. It is definitely not granted by the words spoken but with actions taken.

As an engineering manager, it's important to understand that trust isn't granted automatically from day 1. There will be all sorts of questions and doubts from everyone around. Your manager's doubts: "Will you deliver?," "Can you improve the team's collaboration and engagement?" "Will you do the prioritization right?" Your direct reports' doubts: "Will you help me in their career growth?," "Can you be trusted to discuss my personal situation and challenges?," "Can I expect regular feedback on how I work and what to improve?" Your stakeholders' doubts: "Can I trust the timeline committed?" "Will I be informed if there is a delay in delivery?"

You have to show your credibility and invest in building relationships from the ground up. Showing genuine care and empathy for people around you, being committed and consistent in what you say/what you do, and being authentic are exemplifications of trust.

It takes time to build trust (Figure 3-1). It is like playing a cup stacking game. You need patience to stack cups so that they won't fall, but it takes seconds to break. Once a trust is broken, it takes more time to rebuild than you would imagine.

Figure 3-1. *Building trust—a cup stacking game*

© Ananth Ramachandran 2024
A. Ramachandran, *The Complete Engineering Manager*, https://doi.org/10.1007/979-8-8688-0267-6_3

Building Trust

Building trust is all about being consistent in your behavior, sticking to promises made, and ultimately delivering them. Can one deliver every time as per promise made? Maybe not. Especially not in the engineering world. That's where transparency, overcommunication, and being vulnerable will increase your trust score.

The best feeling you can give people is that you're one of them and not someone who works at a different level and always has other priorities and your own problems.

Get to Know Each Other Better

The meaning of every relationship starts from getting to know each other better. If you haven't introduced yourself to your team, book that meeting now. As a new EM, it's a no-brainer to start with introducing yourself. But if you have been EMing your team for years, you might ask "Why should I express myself? My teammates know me." Is that the case? Do they know the values that you believe in? Do they know how you make decisions? Do they know how you share feedback? How technical are you? It's always good to talk about it.

Also, get to know them better. What are their challenges and where do they need help? How do they want to receive and share feedback? Do they prefer autonomy over hand holding? What are the personal priorities in their life?

One-on-one meetings are a great opportunity to build that trust and spend time getting to know each other. Need fancy options? Go for lunch together. It's a great way to start building relationships from food. You just can't go wrong.

Be Vulnerable and Empathetic

We managers are the most uncertain and vulnerable creatures in the world. Don't get me wrong. It's not that you're uncertain as a person but uncertain in how your job is defined and the work that you do. Your job is not to write a program that gives certain output but to see growth in your people that takes time, define efficient processes, and pray that it will work in every circumstance, commit to deliver projects even though you and your team never had that time to estimate every piece and foresee challenges that could come.

To make it even more challenging, there are no clear signals to detect your uncertainty unless you express yourself. It is not like the technical systems that your engineers work with that show at least the state whenever it's unstable and uncertain. It is not like the dashboards your product managers use to show improvements in North Star metrics and to make data-driven decisions.

The first person to come out and show uncertainty in our teams is us. We have to show uncertainty in the decisions we made, commitment we had with our stakeholders, and the scope and depth of technicality that we don't get to work with every day like our engineers do.

Be Transparent

Being transparent to your team and stakeholders in whatever you do will let them trust you. Let it be on prioritization, project statuses, feedback, performance reviews, and how you make decisions. Your team will appreciate your intention and attitude toward transparency and for letting them understand your thought process.

Here are some actions you can take to be more transparent:

- Regularly share updates on the status of ongoing projects, including successes, challenges, and any changes in timelines. Be open about the project's progress, and if there are delays, provide the reasons behind them.

- When making significant decisions that affect the team, communicate the rationale behind the decision-making process. Share relevant information and factors considered, ensuring that the team understands the context.

- Acknowledge your own mistakes and failures when they occur. Discuss what went wrong, why it happened, and what steps are being taken to rectify the situation. This openness fosters a culture of accountability.

Be Their Ally

Have you rubber ducked with your engineers in difficult situations or paired with them to resolve any technical challenge? I did it a few times.

There was one rubber ducking session that stood out. After 15 minutes of discussion, we resolved it and I was thanked. Trust gained. Mission accomplished. But I didn't say to you what I did on this occasion and how we resolved it. I did "nothing." Yes, I just listened to the engineer, said "mmm" twice and "umm" thrice, the engineer found the root cause of the problem, and summarized it to me and resolved it themself.

The moral of the story? Be their ally whenever you get a chance. Helping them to resolve their technical challenge with your expertise or just listening to them even though you have nothing to say will gain their trust.

Let Them Do

Trust is reciprocal. If you don't trust engineers in your team to do the job, they can't trust you as a manager. Doing their job yourself to finish a project on time or playing the middleman in communication with others will not let them learn and grow. Instead, you should let them do it and act autonomously, but give them constructive feedback on a regular basis and guide them on how to do it efficiently. If you see a gap in their ability, suggest learning resources or give space to learn from mistakes.

Be open about ways of working together right from the start and ask them what's the ideal time to have the alignment regarding the work. Insist they reach out to you proactively instead of you reaching out to them every time to check on their progress. Once these boundaries are defined, it will be easy to work and trust each other.

Praise in Public; Criticize in Private

Should you criticize in private or public? First let's understand what criticism is and the need for it.

Whenever I hear the word *criticism*, "movie critics" come to my mind. I love to read reviewers when they analyze the acting, plot, writing, storyline, and share their perspective in detail. The most interesting aspect here is that reviews are shared to the public and not necessarily to the movie makers directly.

Can we apply the principle of movie critique to criticize individuals in your team in public setup? Will it be effective, and most importantly will it serve the purpose? Sadly not. Criticism in teams is the opposite to that of movie critics. It should reach the individual first before reaching the wider audience. Sometimes it doesn't have to reach wide unless it can be resolved by everyone together, or it's a team problem rather than an individual's.

Criticizing in private shows that you care about the individual's opinion, and the focus is to listen to their perspective and find a solution rather than placing blame. When it's one-on-one, they will not feel as defensive and may openly come forward for suggestions if the criticism is valid and sensible. Wrapping criticism with constructive feedback is more powerful and can earn their trust for being mindful.

You want to praise someone in public? Absolutely, go ahead. There's no better way of recognizing their efforts and contribution, and they will absolutely love it.

Be Invested

Show genuine investment in your team members' goals and successes. This means actively engaging in their professional aspirations and nurturing the relationships you build with them. Your commitment should be evident in all your interactions and decisions, reflecting a long-term dedication to their development.

The return on this investment? You'll cultivate trust and commitment from your team. When they see that you are genuinely invested in their growth and well-being, they are more likely to reciprocate that trust and engage fully in their work. This creates a positive cycle of support and collaboration that benefits everyone involved.

When Trust Breaks?

Breaking trust is relatively easier than building. What does it take to bring down a stack of cups that you built over time? A slight fumble, boom! The entire cup collapses. It takes literally seconds. The same goes with trust.

And if you're an engineering manager, it's a lot easier. There are many ways to break trust, and here are the most frequent ones:

- *Say X, do Y*: Being inconsistent with what you say and what you do

- *Over-promise and under-deliver*: Making commitments exceeding what you can realistically deliver and failing to meet those expectations

- *Not talking about mistakes and avoiding ownership*: Not talking about mistakes and failures at all and avoid taking ownership for the results

- *Team < Self*: Focusing on your own goals, needs, and perspectives as an engineering manager and not caring about the team and others

- *Micromanagement*: Being involved in every tiny detail and taking decisions on behalf of others

Say X, do Y

"Say X, do Y" is when you say something but do something else. As an engineering manager, you're expected to keep your integrity high in what you say and commit. When your actions contradict your words, you create a bad reputation for yourself and also for your team with external stakeholders.

Quality versus speed is always a debatable topic in engineering, and I love it. Telling your team to focus on quality but constantly pushing them to deliver on time by compromising quality is a classic case of "Say X, do Y." And moreover it leaves your team split when you say the same thing again next time. They know what's coming up: another compromise. Your team will lose trust and motivation on your words and may not engage in discussions if you tell one and do something else.

Over-Promise and Under-Deliver

It is common for managers to be ambitious and commit to unrealistic promises with projects while under delivering in terms of expectation, quality, and timeliness. This will lead to dissatisfaction from stakeholders and a loss of trust in your ability to accurately estimate and deliver on commitments.

Next on the list where managers make a lot of promises is on the promotions to their direct reports. I enthusiastically promised a couple of times when I started as a manager on seeing an individual's good performance within my team, without understanding nuances of promotion and other dynamics that comes along with it. At the end of the promotion discussion, it was decided that the individual in my team will not be promoted because of factors such as limited available positions, superior performance from individuals in other teams, and not meeting the success criteria for the next level. What was the result? A diminishing trust in me as a manager due to my well-intentioned yet overzealous promises.

Not Talking About Mistakes and Avoiding Ownership

After you make a mistake and walk away by avoiding ownership, your reliability will be questioned and trust goes down. There are 'n' number of opportunities to make mistakes. And for engineering managers, it's n+1. As you're helming the leadership role of your team, you have to make decisions swiftly. It's easy to go wrong anytime. Not owning your decision and consequences that come along with it will damage your reputation and the trust factor.

Team < Self

When you become a manager, it's not about you. It's about them: the team. Downplaying your team and showing that you're more important as an individual than them is a high degree of self-orientation that leads to lack of trust in you.

What's the highest degree of self-orientation? Passing blame when things didn't work as expected. When you represent your team to senior leadership and point fingers outward for any mistakes that happened and point fingers inward for all the success that your team has achieved is a sign of rating yourself higher than the team. It not only impacts your trust factor within your team but also outside of your team.

Micromanagement

The term *micromanagement* evokes the bothersome boss who second-guesses every decision your direct report makes, frets about the font size on the UI, or inspects all of your engineers' pull requests. This type of manager not only frustrates but seriously damages the motivation and morale of the individual.

Every manager out there has micromanaged at least once in their career; it may be during crises in their teams, not relying on an individual's ability or some assumed that's their only style of management and micromanage all the way. It's a clear sign of lack of trust in their teammates. And as we know, trust is a reciprocal effect. If we don't trust others, we don't deserve to be trusted.

We should be mindful of drawing healthy boundaries with our teammates and define the right balance according to the individual needs and preferences on the ways of working.

Rebuilding

When a trust is broken, what follows up after matters a lot.

- *Acknowledge*: First and foremost is to acknowledge specific action or incident that broke the trust by presenting yourself and owning the consequence.

- *Intent*: Show intent to address lost trust and look to rebuild it. Engage in discussions, planning course corrections and showing it in action.

- *Commitment, consistency and open communication*: Work on realistic commitment, exhibit consistent behavior and performance, be transparent and timely communicate about updates.

- *Ask for feedback*: Ask for regular feedback on how things have improved from the time when the trust was broken.

- *Regain trust*: This is the moment when you start to feel the trust has been regained. You look to continue the momentum and learn from the past experience.

The more consistent you exhibit behavior and show intent for rebuilding trust whenever it is broken, the more reliable you'll be regarded among the people that you work with.

Summary

You have seen for yourself that earning trust is hard. As a new engineering manager, you should focus on building trust and continue to build it forever.

By now, you should be able to:

- Recognize trust as a core component of leadership, understanding it's built over time through consistent, authentic actions and communication with your team, stakeholders, and manager.

- Employ strategies for building and maintaining trust, such as transparency, empathy, and vulnerability, to create a solid foundation for effective team leadership.

- Foster personal connections and mutual respect, acknowledging the importance of getting to know your team members beyond their professional roles to strengthen trust and collaboration.

- Balance autonomy and guidance, demonstrating trust in your team's capabilities while providing support and feedback, avoiding micromanagement to promote growth and self-reliance.

- Navigate and repair broken trust, adopting a clear approach to acknowledge mistakes, communicate intentions for improvement, and actively work to rebuild trust when necessary.

With established trust, you're well positioned to drive change that your team needs, be transparent about an individual's performance, and make swift, timely decisions knowing that your team supports you while also openly challenging you when necessary.

CHAPTER 4

Mindful One-on-Ones

Your people are your core asset.

Successful engineering managers are not successful by themselves but by making their people successful. To truly drive success, you need to understand what motivates each team member, what their goals are, and how you can support them in overcoming challenges in their work and, where appropriate, provide flexibility or understanding for personal life challenges.

A mindful one-on-one meeting is a key opportunity to deepen this understanding. It's a chance for you to engage with your team on a personal level, to listen attentively to their concerns, and to provide meaningful guidance. During these meetings, you should aim to uncover what drives them, what they are passionate about, and where they might be struggling. This includes not only their professional responsibilities but also any personal issues that might be impacting their work.

Effective one-on-ones are not just about discussing tasks or project updates; they are about creating a supportive environment where your team members feel heard and valued. By addressing their motivations and challenges thoughtfully, you can offer the support they need to excel. Whether it's through providing resources, adjusting workloads, or simply offering a listening ear, your role is to ensure that your team members have what they need to thrive both professionally and personally.

In essence, your ability to connect deeply with your team and to respond to their needs is fundamental to fostering a successful, productive, and motivated team.

You Care About Being Prepared

Preparation is key to an effective one-on-one meeting. Frequently arriving late or unprepared can signal a lack of respect for your direct report's time and contributions, leading to decreased motivation. Being well-prepared shows genuine care and respect for the meeting and the individual.

© Ananth Ramachandran 2024
A. Ramachandran, *The Complete Engineering Manager*, https://doi.org/10.1007/979-8-8688-0267-6_4

To prepare, review notes and relevant documents at least 10 minutes before the meeting. This helps you track progress and identify key discussion points. Keeping a one-on-one document with observations on performance—both positive and concerning—also ensures you address important issues. Additionally, your mental state and how you start the conversation are crucial. A negative mindset from past interactions can affect the meeting's quality. Approach with a calm, composed demeanor to foster a more productive and positive environment.

Imagine you are preparing for a one-on-one meeting with Sam, a software engineer who has been working on a challenging project. You've noted from previous meetings that Sam has been struggling with meeting deadlines, and there's also been a recent team reorganization that might be affecting their performance.

You: "Hi Sam, thanks for meeting with me today. I reviewed our notes and saw we talked about tight deadlines. How are you managing the project?"

Sam: "It's been quite challenging. The new team structure shifted responsibilities, and I'm struggling to keep up with the new deadlines."

You: "I understand. Can you tell me which aspects of the new structure are the most difficult for you?"

Sam: "The added tasks from the revised roles are affecting my ability to meet my core responsibilities."

You: "Got it. I can review your priorities and deadlines and look into additional support. Is there anything else on your mind?"

Sam: "No, that's everything. Thanks for your help."

You: "We'll make these adjustments and follow up next week. Let me know if you need anything before then."

This conversation illustrates the importance of being prepared for your one-on-one meetings. By reviewing past discussions and coming to the meeting with a clear focus, you can effectively address your direct report's concerns, show that you value their input, and provide meaningful support to help them navigate their challenges.

You Care About Listening to Them

Listening with full attention during one-on-one meetings is the best way to show your direct reports that you value their input. Take notes on their points and let them finish speaking before asking any clarifying questions. Respond thoughtfully after reflecting on what they've shared. This meeting isn't about dominating the conversation; instead, focus on maintaining a conversational tone where your primary role is to listen.

I find this quote about listening particularly insightful: "Listen to understand, not to respond." By truly understanding your direct reports, asking clarifying questions, and responding constructively, you'll make the conversation more meaningful and effective.

You Care About Their Opinion

Creating a safe environment in one-on-one meetings where your team members feel comfortable discussing their opinions is essential for building trust and fostering open communication. As an engineering manager, one-on-one is your opportunity to not just manage tasks but to understand the thoughts, concerns, and ideas of your direct reports on a deeper level. In these meetings, your approach to listening and responding plays a critical role in whether your team members feel secure enough to share their honest opinions.

When a team member shares their opinion during a one-on-one, the first step is to make them feel heard and valued. This means actively listening without interrupting, showing genuine interest in what they're saying, and responding thoughtfully. A simple acknowledgment, like saying "Thank you for sharing that" can go a long way in reinforcing that their input is appreciated. By doing this, you create a space where they know their voice matters.

It's also important to encourage them to share more. You can do this by asking open-ended questions such as "What do you think about the recent changes in our team's scope?" or "Do you have any thoughts on how we could approach this project differently?" These questions invite your team members to express their views and signal that you are genuinely interested in their perspective.

Moreover, when discussing opinions in one-on-ones, your tone and body language should convey that you are open to their ideas and not just going through the motions. If they sense that their opinions are merely being tolerated rather than considered, they may become reluctant to share in the future. Therefore, ensure that your responses are constructive, even if you disagree. Instead of dismissing an idea outright, explore it with them—ask for more details, discuss potential challenges, and brainstorm together on how it could be implemented or improved.

By consistently creating this safe and encouraging environment during one-on-ones, you build a foundation of trust where your team members feel comfortable sharing their true thoughts and opinions, knowing they will be met with respect and consideration. This not only enhances the quality of your communication but also strengthens your team's cohesion and effectiveness.

You Care About Following Up

Following up on previous discussions is a crucial part of any effective one-on-one meeting. It's easy to overlook this step, especially when there are new topics to discuss or pressing matters to address. However, consistent follow-up is just as important as the initial conversation itself. When you take the time to revisit action items or concerns from previous meetings, you demonstrate a genuine commitment to your direct report's progress and well-being.

Imagine that in your last one-on-one, you and your direct report discussed a plan for improving a particular skill or overcoming a specific challenge. If you fail to follow up in subsequent meetings, it can signal that those conversations weren't as important as they initially seemed. Over time, this can lead to disengagement, as your team members might feel that their growth and challenges aren't being taken seriously.

To avoid this, make it a point to start each one-on-one with a brief check-in on how things have progressed since your last conversation. After the initial lighter discussion on how they're feeling or what's on their mind, smoothly transition into following up on previous topics. You might say something like, "Last time we talked about working on [specific skill or task]. How has that been going?" This not only shows that you remember the conversation but also that you're genuinely interested in their development.

By consistently following up, you help to keep the momentum going, ensuring that the goals and action items discussed in one-on-ones don't fall by the wayside. This approach fosters accountability and shows your direct report that you're invested in their continued growth and success.

You Care About Asking Right Questions

Asking the right questions during a one-on-one meeting with your direct report is one of the most effective ways to ensure that the conversation is meaningful and productive. When you pose clear, to-the-point questions, you not only demonstrate your preparation and focus, but you also signal to your team members that you value their time and insights. Good questions have the power to provoke thoughtful discussions, uncover new perspectives, and even bring about realizations that can be transformative for both you and your direct report.

The key to a successful one-on-one isn't just in the answers you provide or the solutions you offer, but in the questions you ask. These questions can guide the conversation, helping your direct report reflect on their work, goals, challenges, and overall well-being. It's important to strike a balance between asking questions and listening attentively, creating a dialogue that feels collaborative rather than directive. Remember, the goal of a one-on-one is not just to check off agenda items but to engage in a meaningful exchange that benefits both parties.

Additionally, encourage your direct report to bring their own questions to the table. This fosters a two-way conversation where they feel empowered to seek clarification, voice concerns, or explore new ideas. When you prioritize questioning and listening over simply detailing your thoughts or interrupting with advice, you create an environment where your direct report feels heard, respected, and supported.

Here are some questions that you can ask during your one-on-ones as an engineering manager, drawing inspiration from a variety of themes:

Growth and Development

What skills would you like to develop in the coming months?

How do you feel about your current career trajectory?

Are there any projects or responsibilities you'd like to take on to grow your skills?

What kind of training or resources do you think would help you achieve your goals?

Is there a particular area where you feel you need more support or guidance?

Current Challenges

What obstacles are you currently facing in your work?

How do you feel about your workload—too much, too little, or just right?

Are there any team dynamics that you find challenging?

How can I help you overcome any challenges you're experiencing?

Is there anything about the current project that's causing you concern?

Feedback and Improvement

What feedback do you have for me as your manager?

Are there areas where you think the team could improve?

How do you feel about the feedback you've been receiving—too much, too little, or just right?

Are there any processes or tools you think we should reconsider or improve?

How can we improve our communication or collaboration?

Well-Being and Work-Life Balance

How are you feeling about your work-life balance right now?

Are there any personal or work-related issues affecting your well-being?

Do you feel you have enough time and space to recharge outside of work?

How can I support you in maintaining a healthy work-life balance?

Is there anything we could adjust to make your workload more manageable?

These questions are designed to be open-ended, inviting your direct report to share their thoughts and feelings more freely. By asking these questions, you create an opportunity for deeper insight, allowing you to support your team members more effectively and strengthen your working relationship.

You Care About Their Career

Your direct reports' career growth is directly tied to your success as an engineering manager. When you invest in their development, you're not just helping them advance professionally; you're also fostering a more skilled and motivated team. To initiate meaningful career conversations during your one-on-one meetings, start by asking them about their career goals and where they envision themselves in a year. This approach gives you insight into their aspirations and allows you to become a supportive partner in helping them achieve those goals.

It's essential to regularly discuss their learning objectives and career ambitions, ideally at least once a month. By doing so, you can keep their career development front and center in your ongoing conversations. Ask them what projects or initiatives would align with their career goals and provide opportunities for growth. This not only helps them build the skills they need but also keeps them engaged and motivated by working on tasks that are meaningful to them.

Additionally, check in on their progress toward these goals. Ask if they need any specific support, whether it's from you directly or from others within the organization who could provide guidance or mentorship. It's easy for team members to lose sight of their long-term career objectives when they're caught up in day-to-day tasks. As their manager, it's your responsibility to remind them of their goals and to help them stay on track.

One important aspect of this is ensuring they have the time and space to focus on their development. If they're overwhelmed with their current workload, consider whether some responsibilities can be offloaded or delegated, allowing them to dedicate more time to learning and career advancement. By actively supporting their career growth, you demonstrate that you are committed to their success, which in turn builds a stronger, more capable team.

You Care About Sharing/Asking for Feedback

Sharing and asking for feedback is one of the most challenging yet essential tasks for an engineering manager. Many new managers struggle with this, often failing to provide the insightful, actionable feedback that their team members need to grow. When feedback is vague such as simply saying, "You're doing well" or "You're not doing well," it's almost as if no feedback was given at all. If you truly care about your direct reports and want them to value your feedback, it's crucial to structure it in a way that is clear, specific, and focused on improvement.

- *Explanation*: Start by explaining the situation where your direct report either didn't perform up to expectations or where there's room for significant improvement. Be specific—describe the context, the actions they took, and the outcomes. This helps to ground your feedback in concrete examples, making it easier for your report to understand exactly what you're addressing.

- *Clarification*: After explaining, check in with your report to ensure they understand the feedback. This is a two-way conversation, so if they disagree with your assessment, listen to their perspective. Understanding their viewpoint is key to making sure the feedback process is productive. If they agree, you can move forward; if they don't, this is an opportunity to discuss and align on the issues at hand.

- *Understanding*: Once the feedback is clarified and agreed upon, delve deeper into understanding the root cause of the situation. Ask questions that help identify whether the issue stems from a gap in technical skills, a misunderstanding of expectations, or challenges with communication, collaboration, or attitude. This step is crucial because it allows you to pinpoint the underlying problem and address it directly.

- *Follow-up*: Feedback shouldn't end with a single conversation. If the issue involves soft skills, observe how your direct report is improving in that area. If it's a technical skill gap, work with them to create a learning plan and check in regularly on their progress in subsequent one-on-one meetings. This ongoing support and attention show that you're committed to their development and are actively helping them improve.

- *Performance Improvement Plan (PIP)*: In cases where performance or attitude continues to decline despite your feedback and efforts to support improvement, it may become necessary to implement a performance improvement plan (PIP). This should be a last resort, but it's an important tool for setting clear expectations and timelines for improvement. If the steps taken don't result in the desired progress, the PIP provides a structured approach to addressing these ongoing issues.

New engineering managers often shy away from giving critical feedback because they fear it might damage their relationship with their direct reports. However, the opposite is usually true. If you withhold critical feedback and only bring it up during formal performance reviews, it can come as a shock, eroding trust and leaving your report feeling blindsided. Regular, detailed feedback during one-on-one meetings helps avoid such surprises and allows your direct reports to grow continuously.

When delivering critical feedback, avoid the common mistake of sugarcoating it. Don't start with a positive comment and then slip the critical feedback in the middle, as this can dilute the message. Instead, be direct and clear, ensuring that the feedback is understood and taken seriously. Your goal is to communicate effectively so that your direct report can make the necessary changes and continue to develop professionally.

You Care About Them as a Person

Understanding your team members as individuals is crucial for fostering a strong, supportive work environment. As an engineering manager, it's essential to connect with your team members beyond their professional roles. Building a genuine, human connection with your direct reports can greatly enhance their engagement, motivation, and overall well-being.

To create this connection, start by showing interest in their personal lives. Begin your one-on-one meetings with casual, sincere questions about their day-to-day experiences. Ask how they've been feeling, what they did over the weekend, or if they've had any recent highlights. These simple inquiries show that you care about their lives outside of work, reinforcing that you see them as whole people, not just as employees.

For example, if you're aware that a team member's child was ill recently, follow up by asking how their child is doing. If you know someone who enjoys traveling, inquire about their favorite travel destinations or tips for planning a trip. These personal touches demonstrate that you are interested in their well-being beyond the workplace.

Connecting on a personal level can foster a more trusting and open relationship, making team members feel more valued and supported. This approach not only enhances individual morale but also strengthens team dynamics, leading to a more positive and productive work environment. By caring about your team members as people, you contribute to their overall satisfaction and success, both professionally and personally.

CHAPTER 5

Managing Performance

Managing performance in engineering teams is a hard nut to crack.

The more you gain experience as an engineering manager and the more you work with diverse individuals, the better you will be at managing their performance. Needless to say, performance is not a constant but an ever-changing aspect. An individual who is performing well today may not perform as expected in the future due to various reasons: new projects, new technology that they haven't worked with before, team dynamics affecting their productivity—you name it.

As an engineering manager, one of your key responsibilities is to monitor an individual's performance in peaks and troughs, and you care about noticing and asking them to understand their perspective and the challenges that they're going through.

In this chapter, I'll give you tools and frameworks to navigate the intricacies of performance management like a pro.

- *People performance dynamics*: Understand people's perspective better and get a 360° view of team dynamics that could impact your people's performance.

- *Performance criteria and calibration*: Define performance criteria to review engineers on the same scale compared to other teams in your organization and how to calibrate.

- *The Writing part*: Write effective performance reviews that's specific, actionable, and relatable.

- *The Conversation*: Have a mindful and forward-looking conversation for you and your direct reports.

First things first—let's understand the dynamics around people, your team and organization, and how it could have an impact on your people's performance.

© Ananth Ramachandran 2024
A. Ramachandran, *The Complete Engineering Manager*, https://doi.org/10.1007/979-8-8688-0267-6_5

Dynamics Around People Performance

Let's start with the old-school definition of what is a performance. Performance is how well one performs their role and responsibilities and achieves goals and objectives set for them in a timely manner with an agreed quality. Not achieving them or falling short is considered low performance.

I have seen people being assessed even without letting them know what the goals and objectives of their role are. How would you expect them to perform their role better or even assess their performance? Start off with having a session with your direct report where you discuss expectations of their role and responsibilities and clarify the success criteria at the very beginning.

Factors Affecting People's Performance

You just had a performance review conversation with a low performer, John. You were recalling from your memory what you conveyed to him, "Hey, John, you didn't perform well this quarter against performance criteria set for you, and there were few concerns on your communication as well, so you've got 2 out of 5." John's expression was clueless and at the same time fearful. On the other hand, you were clueless as well on what was happening with John and what led to his poor performance as you didn't care about asking them now and didn't check in regularly as well.

What could be some reasons that led to John's poor performance (Figure 5-1)?

- The performance criteria was never discussed.

- He had personal health issues that could have impacted his performance.

- His work was always dependent on the team. If someone in the team doesn't perform well, it's impacting his work.

- He had skill gaps that led him and the team to deliver low-quality results later than expected. Skill gaps can be in technical skills, collaboration skills, or communication skills that affect working with others efficiently.

- Too much context switching impacted his performance.

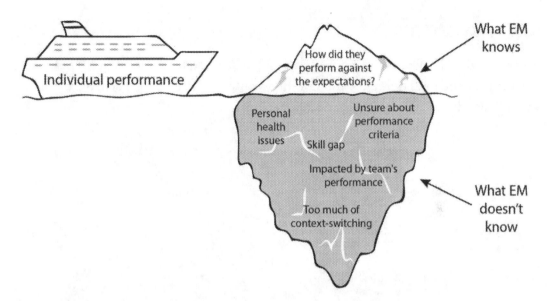

Figure 5-1. Individual's performance—influencing factors

If an individual isn't performing well, you might be part of the problem too:

- Have you discussed the performance criteria with the individual and made them understand well ahead?

- Were they overloaded with too many different topics that could impact their performance?

- Were those performance issues solely because of the individual's inability or due to the team dynamics?

Make sure you understand the factors affecting your people's performance by discussing them regularly in one-on-ones and team retrospectives. Remember, every performance will have a backstory. As an EM, you should work closely with your direct reports to understand their backstory and what has led to their not-so-good performance. An unproductive environment or frequently changing priorities can affect people's performance, and if these issues are left unaddressed, you will be trying to fix something else which may not be the real problem. There's no denying that you have your own share as a manager in your people's performance whether it is a good or bad performance.

Team Dynamics

To assess your people's performance, you need to understand the team dynamics (Figure 5-2), the roles they play, and how they contribute to the larger scheme of things, in other words, the organization goals and purpose.

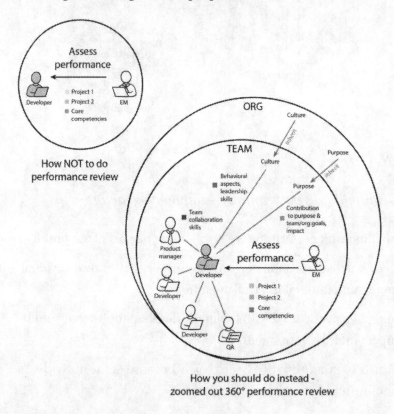

Figure 5-2. *360° Performance review*

Define Your Team

Start by defining your team. Not understanding the team dynamics could have an impact on your people's performance as they may not know the purpose of the team and what their success means to the organization. Remember that the motivation of your people has a direct impact on their performance, and your primary responsibility is to set them up for success.

- *Nature of your team*: Define who you are as a team and what you do. If you are a cross-functional team, you might be focusing on one specific domain or subdomain in your organization. Define that in the very beginning.

- *Your team's core values*: Probably you will inherit core values defined for your organization; however, you can override or extend according to your team's nature.

- *Your team's purpose*: Define why your team exists and how you contribute to the organization's purpose and goals. If you're an infrastructure team, your team's purpose is to enable other internal teams to work efficiently by building tools.

- *Roles and Responsibilities*: Define roles and responsibilities in your team, their dependencies and ways of working together.

Once the team is well-defined, it's important to make everyone in your team understand how the performance of one impacts others and eventually impacts the team itself.

Sum of Individual Performance Is Not Exactly Same as the Team's Performance

All your individuals are performing well, and they have received good ratings in the recently completed performance review. On the other hand, your team's performance is not up to the mark, and you were questioned why that is the case even though individuals are performing well.

Here are some possibilities:

- *Your team might be working on the wrong priorities*: Even though the work is getting completed as expected and everyone in your team is performing well, your team hasn't achieved the intended target for business as your team was working with wrong priorities.

- *Your team often gets blocked by other teams*: Because of the lack of sync between teams, your team's work is always blocked by other teams, and dependencies weren't factored in at the earliest.

Individual 1 performance + Individual 2 performance + … + Individual N performance ≠ Team's Performance

---

The sum of the individual performance doesn't necessarily equate to team's performance, and most importantly you're responsible to align them and lead your team to optimal performance, if they are working on wrong priorities or if they often get blocked by other teams. If the heart is in the right place and performance reviews are done thoughtfully, it can be enriching and contribute to your people's success and growth, ultimately contributing to your team's success.

Goal Setting

Measuring performance without setting clear goals is like asking an athlete to run a race without knowing where the finish line is. Without a defined target, the effort lacks direction, motivation wanes, and there's no solid basis for evaluating progress or identifying areas for improvement. Performance should be seen as the output—an outcome that results from fine-tuning various inputs like role specification, level expectations, and, crucially, the goals that have been set. As an engineering manager, you play a vital role in refining these inputs to guide each individual on your team toward success.

When setting goals for team members, it's essential that the goals serve two primary purposes: they should foster the individual's personal growth and career development, and they should contribute to the success of the team and the organization. If engineers don't perceive the value of these goals in advancing their careers—even if the goals benefit the organization—they will eventually lose motivation. For example, you might assign an engineer to deploy the same script every day, explaining that this task will generate significant revenue for the business. They might carry out the task a few times, but by the fourth day, they'll likely be seeking something more challenging, something that stimulates their curiosity and helps them grow professionally.

So, how do you assist your direct reports in setting goals that are both ambitious and aligned with the organization's needs? Where do you begin? And how can you fine-tune the other input metrics to enhance their performance? The process can seem daunting, but don't worry—you can set, facilitate, track, and achieve goals effectively by following a structured approach.

- *Set*: Using the SMART framework, set goals collaboratively with the individual that are challenging to them and impactful to your organization.

- *Facilitate*: Facilitate the individual in attaining their goals by creating time, resources, and environment.

- *Track*: Identify key performance indicators to track the progress made on goals on a regular basis and course correct based on change in priorities. Be clear about success criteria.

- *Achieve*: Strive for the successful completion of goals, celebrating achievements and learning from failures. Once a goal is achieved, reflect on the process to identify lessons learned and discuss the next steps for continued growth and development. Encourage the individual to set new goals or build upon their recent successes, reinforcing a culture of continuous improvement and ambition.

Set: Establishing Clear and Effective Goals

The first step in the goal-setting process is to work collaboratively with your team members to establish clear and effective goals. These goals should be well-defined, measurable, and aligned with both the individual's career aspirations and the organization's objectives.

- *Clarity and Specificity*: The goals must be precise and unambiguous. Vague goals lead to confusion and lack of focus. A clear goal provides a specific target for your team member to aim for, ensuring that their efforts are directed toward a concrete outcome.

- *Measurability*: It's crucial that goals have measurable criteria. This allows both you and your team member to track progress and determine when the goal has been achieved. Without measurable outcomes, it's difficult to assess performance objectively.

- *Alignment*: Goals should align with the broader objectives of the team and the organization. They should not only contribute to the engineer's personal growth but also advance the company's strategic goals. This alignment ensures that individual success is tied to organizational success, creating a win-win scenario.

- *Challenge and Motivation*: While goals should be realistic, they should also be challenging enough to push your team members out of their comfort zones. The right level of challenge fosters growth, engagement, and a sense of accomplishment once the goal is achieved.

Facilitate: Providing the Support Needed to Succeed

Once goals are set, your next responsibility is to facilitate the conditions that enable your team members to succeed. This involves creating an environment where they have the time, resources, and support necessary to achieve their goals.

- *Time Management*: Ensure that your team members have enough time to focus on their goals. This might involve reallocating responsibilities or shielding them from distractions. Effective time management is crucial for maintaining focus and momentum.

- *Resource Allocation*: Provide access to the tools, training, and resources needed to accomplish the goals. This could include software, mentorship, training programs, or any other resources that will support the individual in their efforts.

- *Environment and Culture*: Cultivate an environment that encourages collaboration, innovation, and open communication. Regular check-ins, constructive feedback, and a supportive team culture can significantly enhance an engineer's ability to meet their goals. Your role is to remove obstacles and create a space where your team members can thrive.

Track: Monitoring Progress and Adjusting Course

Tracking progress is essential to ensure that goals stay on course. Regular monitoring allows you to identify potential issues early and make necessary adjustments.

- *Key Performance Indicators (KPIs)*: Identify the key metrics that will help you gauge progress toward the goals. Regularly reviewing these KPIs will help you and your team members understand whether they are on track or if any changes need to be made.

- *Regular Check-ins*: Schedule regular meetings to discuss progress. These check-ins are opportunities to provide feedback, address challenges, and adjust goals if priorities have shifted. They also help maintain momentum and keep the engineer engaged and motivated.

- *Flexibility*: Be prepared to adjust goals as circumstances change. Whether it's a shift in organizational priorities, unforeseen challenges, or new opportunities, staying flexible ensures that goals remain relevant and achievable.

Achieve: Reaching the Goal and Reflecting on the Journey

The final step is to push for the achievement of the goals and then reflect on the process.

- *Celebrating Success*: Once a goal is achieved, it's important to acknowledge and celebrate the success. Recognition boosts morale and reinforces the value of the effort put in. Celebrations can be as simple as a team acknowledgment or as significant as a formal recognition within the organization.

- *Reflection and Learning*: After achieving a goal, conduct a post-mortem or retrospective to reflect on what went well and what could have been done better. This reflection is critical for continuous improvement. It helps identify strengths to build on and areas for growth, providing valuable insights for future goal-setting.

- *Sharing Success*: Share the success stories within your organization. Highlighting the impact of achieving these goals not only boosts the individual's and team's reputation but also sets a positive example for others. It shows that the goals set are not just checkboxes but meaningful contributions to the organization's success.

Now, it's your turn: Using the principles of setting, facilitating, tracking, and achieving goals, create a structured development plan for the following team members. Answer the questions for each individual to develop their goals.

1. *John: Senior Engineer Aspiring to Become a Staff Engineer*
   Learning Goal:

   - *What specific skill or knowledge does John need to acquire to advance from a senior engineer to a staff engineer?*

   - *How will you measure John's progress in mastering this new skill?*

   - *What resources and support will John need to achieve this learning goal?*

   - *By when should John complete this learning goal?*

   Impact Goal:

   - *What significant project or initiative can John lead to demonstrate his readiness for a staff engineer role?*

   - *What measurable outcomes will indicate the success of this project or initiative?*

   - *What support will John need to effectively lead this project?*

   - *What is the timeline for achieving this impact goal?*

2. *Williams: Mid-Level Engineer Struggling with Performance*
   Learning Goal:

   - *What specific skills or areas of knowledge does Williams need to focus on to address his performance issues?*

   - *How will you measure Williams' progress in improving these critical areas?*

- *What immediate resources, training, or mentoring will Williams need to address his performance deficiencies?*

- *By when should Williams show measurable improvement in these areas to demonstrate that he is on the path to recovery?*

Impact Goal:

- *What critical project or task can Williams undertake that will directly address and improve his performance issues?*

- *What specific, measurable outcomes will demonstrate that Williams has successfully addressed his performance issues?*

- *What types of support and feedback mechanisms will be put in place to assist Williams in meeting these goals and improving his performance?*

- *What is the timeline for seeing significant improvements in Williams' performance, and what are the key milestones to track his progress?*

Use these questions to craft detailed, actionable goals for John and Williams, ensuring they are tailored to their individual needs and aligned with their development paths and organizational objectives.

Performance Review 101

Carrying out a fair and unbiased performance review is not easy. If you're not understanding the system and rationale behind it, it's next to impossible. Individuals' performance in your teams is measured on a *scale* against a set of *criteria* defined for their respective *level* and job *function*. Let's take a look at terminologies first with some practical insights on specific cases and later put it together.

Scale

Get the Basics Right

Before conducting a performance review for your direct reports, ensure you clearly understand the assessment scale (Figure 5-3) being used in your organization. Different engineering managers may interpret performance ratings in various ways. For one manager, a score of 3 out of 5 may indicate that an individual is performing at a mediocre level, while for another, it may mean that the individual has met the established expectations.

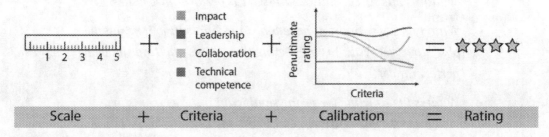

Figure 5-3. *Scale + Criteria + Calibration = Rating*

Start by understanding the fundamentals of the rating scale and what each number signifies in relation to your team members' performance. To rate an individual above a 3, they should have exceeded expectations by going the extra mile—such as mentoring others, helping onboard new engineers, and leading impactful projects. Additionally, consider whether the engineer's contributions are visible to your manager and the leadership group. If they are, that visibility strengthens the justification for a higher rating.

Performing at the Next Level

As the term suggests, these are individuals who are performing beyond their current job level—such as a senior engineer operating at the level of a staff engineer or a mid-level engineer functioning at the senior level. I recommend evaluating candidates not just based on their current level but also in relation to the next level. This helps identify how close they are to achieving it and what skills and behaviors they need to develop.

3/5 Is Not Bad at All

As you can see from the scale, a score of 3 out of 5 is actually quite satisfactory. It indicates that the individual met expectations. This scale differs from a school report card, where a perfect score of 100 out of 100 implies full performance. It's important to communicate this perspective to your direct report as well.

Unacceptable Performance

Unacceptable performance occurs when individuals fail to operate at their expected level, which in turn detrimentally impact the overall effectiveness of the team. This situation may manifest in several ways, including missed deadlines, which can disrupt project timelines, and a noticeable decline in the quality of work produced. Additionally, if there are underlying issues related to attitude or behavior, the impact can be even more pronounced, leading to decreased morale and collaboration among team members. Addressing unacceptable performance is crucial for maintaining a high-functioning team and ensuring that everyone is contributing to their fullest capacity.

Performance Criteria

Performance criteria serve as the foundation for evaluating the contributions of each member within an engineering team. While these criteria can differ from one organization to another, they usually remain consistent across various teams within the same company, reflecting the core values and objectives that drive the business.

As an engineering manager, it's crucial to ensure these criteria are not only well-defined but also manageable. Some organizations make the mistake of piling on too many performance criteria, which can overwhelm the process and dilute its effectiveness. Instead, these criteria should be crafted thoughtfully—comprehensive enough to capture the full scope of an engineer's contributions, yet focused enough to remain practical. Typically, the responsibility for creating these criteria lies with the HR or people management team. However, your role as an engineering manager is pivotal in ensuring that these criteria are relevant, applicable, and aligned with the day-to-day realities of your team. If you ever find yourself questioning how to apply these metrics, your HR team should be your first point of contact.

Let's explore some of the most common performance criteria for engineering teams and consider how they can be applied in real-world scenarios.

Impact

Impact is perhaps the most critical criterion for evaluating an engineer's performance. It's about more than just the work they do; it's about the tangible difference their efforts make to the product, the team, and the organization as a whole. Impact is multifaceted, touching on everything from technical achievements to broader business outcomes.

Consider the engineer who, through sheer determination and skill, finds a way to significantly improve the performance of a key system. Their technical expertise doesn't just solve an immediate problem; it enhances the product's reliability and scalability, creating a ripple effect that benefits the entire organization. But impact isn't limited to technical feats. Think about how this same engineer might mentor a less experienced colleague, guiding them through a challenging project and, in doing so, elevating the entire team's performance. Their influence extends beyond code; it shapes the team's success.

Then there's the business side of impact. Imagine an engineer who plays a crucial role in delivering a feature that customers absolutely love. The release not only meets a critical deadline but also opens up new business opportunities, contributing directly to the company's bottom line. That's impactful—real, measurable, and significant.

Impact also has a cultural dimension. A strong engineer doesn't just blend into the team; they help define what the team stands for. They lead by example, fostering a culture of excellence, collaboration, and innovation. Their impact is felt not just in what they build, but in how they shape the team's identity.

Leadership

Leadership in an engineering context goes beyond traditional notions of management. It's about how an individual steps up when it matters most—whether that's leading a high-stakes project, navigating a crisis, or guiding the team through a complex problem. Leadership is shown in those moments when an engineer takes charge, not because they have to, but because the situation demands it.

Picture an engineer leading a critical project. They are the one who ensures that everything runs smoothly, that deadlines are met, and that quality is never compromised. When challenges arise—as they inevitably do—they don't shy away. Instead, they face them head-on, rallying the team, making tough decisions, and finding solutions that work.

Leadership also reveals itself in more subtle ways. Consider the engineer who sees a problem that others have overlooked—a gap in the process, a potential risk, or an opportunity for improvement. They don't wait for someone else to address it; they take the initiative. They raise their hand, propose a solution, and lead the effort to implement it. This kind of proactive leadership is invaluable, especially in fast-paced engineering environments.

Cultural leadership is another crucial aspect. It's about setting the tone for how the team operates—how they handle success and, just as importantly, how they handle failure. A true leader doesn't just celebrate the wins; they learn from the losses, turning setbacks into opportunities for growth.

Integrity

Integrity is the bedrock of any effective engineering team. It's about more than just honesty; it's about being dependable, transparent, and committed to continuous self-improvement. An engineer with integrity is someone you can count on, not just to deliver on their commitments, but to do so in a way that aligns with the team's values and goals.

Imagine an engineer who is facing a particularly tough challenge. They could take the easy route—cut corners, cover up mistakes, or shift the blame. But instead, they choose the harder path. They acknowledge the difficulties they're facing, are transparent about the challenges, and work tirelessly to overcome them. They're not afraid to admit when they don't have all the answers and are always willing to ask for help or offer support to others. Their commitment to doing the right thing, even when it's not the easiest thing, sets a standard for the entire team.

Integrity also involves a deep sense of responsibility. This engineer is team-oriented, always thinking about the bigger picture, but they also know the importance of self-care and personal growth. They're constantly seeking ways to improve, both as an individual and as a team member, ensuring that their contributions are sustainable and aligned with the long-term goals of the team and the organization.

Collaboration

In an engineering team, collaboration is not just a nice-to-have; it's essential. It's about how well an individual works with others to achieve common goals. Collaboration goes beyond mere cooperation—it's about being an active, engaged member of the team, someone who not only shares knowledge but also amplifies the abilities of those around them.

Think of an engineer who excels at collaboration. They're not just focused on their tasks; they're always looking for ways to support their colleagues. Whether it's through mentoring, code reviews, or simply being available to discuss challenges, they're a force multiplier, making the whole team better through their contributions.

Cross-functional collaboration is equally important. This engineer knows how to work effectively with stakeholders from other teams—product management, design, operations—ensuring that everyone is aligned and moving toward the same goal. Their communication is clear and effective, whether they're writing a technical document or presenting an idea in a meeting. They understand that successful engineering is as much about communication as it is about code.

As an engineering manager, your role is to assess these criteria based on real, tangible examples from your team's work. These evaluations shouldn't be rushed or left to the last minute. Instead, they should be an ongoing conversation, woven into the fabric of your day-to-day interactions with your team. While the criteria outlined here provide a solid foundation, it's essential to tailor them to the specific needs and dynamics of your team. Set clear expectations with your direct reports, and ensure that everyone understands what success looks like in your unique context.

Can a Skill Be a Performance Criteria?

It's important to distinguish between skill and performance, as they are not the same thing. While skills are undoubtedly valuable, they are not, by themselves, a direct measure of performance. A highly skilled engineer may possess an impressive array of technical abilities, but if they do not apply those skills effectively within the context of their role, they may not meet the performance criteria set for them. Conversely, an engineer with more modest skills might exceed expectations by leveraging their abilities in ways that significantly contribute to the team's success.

This distinction is crucial for engineering managers to understand. Performance is not merely about the depth or breadth of an engineer's skill set; it's about how those skills are applied to deliver results that align with the team's and the organization's goals. An engineer might know every programming language under the sun, but if they struggle to work within the team, meet deadlines, or solve problems effectively, their performance will fall short.

Think of it like a dancer. It's not about how many dance moves they know but how they execute those moves when it matters—on stage, under the spotlight. The true measure of performance is in the delivery, not just the potential. In the same way, an engineer's value to the team is ultimately judged by how they perform in real-world scenarios, not just by the skills they've mastered.

So, while skills are important, they are not performance criteria in themselves. Performance is about taking those skills and translating them into meaningful contributions that drive success. As an engineering manager, your focus should be on how well an engineer uses their skills to make an impact, rather than on the skills alone.

Calibration

Calibration is the process of standardizing the performance ratings of engineers across multiple teams by applying a consistent set of criteria. Different engineering managers may have varying perspectives on how to rate performance, so after you've completed your initial assessment of your direct reports, you'll meet with other EMs within the same organizational unit to review and discuss the ratings each of you has given, along with the reasoning behind those decisions.

These discussions are particularly important when it comes to evaluating outliers—those who receive the highest or lowest ratings, as well as cases where promotions are being considered. For instance, there might be situations where two EMs have proposed promotions for their respective team members, but only one promotion slot is available. Calibration helps ensure that these decisions are made fairly and consistently across teams.

The goal of calibration is not to rank engineers against each other across different teams, but rather to establish a common understanding and resolve any discrepancies or disagreements among EMs. If you're a new EM, your first few calibration sessions can be challenging as you learn the process. You might worry about making mistakes or feel uneasy if your proposals aren't accepted. It's important to approach these sessions with an open mind, understanding that the purpose is to collaborate with your fellow EMs to reach a fair and unbiased decision, rather than feeling judged.

It's also crucial to remember that calibration discussions are confidential. They are meant to help EMs conduct an impartial and fair performance review across teams and not necessarily have to be shared with your direct reports.

The Writing Part

And you open your calendar one fine morning to find that performance review discussion with your direct report is happening the next day. You've realized that you can't postpone writing it anymore and the time has come. To make it worse, you don't have quick notes and data to back up writing the performance review. It's going to be hard. Chances of ending up writing a generic and not-much-to-say type of review is quite high unless you defy the odds and go onto write one that is specific, actionable, and relatable to their actual performance backed up by data.

Writing a performance review doesn't happen in a day. In fact, it can. Only if data that you infer, perspectives that you build about their performance, specific cases, and next steps are readily available. Where do you start? What to write? How would you convey "the good, the bad, and the ugly" parts in writing? What tone and word choices will you go with? Believe it or not, performance reviews are emotional and personal to the individuals. Putting some effort and thought into it and being mindful of how you express your feedback in writing will be much appreciated.

Writing a performance review is a three-step process (Figure 5-4): **Prep up, write up, and wrap up**. Prep up is a phase that happens before sitting to write a performance review gathering references and sources to consider. In the write-up phase, you write a meaty performance review that is specific and relatable. You wrap up by writing actionable next steps and what follows up after the performance review in the wrap-up phase.

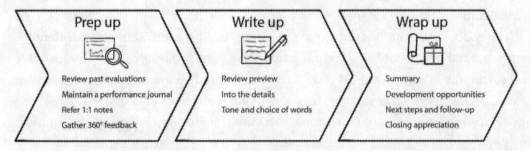

Prep up	Write up	Wrap up
Review past evaluations	Review preview	Summary
Maintain a performance journal	Into the details	Development opportunities
Refer 1:1 notes	Tone and choice of words	Next steps and follow-up
Gather 360° feedback		Closing appreciation

Figure 5-4. *Performance review: three-step process*

Prep Up

Preparation to write a performance review starts from day 1—not one day before performance review discussion. Having enough data and references to write the performance review will make your life easier and also yield a quality write up afterward. How can you be prepared way before the performance review? What are the data and references that you can look up to? What are the individuals' hits and misses? Have you inferred the goals set and feedback shared in the last performance review?

- *Review past evaluations*: If you're managing this individual for the first time, examine earlier performance assessments to grasp the discussions, commitments and areas for improvement. Consult directly with individuals to gather their sentiments, understand planned improvements, and assess their progress to date.

- *Maintain a performance journal*: A performance journal is a record of the performance of every individual on your team, capturing both their achievements and areas where they may have fallen short of the goals set for them. Once you build it with references and data over time, it will act as a valuable source when writing performance reviews, allowing you to cite specific examples from it.

  How frequently do you input notes into the performance journal? Whenever you prefer. It's challenging to recall everything during the performance review season. It is advisable to document observations of an individual's performance—whether positive, negative, or noteworthy—immediately as they occur.

  Can the performance journal be shared to individuals or even with your manager? The decision is yours. It is advisable to maintain a personal journal and share concise notes during your one-on-one meetings with the individual. Seek clarification on their perspective and discuss potential next steps.

- *Refer to one-on-one notes*: It is advisable to document feedback and perspectives on their performance discussed during your one-on-one meetings. These notes will later serve as a valuable reference when composing performance reviews. Through these discussions, you might discover instances where your interpretation of their performance differs, and they can provide additional data, enabling you to write more constructive and accurate performance reviews.

- *Gather 360° feedback*: Gather feedback and recognitions from colleagues, stakeholders, and your manager regarding an individual's performance in handling situations and collaborating closely with others. Regularly share this feedback with the individual, prompting discussions about their perspective and potential areas for improvement.

Write Up

Write up is the written evaluation and forms the essence of the performance review process. If you've executed the prep up phase effectively, write up involves consolidating well-prepared notes in a compelling and constructive manner, aiming to create the desired impact on your direct reports' performance. Let's see the nitty-gritty of the write up:

- *Review preview*: Write a preview on how you see the individuals' performance in the current performance cycle and give a sneak peek on what's coming up in the detailed review up next. Start by thanking them for their contribution so far and the journey that you had together as a team. Callout crucial projects that they led or part of and the impact they created. It's equally important to shed some light on major concerns and areas of improvements in the preview section and save the details for the rest.

- *Into the details*: Into the details section is the meaty part of the performance review where you explain in detail with references to what the individual did well and areas for improvement against set performance criteria.

- *Tone and choice of words*: Depending on what you want to convey you have to choose the right tone and choice of words in your writing.

If the individual outperformed in all areas and set out to take more ownership, use an affirmative and encouraging tone with phrases like "Instrumental role in the success of...," "A team player who consistently goes above and beyond," "Set to take more ownership."

If the individual had personal challenges and other issues but still managed to perform well, use an empathetic tone with phrases like "Recognizing difficulties," "Navigating challenges," or "In spite of your stressful times."

If the performance is a mixed bag, use a balanced tone with phrases like "Balancing strengths and opportunities," and "Improvement areas."

With poor performance, it's important to maintain a focused and constructive tone and not to sound as falsely positive or too harsh. It's important to communicate the importance and why the individual should focus on them. Use phrases like "There have been challenges in meeting the expected standards," "Collaboration with fellow engineers aren't up to the mark and can be strengthened to drive effective outcomes," and "It's essential for us to discuss candidly some concerns that have surfaced during this period."

Wrap Up

The wrap-up section should encapsulate key takeaways and outline actionable steps to set the tone for the period following the review and the path forward for the individual. Without a wrap up, performance review will end up hopeless and leave your individual stranded in the middle of the sea. It's recommended to write the wrap up section of the performance review after the conversation with the individual happened, once both of you agree upon the next steps.

Here's what you can write in the wrap up section and actions following up after performance review:

- *Summary*: Provide a balanced overview of the individual's performance during the review period.

- *Development opportunities*: Write potential areas for professional growth and development. This could involve training programs, mentorship, or opportunities to take on new responsibilities. Align development opportunities with the individual's career goals and the needs of the team or organization.

- *Next steps and follow-up*: Clearly write and communicate what steps will be taken next. This could involve additional meetings, check-ins, or specific actions to address identified areas of improvement. Set a timeline for follow-up discussions and performance check-ins.

- *Closing appreciation*: End the wrap-up section with a sincere expression of appreciation for the individual's dedication and commitment. Also take a moment to ensure your commitment toward their growth and performance.

Let's take two extreme cases: Alice, a high-performing engineer who exceeded expectations set to her level, and Bob, a low-performing engineer who struggled to meet expectations and showed no intent for improvement, and see how you can write performance reviews for them.

Let's start with Alice.

[Performance Review: Preview]

"Dear Alice,

It's a moment to recognize your exceptional achievements and the impactful role you played as a high-performing engineer. You have consistently demonstrated a remarkable blend of technical expertise, leadership prowess, and a keen sense of ownership in your responsibilities.

Throughout this performance cycle, You have not only met but exceeded expectations in every project that you undertook. Your innovative solutions, proactive approach, and collaborative spirit have significantly contributed to the success of our team and the broader organization. What stands out is your ability to take ownership of challenging tasks, driving them to successful completion with precision and dedication.

In the next section, let's delve into these achievements, recognizing the profound impact of your work on our projects and goals. As we look forward, there is a clear opportunity for you to take on more significant responsibilities and ownership within our team. We'll explore avenues for you to lead initiatives, mentor colleagues, and further enhance your influence in shaping the direction of our projects.

Let's chart a course for you to assume even greater ownership and leadership in your role."

[Performance Review: Into the Details]

Alice, your performance during this review period has been truly exceptional, showcasing your dedication, technical prowess, and collaborative spirit. Your contributions have been invaluable, particularly in the successful execution of Project Alpha. Let's delve into the specifics.

Your leadership in Project Alpha was exemplary. As the project lead, you not only met but exceeded the project goals. Your ability to guide the team, make critical decisions, and ensure that each team member was aligned with the project objectives contributed significantly to its success.

Your innovative problem-solving skills stood out during the challenges faced in Project Beta. When unforeseen issues arose, your quick thinking and strategic approach not only resolved the problems promptly but also prevented any major setbacks to the project timeline. Your ability to adapt to unexpected situations is a commendable asset.

In addition to your technical acumen, your collaborative efforts have created a positive impact. Team members appreciate your willingness to share knowledge and provide support when needed. Your collaborative approach has fostered a sense of teamwork that extends beyond individual projects, enhancing the overall team dynamic.

One notable aspect of your performance has been your proactive approach to taking on additional responsibilities. Your initiative in spearheading the optimization of our development processes has significantly contributed to the team's efficiency. It reflects a deep understanding of our goals and a commitment to continuous improvement.

While celebrating your strengths, it's important to remain mindful of areas for potential growth. Continued focus on enhancing leadership skills, particularly in delegating tasks and guiding less experienced team members, will further elevate your impact within the team.

To leverage your strengths and address areas of growth, we will work together to create a tailored development plan. This may include leadership training and targeted mentorship. Regular check-ins will provide a platform for ongoing feedback and collaboration to ensure your sustained professional growth.

Your outstanding performance is a testament to your commitment and expertise. The team values your contributions, and your leadership has set a benchmark for excellence. I'm confident that your continued growth will not only benefit you personally but will also contribute significantly to the team's success. Thank you for your dedication, and I look forward to witnessing your continued achievements in the upcoming review periods.

Now onto writing the performance review for Bob, a low-performing engineer who struggled to meet expectations and showed no intent for improvement.

[Performance Review: Preview]

"Dear Bob,

I want to extend my appreciation for your efforts over the past year while also addressing some areas that warrant our attention.

Thank you for your contributions to the team during this performance cycle. Your participation in projects and day-to-day tasks has not gone unnoticed, and I appreciate your dedication.

However, it's essential for us to discuss candidly some concerns that have surfaced during this period [Mention specific concerns such as not meeting project deadlines, collaboration issues, or any other relevant issues]. Recognizing these challenges is a crucial step in our collective journey toward improvement as it impacts the team's overall goals.

Let's collaboratively explore strategies to address these concerns and work toward improvement. This may involve additional support, training opportunities, or adjustments to our current workflow. Your input on how we can best approach these improvements is valuable.

Our goal is to create a constructive and supportive environment that facilitates your professional growth. I believe that, with the right strategies and support, we can overcome these challenges together.

In the next section, let's openly discuss both your achievements and the areas where you can improve on your collaboration and effectiveness. Your commitment to improvement is crucial, and I am here to support you in this journey."

[Performance Review: Into the Details]

"Bob, your performance over the course of this review period has been a matter of concern. Despite the opportunities for improvement discussed in

previous reviews, there hasn't been a notable shift in your output, particularly in the areas of project delivery and collaborative efforts.

One of the major challenges observed was with Project X. The project timeline stretched significantly beyond the initially agreed-upon deadline, affecting not only your deliverables but also causing a delay in the entire project cycle. This lapse in meeting deadlines is a critical aspect that needs urgent attention.

In the collaborative aspect, the communication gaps were evident in Project Y. Feedback from team members highlighted instances where clarity in your communication could have avoided misunderstandings and rework. Collaborating efficiently with team members is an essential part of our collective success, and it's an area where improvement is imperative.

Moreover, the quality of your code in Project Z raised concerns. The debugging phase took longer than anticipated, impacting the overall project schedule. It's crucial to ensure that the code meets the defined standards to avoid rework and delays.

While these challenges exist, it's essential to recognize areas where you have demonstrated strength. Your problem-solving skills were evident in troubleshooting issues during the testing phase of Project Z. This strength, however, needs to be consistently applied to all aspects of your work.

To address these concerns, a focused effort is needed on meeting project deadlines, enhancing collaboration with team members through improved communication, and elevating the quality of your code. Seeking feedback during code reviews and implementing best practices in coding standards are crucial steps in this direction.

To support your growth, we will schedule regular check-ins for a more detailed discussion on your progress. This will provide an opportunity for you to share your perspective, and for us to jointly chart a path forward. Identifying specific action items and a timeline for improvement will be a key focus in these sessions.

Recognizing the challenges, it's important to acknowledge your commitment to the team and the main intention is to ensure your professional development. Your dedication to improvement is crucial, and I appreciate your willingness to engage in this process. I look forward to seeing positive changes in the upcoming review periods."

Don'ts of Writing a Performance Review

So far you've seen how to write a performance review; it's equally important to know how not to write it. Writing a performance review that's overly negative or positive, biased, and doesn't consider an individual's perspective will set you on a path to fail. Let's take a look at common mistakes that engineering managers make when writing a performance review so that you don't have to repeat the same:

- *Don't write generically*: If your writing is too generic and does not mention the details of an individual performance, the intended message will not be conveyed. Be specific and provide concrete examples to support your assessments. This clarity helps the individual understand their performance better.

- *Don't be overly positive or negative*: Avoid using overly critical language that might demotivate the individual. Instead of focusing solely on weaknesses, provide constructive feedback with actionable steps for improvement.

- *Don't be biased or opinionated*: Ensure consistency in your evaluation. Treat all team members fairly and use a standardized approach to performance assessment. Inconsistencies can lead to perceptions of bias and unfairness.

- *Don't assume but confirm*: Refrain from making assumptions about the individual's intentions or motivations. Stick to observable behaviors and outcomes. If there are concerns, address them directly and seek the individual's perspective.

- *Don't rely solely on recent events*: Consider the individual's performance over the entire review period, not just recent events. A balanced assessment requires a comprehensive view of their achievements and challenges throughout the performance cycle.

The Conversation

The conversation is about to start.

Conversation that will decide the course of action. A course that either propels your direct report further up in their career or that calls out a close collaboration to work on improvements to address identified performance concerns.

Once you and your direct report are done writing the performance review, it's time to read each other's write-up. You read their self-assessment and they read your review written for them. Let's take a look at each other's point of view (Figure 5-5) to see how the review and differences will be perceived and emotions that will be at play.

Your Point of View

As you read their self-assessment, you might start to find some perspectives different from yours on their performance. Either you will come to know their contributions that you weren't aware of or they haven't completely realized their shortcomings. Make a note of them, do your homework, and get prepared. Armed with insights from both perspectives, you're now ready to navigate the performance discussion and collaboratively shape the future course for your direct report.

Even though the conversation is about past performance, you need to be mindful of spending some time to discuss the future of the individual as well. Forward-looking discussions will encourage them to work on improvements by setting realistic goals and contribute better toward the team's success.

Their Point of View

It's time to change sides. As a direct report reading your assessment written for them, it can invoke various emotions for them based on the individual, result, expectation, and their mindset. Let's take a look at different possibilities of reviews and how emotions could play a part in it (Figure 5-5).

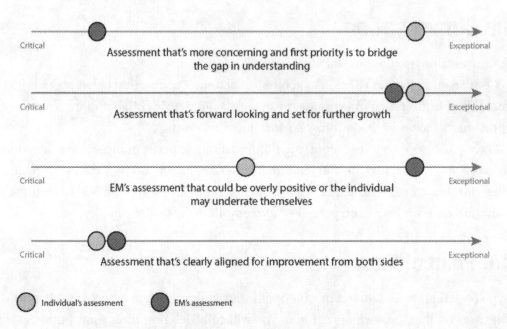

Figure 5-5. Performance review: your and their point of view

EM inclined toward the critical side; individual on the exceptional side

- *Initial impression*: This possibility of assessment is more concerning, and the main priority would be to bridge the understanding. The individual's first question will be on why they were rated critical even if they think they did an exceptional job.

- *Emotions at play*: Their emotions can range from disappointment and frustration to anxiety and resentment to motivation for improvement and some may request for additional support.

- *What should you do?*: It's important to acknowledge and empathize with their emotions and thoughts at first. Effective communication and follow-up discussions are crucial in such situations. You should provide clear, specific, and constructive feedback, offer support for improvement, and collaboratively set goals to ensure the direct reports understand the path forward. Open dialogue and a supportive approach can help turn a challenging review into an opportunity for growth and development.

EM and individual both inclined toward the exceptional side

- *Initial impression*: With this assessment result, it's forward looking and sets the individual up for further growth.

- *Emotions at play*: Their emotions can range from satisfaction and motivation to sense of accomplishment and pride.

- *What should you do?*: It's important to acknowledge their efforts and appreciate them for their achievement and success. While positive feedback is valuable, it's essential for you to provide a balanced and constructive review. To leverage their strengths and address areas of growth, work together with them to create a tailored development plan. This may include leadership training and targeted mentorship. Provide regular check-ins for ongoing feedback and collaboration to ensure their sustained professional growth.

EM inclined toward the exceptional side; individual toward the critical side

- *Initial impression*: With this assessment result, it's important to pause for a moment and understand whether you are overly positive on the individual's performance. On the other hand, the individual will be curious to know your perspective.

- *Emotions at play*: Their emotions can range from curiosity and motivation to a sense of accomplishment and understanding.

- *What you should do?*: You should look to read their self-assessment in detail and be all ears to them during the conversation to review areas where the individual assessed themselves lesser than yours. Being overly positive without addressing genuine concerns can lead to a lack of credibility and may not provide the necessary guidance for professional development.

EM and individual both inclined toward the critical side

- *Initial impression*: With this assessment result, individuals are looking for your support and open for feedback to improve on their self-critical performance.

- *Emotions at play*: Their emotions can range from concern and stress to determination and motivation to commitment and request for additional support. As they themselves realize their low performance, there will not be a moment of frustration or resentment. They were hopeful that you can support and work with them to help them perform better.

- *What should you do?*: It's important to acknowledge and empathize with their emotions and thoughts at first. Effective communication and follow-up discussions are crucial in such situations. You should provide clear, specific, and constructive feedback, offer support for improvement, and collaboratively set goals to ensure the direct reports understand the path forward. As they assess themselves critically, they will be keen to look for learning, opportunities for growth and development.

A significant difference in assessments from each other's perspectives indicates a misalignment in expectations and success criteria, highlighting the necessity for more frequent and ongoing feedback.

Conversation Starts

Your turn: Like any conversation, greet the individual and after casual discussion, start the actual performance review conversation by thanking them for the contribution they have made in that performance cycle. As a conversation preview, tell about the impactful projects that they have led or part of and recognize their effort. Next up, mention areas of improvements without going much in depth and save it for later in-detail discussion.

End on a positive and supporting note assuring that you're there to help them out:

"Recognizing these challenges is a crucial step in our collective journey toward improvement as it impacts the team's overall goals.

Let's collaboratively explore strategies to address these concerns and work toward improvement. This may involve additional support, training opportunities, or adjustments to our current ways of working. Your input on how we can best approach these improvements is valuable. Our goal is to create a constructive and supportive environment that facilitates your professional growth. I believe that, with the right strategies and support, we can overcome these challenges together."

Once you give a short preview to the performance review conversation, give them the stage to express their perspective on their performance.

Their turn: Based on the personality and the kind of emotions they're going through on seeing the assessment result, they might be anywhere in the scale of positivity.

They might be highly positive and motivated on seeing an exceptional rating. If they are satisfied and motivated you might hear the following phrases:

"I want to express my sincere gratitude for the positive feedback in the performance review. It's truly motivating to see my efforts acknowledged, and I'm thrilled to know that my contributions are making a positive impact. This recognition inspires me to continue giving my best and to explore further opportunities for growth within the team. Thank you for your support and encouragement."

They might be having a sense of resentment or determination to learn and perform better on seeing a critical rating—it's purely based on the individual. It's important that you don't interrupt them but *listen* to their point of view. If they are in resentment, you might hear the following phrases:

"I can't help but feel frustrated and disappointed after reading the performance review. I expected a more balanced assessment of my efforts, and it's disheartening to see such a negative perspective. I believe there are areas where the review doesn't accurately reflect my contributions. I'm open to discussing this further, but I can't deny my disappointment in the evaluation."

As you both took turns and set the context for further discussion, it's time to get into the details.

Conversation Progresses

The meaty part.

Your turn: As you and your direct report are entering the core part of the conversation, explain the review in detail and mention specific projects or scenarios based on what the performance was reviewed. Be clear, specific and constructive in sharing your perspective without getting too personal or blaming the individual. Give them a glimpse on the impact it created and how something could have been done better. Instead of going through all the details at once, you can pause after sharing feedback on a specific project or scenario and ask for their perspective. Here is an example phrase:

> *"One of the major challenges observed was with Project X. The project time-line stretched significantly beyond the initially agreed-upon deadline, affecting not only your deliverables but also causing a delay in the entire project cycle. This lapse in meeting deadlines is a critical aspect that needs urgent attention.*
>
> *While challenges exist, it's essential to recognize areas where you have demonstrated strength. Your problem-solving skills were evident in trouble-shooting issues during the testing phase of Project Z. This strength, however, needs to be consistently applied to all aspects of your work."*

Their turn: They explain their perspective and they may agree and add some notes on top of your perspective. Or they might disagree and provide you more data points. Listen to them and clarify any questions you might have at this point.

> *"I appreciate the feedback on Project X, and I acknowledge the challenges we faced with the project timeline. However, I would like to provide additional context to the situation. Several external factors, beyond my control, significantly contributed to the delays. I believe a more comprehensive understanding of the challenges we encountered would provide a fairer assessment. On the positive note, I'm grateful for the recognition of my problem-solving skills in Project Z. Moving forward, I am committed to applying these strengths consistently across all aspects of my work and addressing any concerns raised."*

You exchange turns until you finish discussing performance criteria and specific assessment in detail. With better understanding than from the time you started the conversation, you move toward the lateral part of the conversation which should focus on next steps, agreements and reassurance.

Conversation Ends

As the conversation approaches its conclusion, take a moment to recognize their efforts once more. Acknowledge the hard work and dedication they've demonstrated, reinforcing that you value their contributions. Assure them of your ongoing support as you both embark on the next steps toward continuous improvement. Invite them to share any final thoughts or feelings they may have about the discussion, creating space for open dialogue.

Regarding the topic of salary, while it may not need to be addressed immediately, it's likely on their mind, especially in relation to their current compensation and potential promotions. Be aware of this and suggest scheduling a follow-up meeting specifically to discuss salary considerations and any decisions related to promotions or other opportunities for advancement. This approach ensures that their concerns are addressed thoughtfully and that they feel supported in their career growth.

Summary

Congratulations on successfully navigating the complexities of performance management within an engineering team. This chapter has equipped you with essential tools and frameworks, helping you understand the dynamics that influence individual performance, set meaningful goals, and conduct insightful performance reviews.

You're now equipped to:

- *Grasp People Performance Dynamics*: You've learned to see beyond surface-level performance, considering individual motivations and the broader team dynamics affecting outcomes.

- *Set Clear Performance Criteria*: You understand the importance of establishing transparent performance standards and calibrating these criteria across teams for fairness.

- *Master the Art of Performance Reviews*: From writing reviews that are specific and actionable to holding constructive discussions, you know how to make performance conversations both meaningful and forward-looking.

- *Lead with Empathy and Precision*: Above all, you've gained the insight to manage performance with a blend of empathy and strategic focus, ensuring you and your team grow together in alignment with organizational goals.

Armed with these insights, you're set to foster an environment where your engineers can truly excel, tackling performance management challenges with confidence and grace.

CHAPTER 6

Working with Your Manager

Everyone is living in their own world, which is part of someone else's world.

Your world as an engineering manager (Figure 6-1) consists of worlds of your direct reports, your success, and your worry. Cross-functional experts from the product, design, and data departments are part of your world too as you work together as one team closely on a day-to-day basis.

Rarely can a team deliver value on their own without coordinating with peer teams within the same domain or a business unit—they play a part in your world too. However, the coordination has been considerably reduced over the past decade as teams tend to be autonomous at the same time supporting each other to work toward the bigger picture.

Your Success

Remember your definition of success as we discussed in Chapter 1? It is success to your business delivered through your team along with the success of your people.

Your Worry

Your worries could be the ones that are blockers to attain your success:

- *Team Performance Concerns*: Worries about the overall performance of your engineering team, such as productivity issues, quality concerns, or missed deadlines, can impede success.

- *Communication Challenges*: Worries related to ineffective communication within the team and with stakeholders can hinder success.

- *Scope Creep and Changing Requirements*: Concerns about scope creep or frequent changes in project requirements can be challenging.

111

© Ananth Ramachandran 2024
A. Ramachandran, *The Complete Engineering Manager*, https://doi.org/10.1007/979-8-8688-0267-6_6

- *Prioritization Challenges*: Struggles with prioritizing tasks and projects effectively can lead to delays in delivering high-priority features or addressing critical issues.

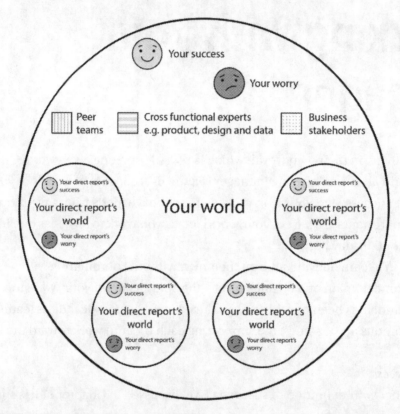

Figure 6-1. *Engineering manager's world*

Having clarity on your success and worry can help take ownership and discuss solutions, not just bring only problems to your manager.

Your Manager's World

Depending on the size of your organization, your manager can be anyone ranging from the CTO to senior engineering manager. If you're an engineering manager of the only team in a startup, your manager will be a CEO or a CTO (if your startup can afford one) who looks after the entire engineering department so to speak.

If you're part of a medium-sized to large organization, your manager will be someone like the head of engineering or director of engineering or a senior engineering manager, and they might be looking after multiple engineering teams in a domain—which is a slice of business that has its own priorities, goals, and strategy contributing to the organization itself. See Figure 6-2.

Figure 6-2. *Manager of manager's world*

To work better with your manager, you have to understand their world better and how it's interconnected with yours and other teams they manage.

If you take a closer look at your manager's world, your world is compressed into theirs, plus the worlds of other managers they manage. They make sure all the worlds of managers within their world don't collide but work in harmony as oneness to contribute to the bigger picture, which is for the organization's success. Besides that, they work with their peers in senior leadership from product, design, data, and business stakeholders but on a strategic level.

Zooming out further, your manager's world is part of the organization's world (Figure 6-3) with executives, leadership, and big clients. Here is where you can find other functions like finance, the people team, and other domains as well.

Figure 6-3. *Organization's world*

Their Success

Your manager's success is nothing but success of all the teams they manage, through which ultimately delivering success to the organization. Success of every team should be aligned with your manager's—you should ensure that's true from your team's perspective as well.

Their Worry

Same as success, worries of all their teams are theirs, but—there's a big but. If your worries are genuine and they can't be resolved by yourself, as it is outside your team's context and responsibilities, you should report to your manager. It can be organization structural concerns, frequently changing priorities from the leadership and business, or lack of people in your team who can achieve team goals.

If your worries are an individual's performance issues, misalignment of your team's priorities to overall strategy, lack of collaboration with sister teams, or lack of skills within your team, these all should be your own worries that you should try to resolve. If you can't resolve it yourself, you can ask for your manager's help, but you should be mindful when you do that. Imagine your manager has two buckets: a success bucket and a worry bucket. Your success can be filled into their success's bucket, and they will absolutely appreciate that. Filling their worry bucket with yours will start to fill it up, and they will soon be overwhelmed.

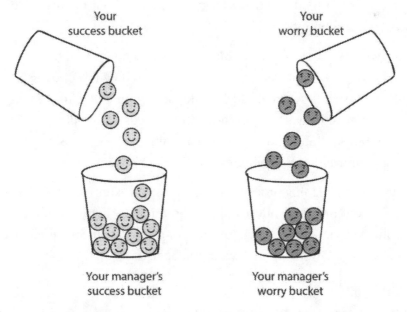

Figure 6-4. *Your manager's success and worry bucket*

Be mindful of what bucket (Figure 6-4) of your manager's that you're filling in. Success bucket or worry bucket?

Building Trust

To establish trust and rapport with your manager, you have to start building it from scratch. Your credibility is your identity. Prove that you can lead your team to success by delivering value, not once, twice, or thrice but reliably over and over again. It definitely takes the time that it deserves, probably a few months or even up to a quarter or two.

What can you do to build trust with your manager?

- *Consistency*: Be consistent in what you say, what you deliver, and how you act. Be deliberate about commitments that you make with them and transparent if you can't take up any unrealistic expectations for you and for your team. Under-promising and over-delivering can work well.

- *Taking ownership*: Stay accountable for the team's results. When things don't go as planned, admit any errors, discuss lessons learned, and outline corrective actions. Demonstrating accountability builds trust and credibility.

- *Keep your manager informed*: Make sure they know about the team's progress, achievements, and challenges. Regular updates create transparency and build confidence in your ability to manage the team effectively. Don't shy away from discussing challenges or roadblocks. Being transparent about difficulties demonstrates honesty and allows for collaborative problem-solving.

Building trust is an ongoing process that requires consistent effort and a commitment to open communication and collaboration. By demonstrating reliability, competence, and a proactive approach to problem-solving, you contribute to a trusting and effective working relationship with your manager.

Aligning on Expectations

Every manager is different.

You are different. I am different. My manager is different. Your manager will be different. And obviously their view on expectations differ, highly influenced by the organizational needs and their leadership style. My very first manager expected me to take up managerial responsibilities up to 70% and be hands-on for 30%. I had a different opinion on it and expressed that I want to be 50-50 with the split. He agreed to it and took over part of the managerial responsibilities on his own, which I got back gradually in a year.

Aligning expectations for each other is important right from the start. From your manager's point of view, they will express what you can expect from them and what they expect from you. From your point of view, you should express what your manager can expect from you and what you expect from your manager. I call it a "cross expectation matrix" (Figure 6-5).

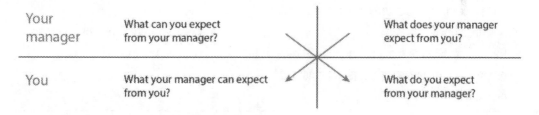

Figure 6-5. *Cross-expectation matrix*

Assuming I'm your manager and you're one of the engineering managers that I'm managing, let's see what a cross-expectation matrix could look like.

Table 6-1. *Cross-Expectations Between You and Your Manager*

What can you expect from me?	*What do I expect from you?*
• Clear direction.	• Building a happy, productive, and high-performing team.
• Career support for your growth in management.	
• Monthly one-on-one to discuss personal topics, concerns, and exchanging feedback.	• Being 70% managerial and 30% hands-on.
• Actively listen to your requests, concerns, and thoughts.	• Manage individual's performance closely and mentor low performers.
• I prefer servant leadership style and give you full autonomy.	• Playing a dual role as both product manager and engineering manager of the team.

(*continued*)

Table 6-1. (*continued*)

What can your manager expect from you?	What do you expect from your manager?
• Building a happy, productive, and high-performing team.	• Weekly one-on-one to discuss personal topics, concerns, and exchanging feedback.
• Being 50% managerial and 50% hands-on.	• Career support.
• Managing an individual's performance and reporting to the management.	• Giving full autonomy leading the team.
• Be a sparring partner to the product manager and build a compelling roadmap delivering against business goals.	• Clear strategic point of view and direction to the team.
• Regular updates to the management about progress on initiatives, change in plans and new goals.	

Once the cross-expectation matrix is mapped, discuss commonalities and differences. Make a note of commonalities, which is a green signal for you to move ahead and continue working towards it. With differences in expectations, discuss each other's point of view and decide on what works best for both of you and for the organization as a whole.

What is your cross-expectation matrix looking like with your manager? Have you done such an activity before? I assure you it's totally worth it. Revisit the expectations matrix whenever there's a change in dynamics or style of working with your manager.

All They Care About

As an engineering manager, understanding what your manager cares more about is crucial to align your success with theirs, leading you to establish a successful working relationship with them.

Here are some of the aspects that managers of managers care more about:

- *Outcome*: Value that their teams are delivering. If you ask them to pick one thing that they care the most, "outcome" will easily end up top in the list. Make sure you're delivering value from the initiatives that your team is prioritizing.

- *Strategy Alignment*: Your team's strategy is aligned with overall domain or organization strategy.

- *Progress and Reporting*: How is your team progressing on goals set and how is it being reported?

- *Collaboration and Reputation*: How is your team collaborating with other engineering and non-engineering teams in the organization? Are there any silos between teams? Are the goals aligned? Are they enabling or blocking each other?

- *Your Team's Adaptability*: As in the ever-changing landscape, your team should be capable of adjusting to the change in priorities and scope.

- *Budget Planning*: They do budget planning for people they need in their engineering teams (including yours) in the short and long term, costs involved in operating the infrastructure, and build versus buy decisions.

- *Culture and Environment*: It's all about how your team fits into the overarching culture and environment that you're in. It also brings your perspective to the table as your manager will welcome any suggestion that you have to improve overall culture.

All They Care "Less" About

While your manager is there to support you, there are certain aspects they are less worried about, allowing you to lead your team autonomously and effectively. In other words, they won't worry about everything that's concerning you and your team. That's why you're there as an engineering manager. To a certain degree, it's your team and your worry, until it gets bigger and impacts the organization or is more challenging for you to resolve.

They have trust that you can do the job and are giving you the autonomy that you deserve. That's the practicality of them being a manager of managers and having bigger problems for them to solve for organization.

Here are some of the aspects that your manager worry less about:

- *Your team's processes*: They don't pay lot of attention to how you estimate, whether you're using agile or kanban, how you do code reviews, or any of your team's processes unless they are enthusiasts of a specific process. They care about the outcome rather than getting into the details of "how."

- *Every individual's performance details*: The performance details of each and every individual that you're managing don't need the direct attention of your manager. Occasionally you can share how each of them is doing overall or can talk about a specific case that your manager might be interested in. But you don't need to share every detail that you observe, especially if there are discussions in progress with individuals. You need to involve your manager only if something is decisive, e.g., having an individual in a formal Performance Improvement Plan (PIP) or discussing a possible promotion of your direct report.

- *Detailed technical aspects*: Detailed technical aspects like management of technical debt, architecture patterns, and best practices will not worry your manager until they turn into a strategic initiative that the whole domain or the organization might care about. You're accountable for technical decisions that your team is making, and your manager might worry only about how that could affect behavior of the product and impact to the business if any.

- *Planning capacity and resource allocation*: Allocating engineers to the projects and planning team's capacity for a quarter or two is on your shoulders, and you may find your manager less interested in it in your one-on-ones or any interaction you have with them. Do you need more people in your team? Well, that can increase their curiosity a bit. Their response will be like "Now, tell me more about it."

- *Day-to-day operations*: The day-to-day operations of your team are not their epicenter. You decide how your team should operate on a day-to-day basis like change in the day-to-day priorities, resolving a technical incident, software releases, and regular deployments.

- *Internal team communication*: It's up to you to define your team's communication patterns and preferences that work best for them. How they touch base with each other, with other teams, and with stakeholders are solely up to you.

You may find your manager more involved in some of these aspects depending on the need, your ability as an engineering manager to manage on your own, their leadership style, or some of them might be just curious to be part of it. If you're a new engineering manager, you may find your manager more involved to help you from the sideline or to share feedback on how you're doing your job. As an experienced engineering manager who has worked closely with your manager for some time, you will have greater autonomy.

It's wise to discuss ways of working and what they care more about the most at the earliest so that you can avoid any misunderstanding that may arise in the future.

Help Your Boss Help You

Your manager is there to help you—whenever you need it. But they may not have a secret power to know when you might need help. It's on you to raise your hand and ask for it. You might be burned out or you're in need of more resources for your team or you need to gain more product and business context to do prioritization right or need a helping hand to resolve a critical conflict in your team. With well-established trust and rapport with your manager, asking for help isn't a second thought.

- *Encourage skip one-on-ones*: It's an opportunity for your manager to get a pulse of what's happening in the team by directly speaking to your direct reports. Through skip one-on-ones, your manager shall give you a different perspective of the dysfunctions in the team, what's working well or not, and feedback about you. This could greatly help you perform your role as a manager.

- *Ask context for prioritization*: Your manager is the right person to ask for business context and goals to prioritize initiatives for your team.

- *Channelize 360° feedback*: Request your manager to channelize feedback from everyone you're working closely with.

- *Working in pairs*: Some managers would be open to pair with you for whatever reasons that you would like to. Once, my manager paired with me to do a mock exit interview as we did a role play and he acted as an underperformer to let out emotions and see how I would handle that in the real conversation with the individual. It greatly helped me in carrying out my job as an engineering manager better.

Help Your Boss

Now it's your turn to help your manager.

You might ask, "Are you sure that I can help my manager?"—yes, I'm sure. Every manager of managers needs help. It's a matter of asking them what their biggest pain points are, where they are overloaded with, and where they lack visibility into your team's work.

You help your boss to:

- *Succeed*: Your success is their success. Helping them to succeed doesn't only make them look nicer but also foster a trusted relationship with you.

- *See your team's accomplishments*: Not every senior manager gets to see their team's accomplishments often as they should be. You can showcase the success of your team on a regular basis about what has been achieved, who went the extra mile, and what impact has been delivered.

- *Delegate to you*: Ask them where they are overloaded with and if you can provide your support. It could be defining and setting up delivery metrics or representing external client meetings on behalf of them. Look for opportunities that you can take something out of your manager's plate

- *Improve by providing feedback*: Like you, your manager depends on your feedback on how they are setting strategic direction.

Having the helping attitude is equal to saying to your manager, "I got your back. We're in this together."

If Things Aren't Rosy

There will be times when you have a differing opinion compared to that of your manager. If things are not going well, it's important to address the situation proactively and professionally.

In the context of a quarterly planning discussion, I was tasked with determining the priorities of upcoming engineering and product initiatives. Projects ranged from addressing technical debt to rolling out new features, each with its own set of implications for the team's workload, product roadmap, and overall strategic goals.

My Perspective

As an engineering manager, my focus was primarily on addressing critical technical debt that had accumulated over time. I believed that resolving these issues was paramount to ensure long-term stability, maintainability, and scalability of the product. From my perspective, tackling technical debt would pave the way for smoother future development and reduce the risk of encountering major challenges down the line.

My Manager's Perspective

However, my manager held a different viewpoint. He was more inclined toward prioritizing the introduction of new features that would enhance the product's market appeal and potentially attract more users. His reasoning was rooted in the need for constant innovation and responsiveness to market demands. From his perspective, delaying the introduction of new features might result in a competitive disadvantage.

Conflict Arises

Clash in priorities became evident during our discussion. I was steadfast in my belief that addressing technical debt should take precedence, while my manager argued for the strategic importance of introducing new features to stay ahead in the market.

Navigating the Conflict

Here's how to navigate the conflict:

- *Open Dialogue*: I initiated an open and professional dialogue, expressing my concerns about the potential risks associated with delaying technical debt resolution. My manager, in turn, explained the importance of staying competitive and meeting customer expectations through timely feature releases.

- *Data-Driven Discussion*: Both of us presented data to support our perspectives. I showcased the impact of unresolved technical debt on development speed and long-term stability, while my manager provided market research indicating customer demand for new features.

- *Finding Middle Ground*: Recognizing the value in both perspectives, we worked toward finding a middle ground. This involved creating a hybrid plan that allocated resources to address some critical technical debt while also incorporating a streamlined release of a few key features. We decided on an 80/20 split on building new product features at the same time of settling tech debt in iteration.

- *Continuous Communication*: After the decision was made, I emphasized the importance of continuous communication and feedback loops. This commitment ensured that the impact of prioritization decisions was regularly reviewed, allowing adjustments as needed.

While the initial conflict highlighted differing priorities, the collaborative approach led to a balanced plan that addressed both technical debt and new feature development. Conflict—when navigated with open communication and a focus on shared goals, ultimately strengthened the working relationship between me and my manager, fostering a more resilient and adaptable team culture.

Whenever you're in a conflict with your manager, the following are the steps you might consider taking:

- *Reflect*: Before taking any action, reflect on the specific issues or challenges you are facing with your manager. Identify whether these issues are related to communication, expectations, leadership style, or other factors.

- *Listen*: Actively listen to your manager's perspective. Ensure that you understand their expectations and concerns. This demonstrates your commitment to a two-way communication process.

- *Clarify/acknowledge*: Clarify if you don't understand your manager's perspective in a conflict. At times, in my experience with my managers, we shared the same perspective but expressed it in different contexts. On clarifying it further, we resolved our conflict and were on the same page. Acknowledge if you understand their thoughts with phrases like "I understand your viewpoint," "I got it where you are coming from," and "I agree with what you say however...."

- *Express*: When expressing your concerns, use "I" statements to communicate your feelings and observations without sounding accusatory. For example, you can say, "I feel there is a communication gap" rather than "You never communicate effectively." Support your concerns with specific examples to help your manager understand the context of your observations.

- *Ask for a moderator*: If the conflict doesn't seem to resolve and both of you have strong opinions, it's better to ask another person to moderate. Probably another engineering manager or product manager within your organization. You need to find a trusted partner who can be involved in such discussions.

See conflicts as opportunities rather than confrontation. This changes the entire dynamics of approaching conflicts with your manager.

Summary

Wrapping up this chapter, you've navigated the intricate dynamics of working effectively with your manager, a journey that underscores the mutual worlds of leadership and team management. Here's a succinct summary of the insights and strategies you've acquired:

- *Understand the Interconnected Worlds*: Your world is part of your manager's. To work better with your manager, you have to understand their world better and how it's interconnected with yours and other teams they manage. Imagine your manager has two buckets, one for success and another for worry. Be mindful of what bucket you're filling in.

- *Build Trust and Rapport*: Establishing trust with your manager involves demonstrating consistency in what you say and do as a leader, taking ownership of your team's outcomes, and keeping your manager informed.

- *Clarify Success and Address Concerns*: Success for you and your manager is deeply intertwined, defined by the achievements of your team and the broader business goals. Identifying and proactively addressing potential worries or blockers is key to maintaining this aligned path to success.

- *Align on Expectations*: Engage in open dialogues to clearly define and align expectations. Utilize the "cross expectation matrix" to map out mutual expectations, addressing any differences to ensure both you and your manager are working toward common goals with a shared understanding.

- *Navigate Conflicts Thoughtfully*: Conflicts are inevitable, but they offer opportunities for growth and clarity. Approach disagreements with an open mind, focusing on understanding your manager's perspective and seeking solutions that align with both your viewpoints and the organization's objectives.

You're equipped not just to coexist but to thrive in the shared world with your manager, fostering an environment where open communication, mutual respect, and aligned goals pave the way for collective success. As you move forward, remember that your relationship with your manager is a dynamic journey, one that evolves with each project, challenge, and success story you share.

PART III

Managing Processes

A bad system will beat a good person every time.

—Edwards Deming

In the previous part, you got to see the importance of people in your engineering teams and how to make them great. But still somehow when they work as a team, it feels inefficient and falls short of achieving expected results. On digging deeper, you found that processes that you have in place are letting them down.

Processes are systems that let your team collaborate, build, and deliver software efficiently; after all, it is a team sport. Processes should never be brakes that slow down how your team operates but rather as lubricants that let your team perform better and smoothly.

In recent years, the thinking around engineering processes has evolved to support modern application development and speed. Everyone wants to produce software, test hypotheses, and make decisions faster, even if it means failing at it. "Fail fast, iterate, and pivot" should be your mantra, and your engineering processes should support that. This could mean moving to agile from the waterfall methodology, embracing failures, looking at the preparedness of your engineering systems, using feature flags, or implementing iterative releases. A lot has changed and will continue to change as you read this book (believe it or not, estimations are still a hot potato).

Software Engineering Processes 101

Every process is designed to take an input and produce an output. The manner in which a process transforms the input and the nature of its output define the essence and purpose of the process. Let's apply this idea to the context of software development.

In software development, a series of interconnected processes (Figure 1) enables a team to collaborate, build, and deliver software effectively. However, the process doesn't stop at delivery. Equally crucial is the ongoing maintenance and support of the software to ensure it continues to function as intended. Maintaining and updating software is as vital as the initial development and deployment phases.

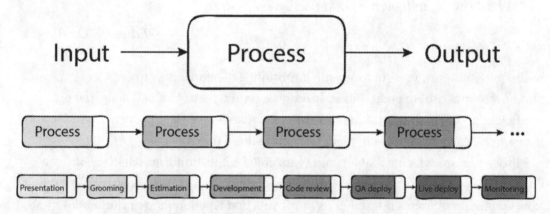

Figure 1. *Chain of processes involved in producing software*

This illustration represents a typical sequence of processes used to build and deliver software. It's important to note that this sequence isn't one-size-fits-all. Different teams will have different processes based on their specific needs and constraints. For instance, a machine learning (ML) team may adopt an iterative and rapid development process tailored to their need for continuous experimentation. On the other hand, a software development team in a traditional banking institution will have to navigate stringent regulations and security compliance, which shape their software development process.

As a leader, your role is to understand these dynamics within your engineering team and tailor the processes to fit both your team's context and your organization's requirements.

Defining and implementing processes in your team isn't about complicating life or imposing rigid structures. On the contrary, well-designed processes aim to simplify workflows, making it easier for your team to work efficiently and predictably. While stakeholders might not be concerned with the intricacies of your processes, they are focused on the results—"when" the software will be delivered and "what" features or fixes will be included, as simple as that.

Your objective is to create processes that streamline your team's work, enhance productivity, and ensure consistent output, thereby aligning with the broader goals of your organization and meeting stakeholder expectations.

Great people need great processes to achieve greater results. And *voila*! You as an EM are responsible for achieving such greatness. In this part, you'll see how to make your engineering processes great again.

- ***Evolving Processes and Bringing Change:*** Defining a process using 4-Key Elements, Evolving your engineering processes, Effecting A Change, Know Your Influencers: Champions, Nay-sayers, Fence-sitters.

- ***Development and Delivery Processes:*** Navigating Conundrum phase—Requirements, Grooming and Estimation, Development phase—implementation, code review and quality, and the Delivery phase.

- ***Technical Processes:*** Processes for your technical systems, Proactive—Operational Review, System Review, Decision Making and Reactive—Incident Management Process, Role you play in technical processes.

CHAPTER 7

Evolving Processes and Bringing Change

When I first proposed using feature flags to my team back in 2016, the reaction was immediate and clear. The room went silent, arms crossed defensively, brows furrowed in confusion, and skeptical glances were exchanged. One senior developer, deeply accustomed to our traditional process, leaned back with a smirk that clearly conveyed, "Here we go again with another one of management's bright ideas."

Our long-standing process involved rigorous testing of code in a sandbox environment before it was deployed straight to production. We didn't use incremental rollouts or release features to specific customer groups. This method has always provided us with a strong sense of control and security. The introduction of feature flags, which enables gradual feature rollouts and on-the-fly toggling in production, seemed like a significant departure. It was more than just adopting a new tool; it represented a fundamental shift in our approach to software deployment.

Introducing such a change presented clear challenges. Mandating a new process without team involvement often leads to resistance. Change imposed from the top can breed resentment and superficial compliance rather than true acceptance. I was aware that pushing too hard could drive the team further away from embracing the new approach.

The benefits of change aren't always immediately apparent. Even though the technical advantages of feature flags were clear, the team needed time to see how this new method would integrate with their existing workflow. Their initial skepticism wasn't solely about feature flags' practicality but about challenging deeply held beliefs regarding our testing and deployment process.

© Ananth Ramachandran 2024
A. Ramachandran, *The Complete Engineering Manager*, https://doi.org/10.1007/979-8-8688-0267-6_7

Changing a deeply ingrained process or belief is no small feat. For our team, moving from a sandbox-only approach to feature flags meant confronting fears about code safety and unforeseen issues. This wasn't just about changing procedures; it was about rethinking a trusted methodology.

Navigating these challenges required acknowledging their concerns, addressing psychological barriers, and adopting a collaborative approach to introduce the change.

Four Key Elements of a Process

Reflecting on my early days as an individual contributor, I realize now that the processes in place within my engineering team felt more like arbitrary rules than tools for success. Without a clear understanding of their purpose, these processes seemed burdensome, and truth be told, my colleagues and I often disregarded them when our manager wasn't around. We simply didn't see the point—why do processes exist? What benefits do they bring? What role do we play in them?

If you're in the position of (re)defining processes for your engineering teams, it's crucial to first grasp the fundamentals. What is the primary purpose of each process? How can you ensure that it delivers tangible benefits? And most importantly, do your engineers fully understand their role within it?

If these questions seem daunting, worry not—the 4-Key Elements Framework can guide you in creating processes that provide clarity and a genuine sense of purpose for your teams. See Figure 7-1.

- *Purpose & Goal*: Start by clearly defining why the process exists. What are the specific goals it aims to achieve? Understanding the purpose helps align the team and ensures that everyone knows the 'why' behind their actions.

- *Output & Artifacts*: Consider what the process will produce. What are the tangible outputs or artifacts that result from following this process? These outputs provide a measure of success and a way to evaluate whether the process is functioning as intended.

- *Roles & Guidelines*: Identify who is involved in the process and clarify their roles. What responsibilities does each team member have? Additionally, establish clear guidelines to help everyone understand how to follow the process correctly and consistently.

- *Operation & Consistency*: Determine how frequently the process should be carried out and whether the team can execute it independently. Consistency is key to ensuring the process becomes an integral part of your team's workflow rather than a one-time effort.

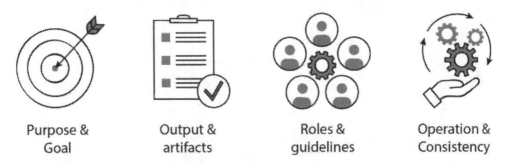

Purpose &
Goal

Output &
artifacts

Roles &
guidelines

Operation &
Consistency

Figure 7-1. *Four key elements of an engineering process*

Ready to give it a try? Take any existing process within your engineering teams and redefine it using the 4-Key Elements Framework. This can also be done collaboratively in a workshop setting with your team. It's an exercise that's well worth the effort. Once you've nailed down the details, bring it back to your team for discussion. You might be surprised at how valuable these conversations can be.

Evolving Your Engineering Process

The framework gives you a foundation to define your team's engineering processes. But I urge you to take a step back for a moment and immerse yourself into the motivation of defining a process in the first place. Is it because there was never a process in place to address a concern and you think it would make sense to have one? Or you redefined it as it didn't serve the purpose? You need to know where you're coming from and at what stage (Figure 7-2) the process is in.

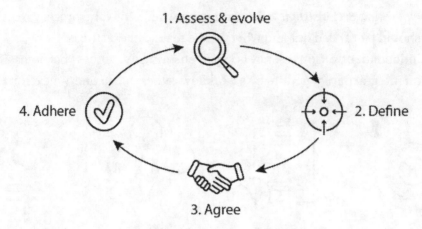

Figure 7-2. *Evolving your engineering processes*

- *Assess*: Start by evaluating the current situation or process. Identify what works, what doesn't, and where there are opportunities for improvement. This assessment provides the necessary insights to inform your next steps.

- *Define*: Based on your assessment, either create a new process or redefine an existing one. Ensure that the new or revised process addresses the identified issues and aligns with your team's needs.

- *Agree*: Ensure that everyone involved in the process comes to a common agreement. Achieving consensus is critical for the successful implementation of any process. When team members buy into the process, they are more likely to commit to and support it.

- *Adhere*: Once an agreement is reached, focus on adherence. It's not enough to have a process in place; the team must follow it consistently. Adherence is as important as the process itself for ensuring its effectiveness and achieving desired outcomes.

Success in any process boils down to two essentials: agreement and adherence. Getting both right is essential for making real, lasting changes. But achieving this isn't an overnight task. It's a gradual process that demands careful attention and steady effort. First, you need to build an agreement with your team. This means having open conversations, addressing concerns, and clearly explaining why the new process is necessary. Expect this to take time—weeks or even months—as your engineers get on board and start to see the value in the change.

Once you've got everyone on the same page, the next challenge is ensuring adherence. This requires ongoing support and resources to help your team integrate the new process into their daily routine. Regular check-ins and feedback are vital to keep things on track and to tackle any issues that pop up along the way.

As an engineering manager, you're at the heart of this transition. Your role is to guide your team through the change, making sure they understand the benefits and feel supported throughout the process. Your leadership is about more than just introducing a new process; it's about embedding it into the team's workflow and making it a natural part of their workday. By staying engaged, providing continuous support, and addressing challenges as they arise, you help turn the process into a success story for your team.

Effecting a Change

Effecting change within a team, particularly concerning processes, is a task fraught with challenges but also rich with opportunities for growth and improvement. Change often brings discomfort because it disrupts the status quo and introduces uncertainty. However, it is an essential component of progress and can lead to significant enhancements in a team's performance and overall efficiency. For an Engineering Manager, mastering the art of implementing and managing change is essential. It enables you to refine processes, resolve issues, and adapt to new challenges effectively, thereby driving the team toward greater success.

When faced with a process that requires adjustment—whether due to inefficiencies, emerging challenges, or evolving goals—it is vital to approach the situation with a structured and thoughtful strategy. The first step in this process is to closely observe how the current process operates. This involves not just a surface-level examination but a deep dive into how each component functions, where bottlenecks or issues arise, and how these affect the team's productivity and morale.

A Real Challenge

To illustrate how to effectively implement change, let's consider a real-life scenario involving the release and monitoring process of a mobile app. This example will demonstrate the challenges teams often face with disorganized processes and highlight how a structured approach can lead to meaningful improvements. By examining this case, you'll gain insights into the steps needed to identify issues, propose solutions, and successfully implement changes to enhance team performance and product quality.

In any software development environment, the effectiveness of your release and monitoring processes plays a part in the overall success of your product. However, when these processes become disorganized or ineffective, they can lead to significant delays and quality issues that impact the user experience and the team's efficiency.

Imagine you're facing a situation where these problems are becoming increasingly apparent. Delays in releases and frequent bugs cropping up post-release have been a recurring issue. You decide it's time to address these concerns head-on.

You gather the team to discuss the current release and monitoring process. As you sit down with your team—let's call them Alex, the senior developer; Priya, the QA engineer; and Jordan, the product manager—you open the discussion by highlighting the concerns you've noticed.

You start by asking, "Let's discuss the current release and monitoring process. I've noticed delays and frequent bugs post-release. What's your take on this?."

Alex (the champion):

Alex, the senior developer, jumps in immediately. *"The process feels disorganized. We lack clear ownership, and bugs often go unnoticed until users report them. I've been thinking about how we can streamline this, maybe even automate some parts of the process to catch issues earlier."*

Priya (the naysayer):

Priya, the QA engineer, nods but adds with a hint of skepticism, *"I agree with Alex, but I'm not sure how much of this is really fixable. Our monitoring tools don't seem effective, and we've tried upgrading them before without much success. We often find out about issues too late, which impacts our response time and quality. I've seen this kind of thing drag on without real improvement."*

Jordan (the fence-sitter):

Jordan, the product manager, chimes in, *"It's impacting our deadlines and the quality of the product. I think a more structured approach could help us get on track, but I'm not entirely sure how we should go about it. We've tried changes before, and it hasn't always worked out."*

You nod, recognizing the validity of their concerns. *"Exactly. I need to understand your experiences better. How do you see your roles in the current setup, and where do you think improvements are needed?"*

Alex (the champion):

Alex expresses a bit of frustration, *"We're not sure who's responsible for what. It's chaotic, especially post-release when we need to monitor the app. But I really think if we assign clear roles and perhaps integrate a new monitoring system, we can turn this around. I'm ready to take on more responsibility if needed."*

Priya (the naysayer):

Priya remains cautious, *"Yes, and we don't have a clear way to track real-time issues. But I'm worried that even with new tools, we might not see a real change unless we address some of the deeper issues. The current tools aren't up to the task, but replacing them might just lead to new problems."*

Jordan (the fence-sitter):

Jordan adds, *"And the lack of clear roles means that no one takes full ownership of the post-release phase. It's causing confusion and inefficiencies. I'm on board with making improvements, but I'll need to see some solid plans before I can fully commit."*

You listen carefully, absorbing the feedback. These discussions reveal a pattern of disorganization and ineffective tools that are contributing to delays and quality issues. The lack of clear roles and ownership in both the release and monitoring phases is a major concern. It's evident that the team needs a more structured approach to manage these processes effectively.

With these insights in mind, you realize it's time to work on a change proposal that will address these issues directly. Your goal is to create a more streamlined process with clearer roles, better tools, and enhanced team collaboration to ensure everyone is aligned and empowered to deliver high-quality releases on time.

Know the Influencers

Processes are meant to serve people, not the other way around. When you're rolling out a new change in your organization, you're not just changing workflows or systems but you're dealing with people, each with their own reactions, concerns, and motivations. And trust me, they don't all react the same way.

First, there are the champions. These folks are like the early spring flowers—bright, eager, and ready to bloom with the new season. They're excited by the possibilities that change brings and might already have a laundry list of ideas on what and how things should evolve. Champions are your natural allies; they'll not only support the change but actively help you push it forward. They're the ones who stay up late brainstorming, who rally others with their infectious enthusiasm.

Then, you encounter the naysayers. These are the team members who've seen it all before but not in a good way. They've been through changes that promised the moon and delivered little more than confusion and frustration. Their skepticism isn't just negativity for negativity's sake; it's born from experience, sometimes painful. They've been let down before, and now, they're protective, wary of getting burned again. A naysayer might say something like, "This will never work," and they'll have reasons, detailed and well-rehearsed, to back that up. It's easy to write them off, but here's the thing: naysayers are deeply invested. If you can win them over, they might just become your strongest advocates.

Finally, there are the fence-sitters. They're like leaves in the wind—unsure of which direction to go, they're waiting for a sign. Fence-sitters aren't necessarily against change; they're just not convinced it's going to happen. Or if it does happen, they're not sure it'll be worth the effort. They prefer to watch from the sidelines, waiting to see which way the tide will turn before they commit. This group is usually the largest, a silent majority that needs a little nudge to get off the fence.

So, how do you deal with these different groups? How do you turn that initial mix of excitement, skepticism, and hesitation into a cohesive force for change?

Empowering Your Champions

Start with your champions. These are the people who are already on your side, so give them the power to make things happen. Assign them meaningful projects, let them make decisions in areas they're passionate about, and give them the resources they need to succeed. When they come to you with ideas, listen. You won't be able to implement every suggestion, but don't dismiss them outright. Instead, explain your reasoning and show genuine appreciation for their enthusiasm. Let them feel that their contributions matter—because they do.

Engaging with the Naysayers

Now, let's talk about the naysayers. It's tempting to try and argue them into seeing things your way, but that's usually a losing battle. Instead, take a different approach: listen. Naysayers often have valuable insights hidden beneath their skepticism. Draw them out. Ask them to share their concerns and experiences. Show them that you're not just paying lip service, but that you genuinely value their perspective. And if you can find a way to address their core issues, you might be surprised to see them become some of your most vocal supporters. After all, a converted naysayer can be a powerful ally as they've already thought through all the reasons something might fail, so when they start to believe in the change, they'll defend it fiercely.

Waiting Out the Fence-Sitters

As for the fence-sitters, don't waste too much energy trying to coax them down just yet. Focus instead on achieving small, visible wins with the help of your champions and any converted naysayers. Once these successes start to pile up, the fence-sitters will take notice. They'll see that the change is real, that it's gaining momentum, and they'll want to be part of it. People naturally gravitate toward success, and when the bandwagon starts to roll, the fence-sitters will hop on board.

The Psychology of Change

It's easy to forget, but all three groups—champions, naysayers, and fence-sitters—believe that their way of dealing with change is the smartest approach. Each response is a rational reaction to the environment they've experienced within the organization. Instead of trying to prove them wrong, focus on showing them that change is not just possible, but beneficial. Make the change visible and tangible. As the situation evolves and they see real results, their attitudes will shift accordingly.

How to Engage and Drive Change

So, how do you get started? Here's a roadmap:

- *Identify Personal Wins*: Begin by understanding what success looks like to each person on your team. What would make the change worthwhile for them on a personal level? Encourage open discussions about their pain points and what would enhance their work life. When it comes to naysayers, challenge them to propose even outrageous ideas, as they might just lead to something practical and transformative.

- *Form Collaborative Teams*: Assemble teams to involve people in shaping the change. Put a champion in charge, and let them lead the initiative. Encourage these teams to test small, actionable changes rather than striving for a perfect, all-encompassing plan.

- *Set Clear Deadlines*: Keep the momentum going by setting firm deadlines for these teams to test their ideas. Structure your meetings to focus on getting things done, not perfecting every detail.

- *Evaluate with an Open Mind*: When your team brings forward ideas, listen with an open mind. If you shut down their suggestions too early, you risk discouraging them from contributing in the future. Building trust takes time, but it can be quickly lost if people feel their input isn't valued.

- *Test changes in Safe Spaces*: Implement the change as minimum viable product (MVP) in parts of the business that are low-risk. This way, even if the experiment doesn't work out, the impact is minimal. Creating a "safe to fail" environment encourages innovation without fear of significant repercussions.

- *Iterate and Improve*: After testing, hold a retrospective with the team to discuss what worked and what didn't. Use these insights to refine the MVP and continue iterating until the solution is strong enough to share with the broader organization.

- *Publicize Real Wins*: When the change yields positive results, make sure everyone knows about it. Share the stories of how change happened and the impact it had. But remember, the wins you publicize need to be genuine—empty slogans about "excellence" or "being the best" won't resonate if they don't reflect reality. Authentic success stories will inspire and motivate, while hollow claims can breed cynicism.

Summary

This chapter provided you with insights on embracing change and effectively managing your team's software development process.

The key takeaways included the following:

- *Embracing Change*: Understanding and navigating the challenges of implementing new processes, and fostering a team culture that is open to adaptation and growth.

- *Empowering Your Team*: Recognizing the roles of different team members—champions, naysayers, and fence-sitters—and effectively engaging each group to drive successful change.

- *Streamlining Processes*: Establishing clear roles, enhancing tools, and refining workflows to improve productivity, quality, and team morale.

- *Continuous Improvement*: Emphasizing the importance of ongoing evaluation and iteration to ensure processes remain effective and aligned with team goals.

With this foundation, you're all set to craft development and delivery processes that work for your team, streamline technical workflows, and drive sustained improvements.

CHAPTER 8

Development and Delivery Processes

Software is not produced in a single day or through a single process but rather through a series of interconnected processes. Every software engineering team is passionate about developing solutions—there's no doubt about that. If you ask them which stage of the software development life cycle (SDLC) they enjoy the most, the answer is almost always the development stage. This phase is at the heart of their work and the reason they were hired. But do they fully understand the why, what, how, and when of their development tasks? And the question that most executives and stakeholders are concerned with: "How long will it take to develop?"

Software development typically progresses through stages (Figure 8-1): from the conundrum phase to development and finally to delivery. The conundrum phase involves thoroughly exploring the problem space through workshops, requirements gathering, and refinement processes before moving on to development and delivery. During the development phase, the focus should be on how to effectively develop, review, and test solutions. In the delivery phase, your processes should allow you to seamlessly deliver your solutions to end users whenever necessary.

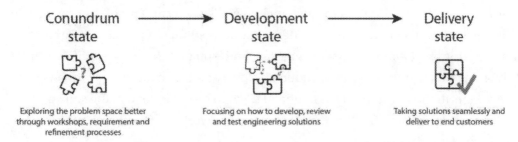

Conundrum state — Exploring the problem space better through workshops, requirement and refinement processes

Development state — Focusing on how to develop, review and test engineering solutions

Delivery state — Taking solutions seamlessly and deliver to end customers

Figure 8-1. *Phases of software development and delivery*

© Ananth Ramachandran 2024
A. Ramachandran, *The Complete Engineering Manager*, https://doi.org/10.1007/979-8-8688-0267-6_8

It's your responsibility to ensure that the right processes are applied at the right stages of software development and that they are executed efficiently. Without a clear understanding of why you're building something and a shared approach to how it's being built, your team risks creating solutions that don't align with the business needs. Over-engineering remains a common issue in many teams, where they invest excessive time and effort into developing overly complex solutions that don't meet client or user expectations. Unfortunately, time spent on over-engineering is time that cannot be recovered.

Conundrum Phase

"Do you often face significant uncertainty before starting the development phase?"

"Does your team frequently challenge the requirements and ask for more context and clarity on why something needs to be developed?"

"Do they express uncertainty about how to approach the development and feel the need to explore further?"

Feeling uncertain at the start of software development is not only normal but expected. It's your responsibility to guide your team through this uncertainty and help them achieve clarity. Let's explore the processes that occur during this conundrum phase, which help your team gain the necessary context and create space for discussing engineering solutions.

Requirement Presentation

This process involves introducing a requirement that may need development or, in some cases, further exploration through technical discovery and proof of concept when a full-scale solution isn't yet needed. These requirements act as problem statements with specific expectations, each with a backstory. If you trace a requirement's origin, it likely spans a long journey—from product discovery and brainstorming with business stakeholders to the negotiations that refined it. This stage is pivotal in the software development cycle, defining the purpose behind the work and its alignment with your team's broader objectives.

Here are some essential attributes to include in every requirement:

- *Background and Motivation*: Describe the current state of the system or product, the impact of the proposed change, and the reasons for implementing it.

- *Problem Statement*: Define the issue the requirement aims to address, detailing specific pain points, inefficiencies, or challenges.

- *Functional Requirements*: Outline the functionalities the system must provide, including features, capabilities, or specific actions required.

- *Nonfunctional Requirements*: Specify criteria related to performance, reliability, security, and other essential aspects that aren't tied to specific functionalities but are crucial for the system's overall success.

- *Acceptance Criteria*: Set the conditions that must be met for the requirement to be considered complete. Ensure these criteria reflect the expectations and needs of end-users or stakeholders.

- *Constraints and Dependencies*: Identify any limitations or restrictions that could affect the requirement's implementation, such as budget, time, or technical constraints. Also, outline any external factors or prerequisites the requirement depends on to manage dependencies effectively.

- *In-Scope and Out-of-Scope*: Clearly define what is included within the scope of the requirement to manage expectations and prevent scope creep. Explicitly state what is excluded to set boundaries and avoid misunderstandings.

Providing these details will make your requirements clearer and more effective. Tailor these attributes to fit the needs of your specific software and system to ensure they are appropriately detailed and useful.

What is your role as an engineering manager in the requirement presentation process?

Ideally, this may not be the first time you encounter a specific requirement when it is presented to the team. You might have previously discussed it with your stakeholders during feasibility consultations or provided high-level estimates. Alternatively, your product manager might have already briefed you for your initial feedback before presenting it to the team.

When the requirements are presented to the team, you need to ensure they fully grasp the purpose, the problem being addressed, and the impact of the change. Encourage your team to critically evaluate the requirements and question their purpose rather than jumping straight into solution mode.

During this phase, you can expect a range of reactions, from uncertainty and doubt to excitement, depending on the nature of the requirement. This stage also offers you a chance to observe team interactions and suggest improvements. Pay attention to how team members collaborate and communicate, especially with non-technical stakeholders. Ensure that the language used is accessible and avoids overly technical jargon, facilitating clear and effective communication.

Technical Grooming

Even if you think you've addressed all the questions during the requirements session, new challenges often emerge when the team begins discussing technical solutions or during implementation. This can lead to delays in delivery and misalignment among engineers during code reviews and later stages of release.

Starting the exploration of these unknowns early will improve both your planning and development processes.

Technical grooming is a session where engineers convene to discuss the technical details of the requirements. It helps mitigate potential blockers and delays that might arise during development. As a manager, this session enables you to obtain accurate estimates from your team, aiding in roadmap and capacity planning. The focus should be on simplifying the solution within constraints to meet the requirements without over-engineering.

Consider applying the four key elements of the process to define your team's technical grooming approach:

- *Purpose and Goal*: The purpose of technical grooming is to make well-informed decisions on the technical solution for a given problem, providing a platform to challenge ideas and get feedback from the team. The goal is to achieve clarity on implementation and align the team on the high-level approach.

- *Output and Artifacts*: The output of technical grooming includes high-level design documents and a breakdown of tasks for progressive delivery of the solution.

- *Roles and Guidelines*: Assign an engineer as the topic owner for each project to drive discussions and draft a technical plan for implementation. As an engineering manager, your role is to ensure the process runs smoothly, foster collaboration, and maintain a constructive environment for open discussions.

- *Operation and Consistency*: The operation and frequency of technical grooming sessions depend on how often requirements are presented. Plan these sessions in detail to ensure consistency.

Here's a sample agenda for a technical grooming session:

- *Reconfirm Requirements*: Review the requirements and clarify any questions or note them for follow-up with the product manager.

- *High-Level Design*: Discuss the architecture, system design, and system interfaces, such as APIs, integrations, and communication patterns.

- *Low-Level Technical Approach*: This is optional and should avoid overly detailed programming constructs while addressing data models, constraints, entities, and relationships. Adjust the level of detail based on the project and requirements.

- *Fault Tolerance and Resilience*: Consider how the solution will handle failures, its impact on clients, and how to ensure a positive user experience.

- *Logging and Monitoring*: Decide how extensive logging and monitoring should be to detect and respond to failures.

- *Milestones and Delivery Scope*: Define milestones and the scope of each milestone. Ensure alignment with the product manager on the approach.

- *Testing Strategy*: Discuss how to test the release, including options like A/B testing or gradual rollout.

- *Risks, Dependencies, and Rollout Plan*: Identify risks, dependencies, stakeholders, and the discovery and rollout plan.

- *Avoid Over-Engineering*: Focus on delivering quality code without over-complicating the solution. Track technical debt and add it to the backlog for future resolution.

Adapt this agenda to fit your team's needs and review it to ensure it suits your specific context.

Do you need technical grooming for every minor decision?: Technical grooming may not be necessary for every small decision. Ensure your team has the autonomy to move quickly when needed. Technical grooming is most valuable for decisions that are complex, irreversible, or difficult to address later in the development cycle.

Estimation

Let's kick off with a quick exercise: "What's the first word that comes to your mind when you think about estimations in software development?".

Your time starts now.

...

...

Beeeep, time's up!

What did you come up with? Does it align with any of the words in the Figure 8-2 or is it something entirely different? That word likely reflects your personal experience with estimations.

Estimations involve predicting the effort, time, and resources needed to develop a requirement. This process requires making educated guesses based on the project's scope, requirements, complexity, and other relevant factors.

As engineering managers, we are the ones keeping a close watch on these estimates. Our role includes reporting to stakeholders about the anticipated time required to develop and deliver requested changes and managing project resources. Our stakeholders, ranging from internal stakeholders to senior leadership, rely on these estimates to make informed decisions and communicate with clients. Clearly, there's a lot riding on these numbers.

Figure 8-2. *Word cloud for estimations*

How many times have you estimated a task to take a few days, only to find it dragging on for weeks? This discrepancy could stem from inaccurate estimations or issues with project execution. Misestimation is common in the industry; research from HBR reveals that one in six software projects experiences cost overruns of over 200% and delays of nearly 70%. Estimations are inherently challenging—there's no denying it.

When an estimation could go wrong?:

- *Incomplete Understanding of Requirements*: Estimations are prone to error when there's a lack of clarity or a misunderstanding of project requirements. If the development team does not have a comprehensive understanding of the scope, complexity, or intricacies of the tasks involved, estimations are likely to be inaccurate.

- *Unforeseen Technical Challenges*: Unexpected technical challenges or hurdles that emerge during the development process can significantly impact estimations. Issues such as unfamiliar technologies, unanticipated integration complexities, or unforeseen dependencies can lead to delays and resource overruns.

- *Overlooking Delivery Efforts*: Estimations may go awry when they focus solely on development efforts while overlooking the time and resources required for testing, debugging, deployment, and other delivery-related activities. Ignoring these aspects can lead to underestimating the overall effort and time needed for successful project completion.

- *Inadequate Contingency Planning*: Failure to account for uncertainties, risks, and potential setbacks in the estimation process can result in inaccurate predictions. Without a robust contingency plan to address unforeseen challenges or changes in requirements, the development team may struggle to meet the initially estimated timelines and resource allocations.

Misestimations come with their own costs—unrealistic deadlines, compromised quality, and team burnout, which can ultimately damage your team's credibility. You have to manage expectations effectively to avoid these pitfalls and ensure that both your engineers and stakeholders remain satisfied.

How to Estimate Better

The closer you take the estimate to reality, the better. How can you do that?

- *Break Down Tasks*: Break down tasks so that it's easy to manage and deliver. The more granular you go, the more accurate estimates will be.

- *Bring Delivery into the Equation*: Factor in the time and resources required for delivery tasks like testing and deployment.

- *Take Uncertainty into Account*: Recognize that some level of uncertainty is always present. Define risks and dependencies, and plan spike tasks to explore unknowns.

- *Challenge Estimations*: Encourage a culture of challenging and discussing estimates within the team. Avoid a "first come, first served" approach and foster group discussions to refine estimates.

#Estimate or #NoEstimate?

You might wonder, "What if we simply skip estimating altogether?" It's a valid question, and there's a growing trend in the industry—the #NoEstimate movement—that advocates for focusing on continuous delivery and iteration rather than precise estimates.

To estimate or not to estimate? This choice depends on your team's preferences and working style. Nonetheless, senior leadership will likely still ask, "How long will it take to complete this project, and what is your team's roadmap for the quarter?"

In many scenarios, providing a clear and accurate estimate is essential. For instance, Sales might need a timeline to secure a major deal, or another team's schedule might depend on a feature your team has to deliver. If your feature is part of a larger product launch, coordinating the release and promotional efforts will likely depend on having a clear estimate. In such cases, providing an estimate is often unavoidable.

You must provide a high-level plan and roadmap for your team while accounting for the inherent uncertainty. With the constant innovation and rapid iterations in today's development landscape, effective management, communication, agility, and adaptability are often more important than the estimates themselves.

Be pragmatic about estimations:

- *Treat Estimates as Estimates*: Avoid letting estimates dictate compromises on software quality.

- *Avoid Deadline-Driven Development*: Instead of rigidly sticking to deadlines, focus on deliverable scopes and plan iterative improvements.

- *Promote Collaboration and Communication*: Encourage open dialogue and collaboration within the team and with stakeholders. Regular updates and transparency can help manage expectations.

- *Iterate and Learn*: Use past projects and post-mortems to refine future estimates. Embrace continuous improvement to enhance accuracy over time.

Collaboration, engagement, and curiosity are essential when navigating the uncertainty of software development. A team that accepts uncertainty and approaches development with an open mindset is more likely to stay motivated and succeed.

Development Phase

It took some time to reach the development phase. Nevertheless, it's totally worth your team's time to make sure you approach the state of conundrum pragmatically so that they're sure why they are developing, the impact, and how they will be developing.

Development

Your engineers thrive on building solutions, don't they? Development is where the real action happens, turning abstract ideas into tangible results. It's the phase where code is crafted, features are built, and the software starts to take shape. For many engineers, this is the most exhilarating part of their job, as they translate concepts into functional products and see their work come to life.

You play a pivotal role in guiding the development process. Your responsibility extends beyond just overseeing tasks; it involves shaping the environment in which your team works. This includes providing the right tools, fostering effective communication, and ensuring that developers have the support they need to perform at their best.

Focus on Developer Experience

Recently, the concept of developer experience (DX) has become increasingly prevalent. DX is centered on creating an environment and providing tools that enhance developers' productivity and satisfaction. It's not just about the technical aspects of development but also about how developers interact with their work environment and tools. A positive DX leads to smoother workflows, reduced friction, and greater overall job satisfaction. This, in turn, contributes to better product quality and more efficient development processes.

By focusing on DX, you help your team to work more effectively, reduce frustration, and improve their overall experience. This makes a significant difference in how quickly and efficiently solutions are developed, ultimately leading to better outcomes for both the team and the business.

What are the DX aspects that you should care about as an engineering manager? GitHub defines developer experience as a combination of developer productivity, impact, and satisfaction (Figure 8-3).

- *Productivity* refers to how efficiently changes can be made to the codebase.

- *Impact* measures how seamlessly ideas transition from conception to production.

- *Satisfaction* evaluates how the development environment, workflows, and tools influence developer happiness.

You can run a DX survey (see Figure 8-3) focusing on understanding the effectiveness and productivity in the development processes on what needs to be improved.

Figure 8-3. *Developer experience survey*

The following are some usual concerns that engineers face:

- *Ineffective Collaboration*: Any communication bottlenecks or silos in your team spell trouble, leading to waste, missed opportunities, and a sluggish development process. Don't ignore the telltale signs of miscommunication, confusion, duplication of effort, and so on.

- *Disjointed Tool Integration*: Fragmented toolsets are nothing but roadblocks for modern developers. When tools don't mesh well, it's a sure-fire productivity killer. Look out for grievances about constant tool switching or manual data transfers.

- *Laggy feedback loops*: Timely feedback is the lifeblood of progress. Without it, you're left with wasted time, rising frustration, and a stalled development process. Pay close attention to feedback delays.

- *Unsatisfactory Documentation and Resources*: A stellar DX requires comprehensive and accessible documentation. If developers are left in the lurch, scrambling for answers, your DX is taking a hit. Keep an ear out for repeated questions or frustrations around information access.

- *Burnout and Attrition*: A dismal DX is a surefire recipe for exhausted developers and a revolving door of team members. Monitor workload levels and well-being to keep burnout at bay.

- *The Hard Truth Shows Up in the End Product*: A suffering DX often manifests as compromised product quality and delayed releases. Keep a close watch on progress and performance as symptoms of underlying DX issues.

You improve developer experience when you reduce friction in software development. Here are the steps you can take to reduce friction and improve productivity:

- *Conduct Regular Audits*: Start by systematically evaluating your existing tools and processes. Identify bottlenecks, inefficiencies, or any areas causing unnecessary friction. Make this analysis an ongoing practice to ensure your environment continues to support, not hinder, your developers' workflow.

- *Upgrade Your Tools*: Select and upgrade tools that enhance collaboration, streamline processes, and reduce redundancies. Remember, the tools should also have robust integration capabilities to limit time wasted on switching contexts or manually transferring data.

- *Refine Coding Standards*: Implement clear, consistent, and well-documented coding practices. This improves code readability and maintainability. Automating code reviews and employing linting tools can help enforce these standards.

- *Automate Tasks*: Automating routine tasks, such as code formatting, testing, and deployment, drastically reduces manual work. This lets developers focus more on creative problem-solving and innovation, boosting productivity and job satisfaction.

- *Establish Robust Feedback Loops*: Encourage constructive feedback within your team. Leverage AI-powered tools to automate feedback, analyze code changes, and spot performance bottlenecks. Instant feedback allows developers to make immediate corrections, leading to a more efficient development process and a higher-quality codebase.

Combine data with empathy and a deep understanding of the personal experiences behind the metrics. The goal is to foster an environment where developers can thrive and feel appreciated. This is the essence of DX and it starts with us, engineering managers. By improving the development environment, we boost developer satisfaction, create better products, and achieve better business outcomes.

Should Engineering Managers Contribute to Development?

The decision for engineering managers to contribute to development work hinges on a balance between the benefits and challenges.

Direct involvement in coding offers several advantages. It provides managers with deeper technical insights, enabling more informed decisions and better guidance. Engaging in development fosters empathy and improves support for team members, leading to a stronger, more cohesive team. Additionally, it keeps managers updated on the latest technological advancements, potentially sparking innovation.

However, managing this involvement requires careful consideration. Time management is a key challenge; too much focus on coding can detract from essential leadership duties, such as mentoring and stakeholder communication. Moreover, excessive technical involvement can disrupt team dynamics and create dependency. Managers need to ensure their coding activities do not overshadow their primary leadership responsibilities.

To address these issues, managers should set clear boundaries for their technical contributions. Focus on strategic tasks like solving complex problems or mentoring rather than routine coding. Encouraging team autonomy and regularly assessing the impact of their involvement ensures that both leadership and development goals are met effectively.

In summary, engineering managers should weigh their contributions to development against their leadership duties. By maintaining a balanced approach, they can enhance both their team's performance and their own managerial effectiveness.

Code Review

In our team, every commit to the master branch must go through a Pull Request (PR) process, and each PR must be reviewed and approved by at least one peer. As an engineering manager, your role is to guide this process effectively, ensuring that it enhances both the quality of the code and the collaboration within the team.

Establishing Code Review Guidelines

Code reviews are essential for maintaining code quality, promoting collaboration, and ensuring that the code meets the team's standards. It's essential to define clear guidelines for what a code review should accomplish. The primary goals should be to ensure that the code adheres to agreed-upon standards, functions as intended, and maintains the overall health of the system.

Every PR should be tied to a specific functionality or purpose, such as fixing a bug, paying down technical debt, or implementing a new feature. This ensures that reviews are focused and relevant. Including references to Jira tickets or similar task-tracking tools can provide context for reviewers, helping them understand the changes being made.

Guiding the Review Process

You can influence the effectiveness of the code review process by ensuring that it is both thorough and efficient. Encourage your team to submit PRs that are small and focused. Large PRs can be overwhelming for reviewers, leading to slower reviews and potential oversights. By promoting smaller, incremental changes, you help maintain a steady flow of code through the review process.

Keep an eye on the pace of code reviews. Set expectations that balance thoroughness with the need to maintain development momentum. For instance, bug fixes and critical updates should be reviewed promptly, while other changes should be reviewed within a day. Ensuring that the review process doesn't create bottlenecks is key to keeping your team productive.

Fostering Constructive Feedback

The way feedback is delivered during code reviews can greatly affect team dynamics. Encourage your team to provide feedback that is constructive and focused on the code, not the person who wrote it. This helps maintain a positive and collaborative atmosphere, where team members feel supported rather than criticized.

Guide your team on how to handle disagreements that may arise during code reviews. Encourage direct communication or mediation if necessary, to resolve conflicts quickly and keep the process moving forward. The goal is to ensure that code reviews remain a tool for learning and improvement, rather than a source of frustration.

Supporting Continuous Improvement

Ensure that the code review process continues to evolve along with your team. Regularly gather feedback from your team on the process and be open to making adjustments as needed. This might include refining the guidelines, adjusting the speed of reviews, or addressing any issues that are causing friction.

By staying engaged with the code review process and supporting continuous improvement, you help ensure that it remains effective and aligned with the needs of your team. This not only improves the quality of the code but also fosters a culture of collaboration and excellence within your team.

What About Quality?

In the fast-paced world of software development, teams frequently face the challenge of choosing between speed and quality. The urgency to deliver quickly might make these goals appear to be in constant conflict. But is this trade-off unavoidable? Can speed and quality coexist effectively? By adjusting our approach, we can find that prioritizing quality does not necessarily slow us down; in fact, it can be the key to sustainable speed and success.

Why Should It Always Be Speed vs. Quality? Can They Coexist?

The debate between speed and quality is one of the most persistent in the software development industry. Often, teams feel pressured to deliver features quickly, fearing that a focus on quality will slow them down. However, this perceived trade-off is a false dichotomy. Speed and quality are not opposing forces; they can, and should, coexist. As emphasized in the book *Accelerate* by Forsgren, Humble, and Kim, speed and stability are complementary outcomes that can reinforce each other.

When stability concerns arise, they act as speed bumps that hinder your team's ability to deliver quickly. For instance, if automated tests are lacking, your team is forced to rely on manual testing, which is not only time-consuming but also error-prone and unsustainable at scale. As the complexity of the project grows, manual testing becomes increasingly unmanageable. This leads to a cycle of doubt and fear—your team begins to question the quality of the deliverable, which in turn slows down the entire process.

Moreover, without a robust testing framework, your team is essentially starting from zero each time a new feature is developed. The lack of tests means that every aspect of the software needs to be re-verified, which significantly delays delivery. In contrast, a well-established suite of automated tests can provide immediate feedback, allowing teams to make changes quickly and confidently. Thus, investing in quality upfront, particularly in the form of automated testing, can actually speed up the development process by reducing the friction caused by stability concerns.

Situations Where Speed May Trump Quality

While prioritizing quality is generally the best approach, there are specific situations where speed may need to take precedence. Understanding these scenarios can help you make informed decisions without compromising your long-term objectives.

- *Prototyping*: When developing a prototype, the goal is usually to explore ideas quickly and validate assumptions. Prototypes are often disposable; they are built to be thrown away rather than to last. In such cases, it may not be necessary to invest in rigorous quality measures. The focus should be on speed—getting a working model in front of stakeholders or users as quickly as possible to gather feedback and iterate. However, it's important to recognize that once a prototype evolves into a production-level system, quality should no longer be bypassed.

- *Fixing Critical Incidents*: When a P0 incident occurs—where a critical bug or failure disrupts production—swift resolution takes precedence. In such cases, restoring functionality quickly might require temporarily bypassing certain quality checks, like writing thorough tests. However, this is a short-term solution. After resolving the immediate problem, it's essential to revisit the impacted code, add the necessary tests, and reinforce the test suite. This approach helps prevent similar issues in the future, ensuring long-term stability.

In both scenarios, the key is to strike a balance. While there are moments when speed is essential, neglecting quality entirely can lead to greater problems down the line. Even in these cases, any shortcuts taken should be temporary and followed by a thorough review and improvement of the quality measures.

The Importance of a Clear Definition of Done

A clear and well-communicated "definition of done" (DoD) ensures that everyone on the team—developers, QA engineers, product owners, and stakeholders—has a shared understanding of what it means for a task, feature, or project to be considered complete. Without a clear DoD, tasks may be marked as done prematurely, leading to incomplete features, bugs, or unaddressed requirements that could disrupt the project's timeline and quality.

The DoD should encompass several key criteria:

- *Acceptance Criteria*: These are the specific conditions that a deliverable must meet to be considered complete. They are typically defined by the product owner in collaboration with the development team and should be clear, measurable, and testable. The acceptance criteria form the basis for testing, ensuring that the deliverable meets the user's needs and expectations.

- *Testing and Validation*: Before a task is marked as done, it should pass all relevant tests, including unit tests, integration tests, and any end-to-end tests. This ensures that the software functions correctly in all expected scenarios. Additionally, the software should be validated against the acceptance criteria to confirm that it delivers the expected value.

- *Review and Approval*: The final step in the DoD involves review and approval by a designated person or group, typically the product owner or QA engineer. This step ensures that the deliverable meets the agreed-upon criteria and that all stakeholders are satisfied with the outcome.

Developers should be fully aware of the DoD before they begin working on a task. If they have concerns about meeting the DoD, these should be raised and addressed early on. This proactive communication helps prevent misunderstandings and ensures that the team delivers high-quality software on time.

Who Owns the Quality?

Quality ownership is a shared responsibility across the entire software development team. However, the distribution of this responsibility can sometimes be unclear, leading to gaps in quality assurance. It's important to clarify that everyone involved in the development process has a role to play in ensuring quality:

- *Engineering Manager (aka You)*: As an engineering manager, you play a pivotal role in fostering a culture of quality. This includes setting expectations, providing the necessary resources for quality assurance, and ensuring that quality is prioritized at every stage of development. You should also lead by example, advocating for best practices in testing, code reviews, and continuous integration.

- *QA Engineers*: QA engineers specialize in defining testing strategies, writing and maintaining tests, and ensuring the software meets quality standards. Their involvement should begin at the earliest stages of the project, such as during design and requirement gathering, to provide feedback and identify potential issues before they escalate.

- *Product Managers*: Product managers own the product and, as such, have a vested interest in its quality. They should work closely with the development and QA teams to ensure that the product meets user expectations and business goals. This includes defining clear acceptance criteria and participating in the review and approval process.

- *Developers*: Developers are responsible for writing clean, maintainable code that meets the project's requirements. They should not view testing as solely the QA team's responsibility. Instead, they should be actively involved in writing unit tests, participating in code reviews, and ensuring that their code meets the DoD before it is handed off for final testing.

The fewer handoffs and bottlenecks in the quality assurance process, the better. Streamlining this process ensures a faster feedback loop, allowing issues to be detected and addressed as close to their source as possible. This approach not only improves the overall quality of the software but also accelerates delivery by minimizing rework and reducing the likelihood of defects slipping through to production.

Keeping the QA Environment Stable

A stable QA environment that closely mirrors the production environment will let your team do effective testing. When the QA environment is unreliable or significantly different from production, it undermines the confidence of developers and QA engineers alike, leading to increased risks of defects making their way into production. To ensure the QA environment remains stable and consistent with production, consider the following practices:

- *Automate Database Management*: Manual insertion of database scripts can lead to inconsistencies and errors that are difficult to track and fix. Instead, use tools like Liquibase or Flyway to automate database changes. These tools allow you to version control database scripts, making it easier to manage changes and ensure that the QA environment is always in sync with production.

- *Sync System Configurations*: Ensure that system configurations in the QA environment match those in production. This includes server settings, environment variables, and any other configurations that could affect the behavior of the software. Consistency in configurations helps ensure that the software behaves the same way in both environments, reducing the risk of environment-specific bugs.

- *Regularly Update Dependencies*: Keep all dependencies in the QA environment up to date with those in production. This includes third-party libraries, APIs, and cloud services. Regular updates help prevent integration issues and ensure that testing is done in an environment that accurately reflects production.

- *Frequent Testing in QA*: The more you test in the QA environment, the more you can identify and resolve differences between QA and production. Frequent testing helps to catch environment-specific issues early, ensuring that they are addressed before the software is deployed to production.

By maintaining a stable and production-like QA environment, you can increase the reliability of your tests, build confidence in the testing process, and reduce the likelihood of defects slipping through to production.

Delivery Phase

At this stage in the development cycle, your team's focus should shift from justifying changes to ensuring smooth and rapid delivery. Once a change has been developed and tested, your delivery processes should empower the team to release those changes to production as quickly and confidently as possible. By "confidence," I'm not just referring to the assurance that nothing will break, but rather the confidence that, even if something does fail, your team can quickly roll back the changes or limit the impact to a small subset of users.

I've been part of teams where delivery was a drawn-out process, involving a lengthy checklist and a series of rituals that felt more ceremonial than practical. These included practices like avoiding Friday deployments, preparing extensive release notes, obtaining sign-offs from various stakeholders, and waiting for approval from senior management. While these processes may have had their place in the past, many teams today have moved beyond such cumbersome pre-delivery rituals. Now, it's possible for an engineer to implement a change, verify it against the acceptance criteria, and release it to the world with minimal delay. How refreshing that is!

As an engineering manager, one of your key priorities should be to simplify the delivery process for your team. The best way to do this is by stepping back and allowing the team to operate autonomously, while you focus on identifying and removing obstacles that slow them down during delivery. Ask yourself: Is the team hampered by dependencies on other teams? Is there a lack of confidence due to quality issues that make them fear failure? Or is the technical setup itself outdated and in need of automation to allow for faster movement?

Simplifying the Delivery Process: Key Considerations

These are some key considerations:

- *Architect Systems for Speed*: Advocate for designing systems that are loosely coupled and easy to maintain. Overly complex systems, built for the sake of complexity, can stifle productivity and directly impact business outcomes. Simplified systems facilitate quicker, more reliable deployments.

- *Build Quality Incrementally*: Ensure that quality is not sacrificed in the name of speed. Neglecting quality during each delivery can create significant roadblocks in the future. By incrementally building and maintaining high standards, your team can avoid these pitfalls.

- *Continuously Evolve Technical Setup*: Invest in evolving your technical infrastructure to keep pace with the growing needs of the business. A modern, well-maintained technical setup can dramatically reduce the time and effort required to deliver changes.

- *Keep Changes Small and Manageable*: While it may sound obvious, it's still a challenge for many teams. Small, incremental changes are easier to deploy and less risky than large, monolithic releases. This approach not only simplifies the delivery process but also enhances the team's ability to respond to issues quickly.

Adapting the Delivery Process to Your Team's Needs

The delivery process will naturally vary depending on the nature of your team and the technology stack you're working with. For instance, if you're managing a mobile development team, the process might be more complex due to the requirements of app marketplaces like the Apple Store and Google Play. In such cases, you may need to involve project managers who specialize in managing the app lifecycle, from submission to approval.

Moreover, the delivery process can differ significantly when dealing with urgent situations, such as releasing a hotfix. In these cases, an expedited delivery process is often necessary to get the fix out faster than your usual procedures would allow.

As an engineering manager, you need to define what delivery means within the context of your team and ensure that the process aligns with your business needs. The goal is to create a delivery process that not only matches the operational capabilities of your team but also supports the broader objectives of the business. By doing so, you help ensure that your team can operate at its best, delivering high-quality software efficiently and reliably.

Summary

This chapter took you on a journey through the essential phases of how software is built, providing you with strategies to enhance your team's effectiveness from the initial stages of uncertainty to the final steps of delivery.

The key takeaways included the following:

- *Embracing the Conundrum Phase*: It emphasizes the importance of effectively managing the initial uncertainty with requirement discussions and technical grooming. This ensures the team fully comprehends the purpose and scope of their projects and sets a solid foundation for development.

- *Refining the Development Phase*: The focus shifts to creating an optimal DX to boost productivity and satisfaction. By evaluating and enhancing tools, processes, and collaboration methods, you lead your team toward a more enjoyable and efficient development experience, along with incorporating good quality practices.

- *Streamlining the Delivery Process*: The chapter discusses the critical final steps of delivering software, advocating for systems designed for rapid and confident deployment. Simplifying the delivery process allows for quicker releases and emphasizes the need for architectural flexibility and maintaining high quality.

- *Accurate Estimation Techniques*: A significant portion is dedicated to mastering estimations, acknowledging the challenges and proposing strategies for more realistic forecasting. It advocates for breaking down tasks, considering delivery efforts, accounting for uncertainties, and fostering a culture of challenging and revising estimates.

- *Continuous Improvement Across Phases*: Throughout, there's an undercurrent of iterative improvement and adaptability. Whether it's refining the development environment, improving code review practices, or optimizing delivery mechanisms, the chapter encourages an ongoing evaluation and enhancement of processes.

CHAPTER 9

Technical Processes

October 4, 2021.

Facebook experienced a massive outage that also took down other Meta services. It took around six hours to restore everything back to normal, and in the meantime, it caused them roughly $60 million in ad revenue and much more. If it happens for an internet giant, it could happen for any software engineering team out there.

Imagine you as the engineering manager of the affected team. What would you be doing at this moment? You might be sweating to resolve it at the earliest along with your team or interfacing your stakeholders so that your team focuses on fixing the problem or you might be reading this in a flash news alert chilling out in the Bahamas enjoying your vacation.

Failures in technical systems are inevitable. How soon they get detected and restored matters the most for your team and your business. The longevity of your software and technical systems directly equates to the longevity of your business.

As an engineering manager, you're accountable for defining processes to evolve and review your technical systems on a regular basis and also for reacting and communicating swiftly whenever something goes wrong. As your engineers take care of technical systems, you as a manager should take care of defining, assessing, and evolving the processes to provide clarity and what is expected out of them. See Figure 9-1.

You need technical processes to let engineers proactively review systems and react to abnormalities and incidents swiftly to keep the system up and running.

- *Review (Proactive)*

    - *Operational Review Process*: Review operational metrics of your technical systems on a regular basis to understand the trends and be proactive about their scale and stability in the tide of surmounting traffic and increasing complexity.

© Ananth Ramachandran 2024
A. Ramachandran, *The Complete Engineering Manager*, https://doi.org/10.1007/979-8-8688-0267-6_9

- *System Review Process*: Review your technical systems and their metrics over time for planning technical initiatives to evolve and sustain them, ensuring they meet future business needs and are easy to maintain.

- *Technical Decision-Making Process*: Make technical decisions in your team that are pragmatic, swift, and unbiased.

- *React (Reactive)*

- *Incident management process*: Detect, communicate, and address technical incidents so that you are quick to acknowledge, recover, and perform a postmortem to learn from the incident.

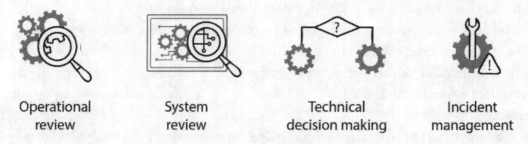

Operational
review

System
review

Technical
decision making

Incident
management

Figure 9-1. *Technical processes for your engineering teams*

Operational Review Process

When I was managing one of the engineering teams, we used to come to the office on Wednesdays and work other days from home. Strangely, we used to face technical incidents almost on that day every week. Either the system would go down or nearly a million background data updates would be waiting to be processed that got stuck in the pipeline. We used to joke that going to the office on Wednesdays is a misfortune and it would be better to work every day from home.

Nevertheless, it was one of the most challenging and stressful times for my team. Our systems were pushed to the limits and unable to cope up with traffic they were handling. We weren't checking the metrics and the trend that was approaching. To make it worse, not everyone in our team understood what was really happening except one engineer. We were keeping our fingers crossed and assuming everything would be fine.

After a brainstorming within our team, we decided we needed a process that let our engineers come together on a regular basis and proactively go through system metrics like scalability, availability, and stability of the services to understand the patterns approaching and any course corrections to be made. We named it the *operational review process*.

Through an operational review process, you can:

- Assess how your apps, systems, and technical services are running right now and for the past few days and weeks.

- Understand whether there are any technical issues happening under the hood and their impact and severity.

- Plan action items to prevent issues from happening or to understand how it could happen in the near future.

How Do You Run It?

To run an operational review process for your technical systems, you need an interface to look into system metrics and trends in the recent past to gauge its health. Based on how and where you deploy your systems, instrumentation and tooling will be provided and available by default. If you're using one of the cloud services like Google Cloud, AWS, Confluent, etc., it comes with a built-in interface to observe system metrics. Third-party tools like Newrelic, Kibana, Datadog, etc., can be integrated as well, which gives you sophisticated monitoring and alerting capabilities based on your application needs.

Once the interface is in place and the metrics are defined, next is to bring your engineers together on a regular basis and set up an agenda for running such an operational review process.

The following can be the agenda of an operational review:

- Start by reviewing the action items committed in the last operational review and discuss its status.

- Review metrics and constraints of your software systems such as memory, processing utilization, and other architectural characteristics such as availability, failure rates, performance of your code, API, database, or any other component as part of your team's scope.

- Make a note of any change in system pattern and the impact it caused. If the change is more than 10%, get a level deeper into what caused it and how it could be prevented next time.

- Plan action items for improvements and assign ownership among engineers.

How long and how often? I could go with an easier answer "It depends." But let me try to explain it better. Ideally such a process can be run once every two weeks for 20 minutes or so. It's recommended for engineers to come prepared and bring up their crucial observations and concerns about the system to discuss with the team. Keeping a running notes of every operational review session will help your team to revisit what was discussed and act as a reference in the longer term to look back.

How does operational review differ from the system review process? Operational review runs more frequently than system review and focuses on day-to-day operations and metrics to incorporate immediate action. Your primary goal is to ensure your technical services remain healthy and stop or reduce the effect of an unforeseen pattern blowing up your infrastructure and systems. System review, on the other hand, is conducted once a quarter or bi-annually from a strategic standpoint, taking mid- to long-term technical initiatives into account when planning and negotiating your quarterly or bi-annual priorities.

When Do You Need It?

You need an operational review process when:

- When your team doesn't understand the pattern on why the issue is occurring nor the root cause of it.

- When your system has faced continuous instability in the recent past and fires are put out almost every week.

- When your team doesn't seem to have the same understanding of what's happening under the hood, and to make it worse, no one seems to take the ownership.

- When your clients are dissatisfied with the quality of your technical system and close collaboration needed among your engineers to keep the system up and running.

You ain't gonna need it (YAGNI) when:

- It's been only a few months since you started building your system and there's no real traffic or abnormalities.

- Your system is pretty stable, and even if it was unstable, your team was on top of it and couldn't recall a time when they looked clueless.

- Everyone in your team has the same level of context about your system and have a common understanding of the technical metrics and its implication.

- There's a high degree of ownership in your teams and your team is proactive in observing patterns and cares about raising concerns before the system blows up.

- You have exceptional monitoring in place, and you can trust it completely.

Our team's situation was a classical case where we felt a need for such a process and it paid us back during the crisis. We were able to proactively flag and address numerous technical incidents that otherwise could have led to major downtime or a mishap. The other benefit of having this process was knowledge and context about our technical system and metrics start to get evened out across our team, which before was in one person's head.

As the entire team started to feel comfortable working with system metrics, taking up ownership became evident. We followed up with building better monitoring and alerting capabilities as we understood our metrics and its baselines better. We were even able to point out specific incidents and why they occurred during the solution design phase and how it could be avoided greatly helped us in designing the system right from the start.

With the technical state of the system getting better daily and everyone assumed ownership, we brought down the frequency gradually from weekly to once in two weeks to once in a month. After all, the goal was not to have a process for the sake of having it but to keep our system healthy and operational without much trouble. We decided to stick to monthly frequency to have healthy technical discussions, and it greatly helped us in reflecting on our systems and avoiding knowledge silos that can form easily in engineering teams.

Technical System Review Process

I'm a leisurely bike rider. I love to explore nearby places with my bike and always had an impression that my bike was in good condition as it never got punctured and I was proud of maintaining it well.

One day when casually discussing bikes with a friend of mine, who is an avid rider, he asked, "How often do you run safety checks on your bike? I'm doing it once a month." I replied, "Hmm well, in fact, I have never done it, and everything is good so far." He replied, "Really? How good?" He introduced me to a bike maintenance chart and made me realize I'd been doing a disservice to my bike all these years. I hadn't lubricated it, I rode it with broken brakes and flat tires, and I'm sure all those vibrations were because of loose bolts, screws, and nuts that I never tightened.

In simple words, I hadn't taken good care of it. The same goes with your code and technical systems. Over time, it tends to deteriorate in terms of performance, scalability, and maintainability if not taken care of. Good care of your technical system means it can evolve and sustain over a period of time to meet the demands of future business needs and ease in maintaining it. How would your team review it and how often? What are the system metrics to care about? What role do individuals and you as a manager play, and how are decisions made? Let's take a look.

How Do You Run It?

The day has come for your team to conduct a technical review of your system. It's pretty exciting and you're unsure what to expect at the same time. What should the agenda be? Do you have a defined software attributes checklist that needs to be ticked? Who are the stakeholders that need to be aware of the results and next steps?

Agenda:

- *Explain your current technical system*: Set the stage for your review by detailing how your system currently performs. Use diagrams to illustrate the overall structure of your architecture, and make a point to explain how the components of your architecture work together.

- *Develop software architecture review goals*: Before you conduct an extensive architecture review with your team, make sure you're aligned toward a common goal. Define software quality attributes that are most important to your team and business. This will help focus your strategy when you review your architecture and plan new projects.

- *Identify software quality issues*: Assess system performance by listing issues with your current architecture and explain how they affect your business or user experience.

- *Plan software quality improvements*: With a clear vision of how to improve your architecture for identified issues, plan the next steps. Prioritize proposed projects and estimate the time, work, and resources needed to complete them.

- *Involve Stakeholders*: Keep relevant stakeholders in the loop about the significance of the improvements planned in terms of how it affects the end user or seek for inputs if there are any to be obtained from them. Product managers and business ops are ideal stakeholders to be informed about the outcome of the system review.

Table 9-1 lists some common attributes associated with general-purpose software systems. If your team's technology is specific and goes into different streams and specializations like data teams, mechanical engineering, AI/ML teams, etc., consider defining technical attributes relevant to your context.

Table 9-1. *Code and System Attributes*

Attribute	Definition	KPI
Maintainability	Time and resource required to repair or refactor a system	Ripple effects of change made, improvement in developer experience
Reliability	System's ability to operate under both normal conditions and unexpected situations	Mean time to failure
Security	System's ability to resist unauthorized attempts at usage	Vulnerabilities, security breaches
Scalability	How effectively the system can scale up to meet increased load	Response time under load, throughput, concurrency, resource utilization
Availability	How much a system is up and running and serving the end users	How long is a service down in a given period, e.g., five 9s uptime in a year equates to less than six minutes of downtime in a year.
API Latency	Time it takes for a request to be processed and a response to be delivered by an API	Response time

How long and how often? Don't get intimidated by the word *process*. It doesn't have to be stringent and tiring. It can be lightweight, and in fact it should be. Once you know what technical metrics to review and instrumentation in place, it's around a half-day activity to review a single technical service. Do you own *n* number of technical services? You know the math. $n \times \frac{1}{2}$ day. Phew!

Depending on the pace at which your system is changing, you can decide on when to have such a technical system review process. Having a full-scale review once every six months and sanity check on every quarter is the right balance for a system review process. But I'll leave it to you to decide the review cadence that suits your team's needs and speed at which your system is changing. It will greatly help you in prioritizing tech initiatives at the right time if your team does quarterly planning by taking the results of system review into account.

When Do You Need It?

It will be too early to run a technical system review process for an engineering team who are just a few months old and who start to dish out feature after feature or too late for a team who are battling almost every day to keep their system up and running. The ideal time for such a review is when your system starts to show signs of wear and tear, probably in a year's time. Here are a few signs that indicate you may need system review is when:

- Development is slowing down and your engineers are complaining about how difficult it is to manage the system and code.

- Your system is under pressure that it couldn't withstand the surmounting scale and availability is compromised more often than not.

- Breaking things in the production becomes a norm for your team.

- Your clients are starting to complain about quality attributes that weren't evident in the earlier phase when your software was rolled out.

Technical Decision-Making Process

Have you ever had a conflict with someone on a technical decision and had strong opinions on your approach? I had that quite a lot when I was an individual contributor. Won some, lost some.

For example, what communication pattern should we go with for a given problem? Should it be event driven or API driven? We were discussing this question for weeks without much progress and ultimately settled with API driven based on voting. On what basis was the voting made? No one knows.

There was no discussion about the pros and cons of both communication patterns, which one was better suited for the given problem statement, and what were the consequences of choosing one over the other.

Engineers who suggested both options were trying to justify their choices with phrases like "We've always used API driven, so we should go with it." Others would say, "Event driven is pretty new and exciting for us, so we should go with that." Some others said, "Another team is using API driven, so that should be our choice too." Decisions were made solely based on personal opinion and randomization rather than achieving team consensus by having a clear and pragmatic process.

It made one thing clear. We weren't sure how to make decisions as one team. We didn't know how to come to a consensus as a team and weren't listening to each other's opinion. To make it more complicated, we didn't have any records of previous decisions and considerations, which had led us to making inconsistent and inaccurate decisions with the processes in place.

Does this sound familiar? You need a process to make technical decisions. The process needs to be lightweight and effective at the same time for your team to make a decision.

How Do You Run It?

Let's see how to adopt a decision-making process in your teams that are pragmatic, swift and unbiased.

Start with a Need

Start with a real product or technical need. Product needs are like building a new feature, adding a capability to a feature, building a whole new product, etc. Even sometimes not every product demands a technical decision like adding a new field, adding a validation to an existing field. It could be a small change so the team can even rule out the decision making process and can proceed with implementation.

Same as a product need, there could be a technical need like refactoring, paying back tech debt, re-architecture to improve some technical characteristics like availability, scalability, consistency, fault tolerance or maintainability of the system. In most cases, technical need demands a decision even if it changes some basic parameters and the nature of your system.

Of course, if you don't have a real product or technical need, you don't have to change anything.

Gather Requirements

Once you're sure with a product or technical need, gather requirements from the respective stakeholders. Requirements for product needs come from a product owner. For technical needs, the technical owner will define the requirements. Even for product needs, nonfunctional requirements like scalability, availability, etc., should be considered.

Apply Constraints

Technical constraints are specifications that enable developers to formalize design rules that technical systems should respect, like the topological conditions of a given architecture pattern or style. Every requirement will have some constraints. Leaving out or not thinking about constraints is a recipe for disaster when making decisions.

Brainstorm Approaches

Every problem statement can be resolved in multiple ways. After understanding the requirements and constraints, it's time to come up with different approaches. At this stage, it's recommended to think of solutions that can be built in house instead of relying on the "off-the-shelf" options. This way, you're providing an opportunity for your team to research, propose, and innovate.

System Dependencies

When making a decision, dependencies with other parts of the system and components need to be analyzed and specified. This helps you to understand the impact of the decision and how to make it compatible with other parts of the system.

Get CERTified

The next step is to get CERTified through Cost, Expertise, Resources, and Time. Your team needs expertise to build an in-house solution and maintain it for life. If your team has the expertise, they need to have a rough understanding of how long an approach takes. If your team thinks they don't have the expertise and are not sure whether they can pull it off, they can develop a proof of concept to gain some confidence in the approach. Cost is another important factor that needs to be considered while weighing your various approaches. If an approach is going to cost a lot, you really have to think about the alternatives. Available human resources to implement an approach also have to be taken into account.

Imagine what would happen if you chose a technology blindly and it ends up costing too much or you don't have the expertise in your team to implement it. That's the result of a hype-driven development. Tools and technologies shouldn't define your architecture. Your architecture needs should affect the decision.

If all the CERTified aspects fail, it means that your team is not ready yet to take up the project. You should reduce the scope of the requirement and redo the CERTified process to understand whether the reduced scope is achievable. Creating a minimum viable product (MVP) and working in multiple iterations will reduce the risk of the project itself as the team can gain an overview as soon as they release some iterations; over time expertise can also be built.

Build vs. Buy

If the team has no expertise and resources for any of the approaches and the organization has a strategy to release as soon as possible, now it's time to think about "build versus buy." With the buy route, you have to evaluate the various options. Comparing the specifications and offerings that each vendor is providing and balancing with the cost that you can afford will result in a good buy. Even a minimal proof of concept can be done with various buy options to understand the integration efforts that might be involved.

Onboarding Stakeholders

Once the decision has been taken, other stakeholders can be onboarded to provide them with clarity on the timeline of the project, the trade-off involved, and the consequences. Every decision in software architecture has some trade-off involved. It's important that those trade-offs aren't ignored, and communicating that to stakeholders will help them in setting the expectations for the user experience.

Documenting Decisions

Documenting architecture decisions can be done in as simple a format as possible. Michael Nygard invented a simple format for recording architecture decisions called architecture decision records (ADRs).

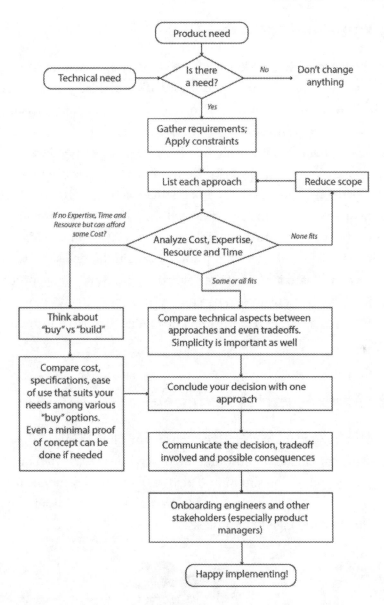

Figure 9-2. *Making a technical decision*

Figure 9-2 shows one view of the process; the steps shown can completely vary from one team to another. Customize the steps as per your requirements and the team's circumstances.

With these decisions, the "why" part is the most important aspect, as one can refer back later as to why certain technical decisions have been made and why other choices were ignored, what the constraints and trade-offs involved were, and what the consequence mentioned was.

When Do You Need It?

You should establish a decision-making process when choices within your team are becoming increasingly opinionated. In such cases, it's essential to create an impartial framework that allows all team members to review options, challenge assumptions, and voice their own suggestions and concerns. This helps ensure that decisions are not solely influenced by personal bias but are evaluated from diverse perspectives.

Additionally, when your team finds itself stuck in continuous discussions without reaching a conclusion, it's often a sign of procrastination or uncertainty. A well-defined decision-making process can help break this cycle of indecision by providing clear steps to follow, guiding the team toward actionable outcomes rather than endless debate.

Finally, if there is historical uncertainty about how similar decisions were made—what factors were considered and what the consequences were—it becomes crucial to have a process in place. This ensures transparency and consistency, allowing the team to learn from past experiences and apply that knowledge to make informed decisions on current challenges.

Incident Management Process

When I think about how we manage and resolve technical incidents in the engineering world, it has striking similarities to how first-aid procedures are carried out when someone faces a life-threatening situation. The 3 Ps of First Aid principle (Figure 9-3) are Preserve Life, Prevent Deterioration, and Promote Recovery. This also applies when designing your incident management process.

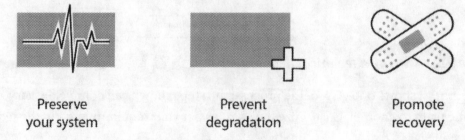

Preserve
your system

Prevent
degradation

Promote
recovery

Figure 9-3. *Three Ps of First Aid principle for your incident management process*

- *Preserve Life*: With any first-aid process, first a person's life should be preserved irrespective of whatever it takes; same goes with your technical systems. You can apply quick measures to your technical systems to recover from failure. Check your system's health by checking its availability, error rates, and responsiveness. Don't forget to dial in to technical subject-matter experts of the system under stress.

- *Prevent Deterioration*: Don't deploy any further changes to stop further deterioration. Contain the service abnormality with rate limiting, feature flag, and circuit breaker techniques and look for a quick fix.

- *Promote Recovery*: Let your system operate with additional resources for a couple of days if that helps. Keep an eye on how system metrics evolve over a period of time. Do a blameless postmortem so it doesn't happen again.

For every piece of software consumed by users, it's advisable to have an incident management process that ensures organizations can respond promptly and effectively to incidents. It can have a significant impact on clients, regardless of whether the business follows a B2B or B2C model. The effectiveness of incident management directly influences how clients experience and perceive the services or products offered by a business and developed by your team.

Especially if you're building a B2B product, you know the retention of your clients will be at stake when you can't ensure stability and if your system continues to face technical issues and downtime. Not only with clients, the dynamics of your internal stakeholders will change, with a bit more agitation and tension going around. Your service-level agreement (SLA) will be your communication protocol with clients, which can be your friend or enemy depending on the context. It safeguards your team if well defined, but in most of the cases it puts pressure on teams if not handled well.

If B2B is all about retaining and acquiring new clients, B2C is more about user experience. In the age of social media, incidents in B2C can quickly become public. Efficient incident management is essential to mitigate negative publicity, preserve brand reputation, and assure consumers that issues are being addressed.

How Do You Run It?

When I was managing a mobile team of a B2B product, I understood what it really takes to resolve a technical incident and why having one process saves everyone's time and lets your team ultimately focus on resolving the issue rather than being interrupted by many stakeholders.

We released a mobile app version with a bug that impacts every iOS user by not letting them enter into the app due to a security issue that happens only when downloaded from the app store. We did all our testing from a local repository that was not a store version and released it. What happened next? I happily went home after dropping a "we rock!" emoji in the team Slack channel.

The next morning, I was invited to a call where the project manager, product manager, CPO, and customer support manager were on the same call. I never saw all of them in one call and guessed there was something big happening. The mere presence of the customer support manager indicated to me I should start worrying. Not to my disappointment, our customer support manager started, "We were reported that none of the users were able to log in to the app and use it. We're getting pressure from our clients, and it's causing a big headache." I responded with a confused expression yet pragmatic, "When did this start to happen?." He replied, "Yesterday evening." It rang a bell loud inside my head, "We did a mobile release." I didn't say anything about it right away but replied, "We will look into it and get back with more findings and next steps." The CEO pitched up and asked, "When can it be addressed? Some clients are calling me directly?." I replied, "Within a day."

That's where it all started.

After digging deeper, we did find the issue, and the resolution wasn't straightforward at all. We had to bring all the internal stakeholders on the same page to make a decision on the next steps and look for an expedited app release process as we still had to submit the app for approval and it would take a day or two to reach the end user. And how can I miss the communication part? We had to strategize how we communicated to users, as we couldn't send push notifications as users couldn't open the app itself. We set up email communication for all iOS users extracted from our system, and on the other hand, our executives managed big clients directly over phones and chats.

I probably don't have to explain why you need a streamlined incident management process. You need a way to detect an incident before a user reports, prioritize it based on the impact, and set up a communication strategy for internal and external clients. Later based on the priority, you need a way to let your team focus on resolving the issue rather than being interrupted by your internal stakeholders.

Here are the steps that you can adopt in your incident management process:

- *Detect*: First things first. You need a way to detect incidents happening in your system, either through automated monitoring and alerting or done manually. If you come to know about a technical incident only through users, you need to work on your process, as your users have other things to care about.

- *Prioritize*: Once you detect an issue, you need to prioritize it by the scale of the impact, nature of the feature (if a user can't log in, it's a P0 issue), and severity of the incident.

- *Communicate*: Communicate and interface with stakeholders about regular updates on the resolution. It's on you as an engineering manager to take care of this responsibility so that your team can focus on resolving the issue.

- *Create*: Create an incident in your favorite project management tool so that it's visible for the entire team and for tracking.

- *Troubleshoot and Resolve*: Provide time for your team to troubleshoot and resolve the issue.

- *Release and Monitor*: Plan and release the resolution for the incident. Monitor to ensure the system runs normally and the reported incident is resolved.

- *Postmortem*: Perform a blameless post mortem on why the incident happened in the first place, how to improve early detection of the incident if possible, and what can be improved.

Having a postmortem is such a crucial step in the entire incident management process so that you ensure your team learns from the incident and focuses on improvement rather than placing blame on a person.

When Do You Need It?

It's good to have an incident management process defined for every piece of software that has been released to the public, even at the early stage when you start to acquire clients. It's a no-brainer to have one if you're building a renowned product and improving it over time. The faster you detect issues, the better the resolution time will be. The better the resolution time, the more satisfied your internal and external clients will be.

Your Role in the Technical Processes

As your team runs technical processes, your role as an engineering manager is to set it up, review it, and be a bridge in communicating the needs of such a process. You also need to get alignment with the wider leadership team. You can participate in any of the technical processes as a volunteer to listen and provide suggestions based on your view.

You can influence the process in the following ways:

- Review the output of the technical process, clarify your questions, or provide feedback to your team.

- Share it with nontechnical stakeholders in their vocabulary about the outcome of a technical process and how it could impact the business and product.

- Help your team to prioritize tech initiatives based on the system metrics and how it could affect the current status quo and future development.

- Prioritize and communicate incident resolution to relevant stakeholders. Drive continuous improvements out of that experience through an effective and blameless postmortem process.

- Improve how the process is conducted and look for improvements in collaboration among participants.

Summary

In this chapter, we explored the crucial role that technical processes play in ensuring the health and longevity of software systems, inspired by the significant Facebook outage on October 4, 2021. This example served as a stark reminder that system failures can strike any team, regardless of size or stature, emphasizing the need for engineering managers and their teams to be well-prepared.

Here's a summary of the key processes discussed:

- *Operational Review Process*: Think of this as your system's regular health check-up. It's about staying ahead of potential issues by keeping an eye on the metrics that matter—scalability, stability, and performance. It's all about being proactive rather than reactive.

- *Technical System Review Process*: This process involves taking a step back to ensure your technical systems are aligned with future business needs and are as painless as possible to maintain. It's about looking at the big picture, identifying improvement areas, and planning for growth and challenges.

- *Technical Decision-Making Process*: Here, the focus shifts to how you and your team make those tough technical calls. It's about cutting through the noise to make decisions that are informed, balanced, and aligned with your project's goals. It's crucial for resolving differences of opinion and making sure that decisions are based on solid reasoning rather than just gut feelings.

- *Incident Management Process*: This is akin to emergency first aid but for your technical systems. When things go south, this process is your playbook for minimizing damage, getting back on track quickly, and learning from the incident to prevent future ones. It covers everything from detecting and prioritizing incidents to communicating effectively and conducting a thorough postmortem.

These processes are more than just bureaucratic steps; they are foundational to building a culture that values foresight, readiness, and continuous improvement. They empower teams to anticipate and mitigate issues before they turn into crises, align technical efforts with business objectives, and maintain high standards of system health and stability.

As an engineering manager, your job extends beyond the technical; it involves facilitating clear communication, aligning technical strategies with broader business goals, and nurturing a culture of accountability and improvement. By embracing and refining these technical processes, you not only protect your technical systems but also drive the sustained growth and success of your business.

PART IV

Mastering Prioritization

Eat. Sleep. Prioritize. Repeat.

Don't be surprised if your routine looks like that. You have to prioritize work for you and your team ruthlessly. If there's only one thing to do, you don't have to prioritize at all. But that's not the reality. Your team will have n+1 things to do, if they were doing n things yesterday.

Product teams work toward bigger goals for their organization—their North Star. From Spotify's "Music for everyone and everywhere" to Airbnb's "Belong anywhere" to Uber's "Setting the world in motion," a North Star is what makes an organization evolve and thrive for continuous success. It is ambitious, game-changing, and visionary. How do you make it a reality? What does the journey toward your North Star look like? Will it be smooth sailing?

Rarely, the path to your North Star looks like a straight line. You will have more than one way to reach your goals in the form of strategic initiatives. And it involves twists, turns, obstacles, and unexpected challenges along the way. If one project doesn't deliver the expected outcome, you resort to another and another and another. However, your North Star remains the same. That's what you call a strategy.

Your product manager leads in defining priorities aligning to your organization's North Star and planning what initiatives to work on. You, as an engineering manager, will be consulted and will lead in pulling it off along with your team, realizing your product manager's vision. To add a flavor and challenge to your role, priorities do change. You play a crucial role in adapting to changing priorities and realigning your team's focus. And there's a people aspect to it.

Change in priorities means that what your engineers have been building all these days will be put on hold or discontinued; they'll need to get onboarded into the new priority initiative and start working on it. It can be frustrating for some and exciting for others, depending on their temperament and how product-minded they are. Nevertheless, you have to put in time and effort to not run off with changing priorities, but rather take time to hear what your engineers have to say and communicate the reasoning behind it with clarity. You know, at the end of the day, they are the ones who are building the product.

Strategic initiatives are your big rocks that move your business forward. To prioritize two to three initiatives, you have to deprioritize at least a dozen others. Fine, how about pebbles and sand? How do you treat ad hoc operational requests and quick wins in the middle of strategic initiatives? An impact-and-effort matrix is a simple yet effective technique that works like a charm. Low-to-medium effort and high impact initiatives are your quick wins, which are your pebbles.

Sand is mostly tech debts or small product improvements that can be done in a couple of days to a week without overthinking. Giving space to your engineers to do such work would greatly increase their motivation and autonomy. Imagine how productive they would feel to cross out three to five small tasks in the backlog in a short span of time? A real productivity booster. On the other hand, ad hoc operational requests and incidents are to be treated based on their urgency as they might have a negative impact with your customers if not resolved on time.

By the way, have you ever said no to a random request from your stakeholders? If not, practice saying it. You have to use it a lot. Remember, prioritization can't happen without deprioritization.

In the midst of ambitious product development, you have to make short-term trade-offs and prioritize speed over quality. The result? Accumulation of technical debts. Tech debts aren't bad until they turn into a nightmare for your engineers and systems, which ultimately slows down product development in the later phases due to maintenance load and increased complexity. Timely prioritization of technical improvements along with implementing new features can help your team to keep a sustainable pace of product development.

Your technical experience can greatly help you in advocating for technical improvements and negotiating with your product counterpart. Prioritizing technical initiatives ahead of product development is a big deal, so make sure it really deserves to be prioritized. Your best bet would be to show the value it brings and what problem you are trying to solve.

You need to focus on what matters most for yourself, your team, and your organization by prioritizing effectively and sustainably. This is precisely what you'll be mastering in this part.

- ***The Bigger Picture:*** Know your organization's big bets, vision and mission, Mastering the Strategy Trio: Business, Product and Engineering Strategy, OKRs in action, Acting as a bridge in top-down and bottom-up approach.

- ***Pragmatic Approach To Prioritization:*** You'll explore prioritization techniques like the Impact-Effort Matrix, MoSCoW, and Rock, Pebbles, and Sand, and avoid common pitfalls, Managing shifting priorities and best practices for deprioritization—including balancing stakeholder demands with strategic goals and maintaining transparency.

- ***Prioritizing Technical Initiatives:*** Managing technical debts and the People Effect, Keeping up-to-date prioritized technical backlog, Advocating for rock-sized technical initiatives.

CHAPTER 10

The Bigger Picture

Why is your team working on building the personalization feature for your users? Why is there a new merger-and-acquisition project? Why are you decoupling your system architecture when you go months without rolling out any new product features? Most importantly, why now? And why not other initiatives?

That's a lot of questions to start with. In the myriad of possibilities, you need a way to know what your team should work on right now to contribute to your organization's success. In short, you need to know the bigger picture.

When it comes to the concept of the bigger picture, few companies illustrate it as clearly as Spotify. With the mission of delivering "Music for everyone, everywhere," Spotify has set an ambitious vision that drives every decision, from high-level strategy down to daily tasks. This vision isn't just a lofty statement; it's a guiding principle that shapes how the company prioritizes its initiatives and measures success.

Spotify's vision reflects a "big, hairy, audacious goal" (BHAG)—a long-term, ambitious target that energizes and unites the organization. This goal is bold and inspirational, for Spotify aiming not just to be a music service but to transform how people experience music globally. But having a grand vision is only the starting point. To turn this vision into reality, Spotify needs a concrete strategy that answers key questions: "What do we prioritize? Where do we focus our resources? What success metrics should we track?"

Defining the North Star Metric

For Spotify, the answer lies in their North Star metric (Figure 10-1): *time spent listening to music by subscribers*. This metric isn't arbitrary; it's carefully chosen because it directly ties back to their vision. The more time users spend listening to music on Spotify, the closer the company gets to achieving its mission of being the go-to platform for music lovers everywhere.

© Ananth Ramachandran 2024
A. Ramachandran, *The Complete Engineering Manager*, https://doi.org/10.1007/979-8-8688-0267-6_10

Figure 10-1. *The North Star metric*

This North Star Metric serves multiple purposes:

- *Guidance*: It provides a clear focus for the entire organization. When teams at Spotify are deciding which features to develop, which markets to enter, or how to allocate resources, they consider how their choices will impact this core metric.

- *Alignment*: It aligns different departments—product, marketing, engineering, and sales—around a common goal. Whether it's improving the recommendation algorithms or launching new artist partnerships, every effort is measured against how it contributes to increasing listening time.

- *Prioritization*: The metric also helps in making tough prioritization decisions. For instance, if Spotify's data indicates that enhancing personalization features could lead to more time spent listening, this initiative might take precedence over others. On the other hand, if a project doesn't directly contribute to this metric, it might be re-evaluated or deprioritized.

Making Big Bets

Spotify's strategy involves making "big bets"—strategic initiatives that have the potential to significantly move the needle on their North Star metric. These aren't small, incremental changes but rather bold moves that require substantial investment and carry a certain level of risk.

Consider Spotify's investment in machine learning and data analytics to power their personalized playlists, like Discover Weekly and Release Radar. These features didn't just happen by chance; they were the result of deliberate, data-driven decisions to enhance user engagement. By focusing on personalization, Spotify aimed to increase the time users spent discovering and enjoying music on their platform. The success of these features not only drove up user engagement but also reinforced Spotify's position as a leader in music streaming.

Another example of a big bet is Spotify's push into podcasts. Recognizing the growing popularity of podcasts and their potential to increase listening time, Spotify invested heavily in acquiring podcast production companies and exclusive content deals. This strategic move was aligned with their goal of maximizing user engagement, and it has helped Spotify expand beyond music, offering a broader range of audio content to keep users on their platform longer.

The Purpose, Vision, and Mission

Every department works toward the bigger goals of their organization. These goals aren't generated by AI yet but are the result of human discussions and decisions based on collective knowledge and experience. As these goals are set, they are communicated through various levels of management (Figure 10-2). You receive goals and priorities from your manager, who received them from their manager, who, in turn, got from their manager.

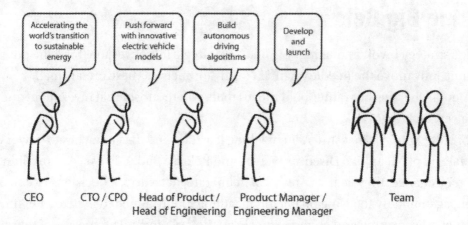

Figure 10-2. *Goals communicated through chains of management*

While goals and strategy are conveyed through people, they are adapted to fit the specific context of each team while remaining aligned with the organization's overall purpose, vision, and mission.

Vision is the long-term aspirational statement that defines where the organization wants to go. It is the big-picture idea that inspires and guides every decision made within the company. *Mission* is the more immediate and practical statement that outlines the organization's core *purpose*—what it does today to achieve its vision. Together, the vision and mission provide a clear direction for the organization, ensuring that all efforts are aligned with these guiding principles.

At a visionary electric car company, the CEO sets the overarching goal of "Accelerating the world's transition to sustainable energy," which encompasses advancing technology and expanding product offerings. This goal is deeply connected to the company's vision of a future powered by sustainable energy and its mission to create innovative electric vehicles that drive this transition. Let's see how that ambitious goal is translated into actionable objectives across different levels of the organization:

- *Chief product officer (CPO) and chief technology officer (CTO)*:
  Work closely together to translate the CEO's vision into actionable objectives. CPO translates these technological advancements into product goals, such as developing new vehicle models that integrate these innovations while remaining affordable and appealing to customers. Simultaneously, CTO focuses on technological advancements, such as improving the performance of autonomous driving systems and enhancing battery efficiency.

- *VP of product management and VP of engineering*: VP of product management ensures that these technological enhancements are incorporated into new vehicle models that meet market demands and align with the CPO's product vision. Meanwhile, the VP of engineering might prioritize the technical development of new autonomous driving algorithms and battery technologies.

- *Head of product and Head of Engineering*: The head of product works on designing the new vehicle models, incorporating the latest technologies and ensuring they meet customer needs. On the other hand, the head of engineering focuses on the technical implementation of new systems, ensuring that advancements in technology are effectively developed and tested.

- *Product Manager and Engineering Manager*: The product manager coordinates these technical developments with the creation and launch of new vehicle models, ensuring that the final products align with the product vision and technological capabilities. The engineering manager leads efforts to develop and refine new technologies, such as autonomous driving systems and advanced batteries.

Effective communication is vital for successful prioritization and alignment within any team. As engineering managers, our role goes beyond simply assigning tasks and managing timelines. If we aren't clear in our communication and strategic in our prioritization, our team members may struggle to grasp the significance of their work. This can lead to confusion and a sense of being "lost in translation," where the connection between their day-to-day tasks and the organization's overarching goals becomes unclear.

You might think prioritization is the first thing that your team should do. But if you want to do it right, it comes after knowing your organization's purpose, goals, and strategy. Without understanding your organizational needs and goals, you can barely prioritize. You have to understand the purpose, vision, and mission for the following:

- *Alignment with Organizational Goals*: Knowing the company's mission and strategic objectives ensures that your team's efforts are aligned with what's most important for the organization. This alignment helps in setting relevant priorities that contribute to the company's success.

- *Contextual Relevance*: Understanding the broader strategy helps you explain to your team why certain tasks are prioritized. When team members see how their work contributes to larger goals, they are more motivated and engaged.

- *Effective Resource Allocation*: With a clear grasp of organizational needs, you can allocate resources more effectively, focusing on initiatives that offer the greatest impact.

You have to implement specific strategies to bridge the gap between high-level goals and daily tasks and to ensure your team remains focused and aligned. These actions will help you communicate effectively, prioritize tasks accurately, and maintain a clear connection between your team's work and the organization's objectives. Here are the key steps for achieving this:

- *Engage in Strategic Alignment Meetings*: Regularly participate in meetings with senior leadership to stay updated on the organization's goals and strategies. This ensures you have the most current information to translate into actionable priorities for your team.

- *Communicate the Bigger Picture*: Clearly explain to your team how their tasks contribute to the company's goals. Share this context in meetings and project briefings to help them understand the relevance of their work.

- *Align Priorities with Strategic Objectives*: Use tools like objectives and key results (OKRs) to set team goals that support the organization's strategic objectives. Ensure that your priorities are directly contributing to the company's success.

- *Implement Feedback Loops*: Establish regular check-ins with your team to review progress and adjust priorities as needed. This helps maintain alignment and allows you to adapt to evolving organizational needs.

- *Foster Open Communication Channels*: Create an environment where team members feel comfortable asking questions and providing feedback. Encourage open dialogue to clarify misunderstandings and ensure alignment.

- *Educate Your Team on Organizational Strategy*: Conduct training sessions or workshops to enhance your team's understanding of the company's mission and goals. This fosters greater engagement and a stronger connection to the broader objectives.

- *Regularly Review and Adjust Priorities*: Periodically reassess and adjust priorities based on team feedback and changes in organizational strategy. This ensures that your team's focus remains relevant and impactful.

Figure 10-3. *Vision to initiatives*

By adopting these practices, you can enhance communication, effectively set priorities, and ensure that your team's efforts are consistently aligned (Figure 10-3) with the organization's strategic goals.

Business, Product, and Engineering Strategy

Strategy is a word that's overused but underutilized in many organizations that deem themselves innovative.

In practical terms, a strategy is the overarching plan that outlines how an organization will achieve its long-term goals. Think of it as the game plan that guides all decisions and actions. It helps you understand what you want to accomplish, how you're going to get there, and what steps you need to take to overcome obstacles along the way. In essence, a strategy is about setting a clear direction and making smart choices to achieve long-term objectives.

To effectively run an innovative organization, strategy is essential for the following:

- *Aligning Vision*: Ensuring everyone is working toward the same goal

- *Guiding Decision-Making*: Providing a clear framework for making consistent and informed decisions

- *Achieving Long-Term Goals*: Outlining how to reach key milestones and sustain success over time

In an innovative organization, strategies from different specializations—business, product, and engineering—must work in harmony. Each strategy plays a unique role but needs to be integrated seamlessly to support the overall vision and goals of the organization.

No other game captures the essence of strategy (Figure 10-4) as effectively as chess:

- *King*: The king represents business strategy. Just as the game's objective revolves around protecting the king, everything in an organization is designed to support and safeguard the core business objectives.

- *Queen*: The queen symbolizes product strategy. With her versatility and power, the queen mirrors the product strategy's central and formidable role in driving market success and advancing the business.

- *Knight*: The knight stands for engineering strategy. Known for its unique movement and ability to navigate complex challenges, the knight embodies the agility, creativity, and problem-solving mindset crucial for effective engineering teams.

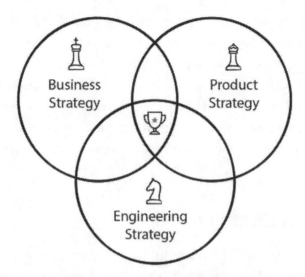

Figure 10-4. *The strategy trio: business strategy, product strategy and engineering strategy*

King: Business Strategy

In chess, the king is the centerpiece of the game—its capture signifies the end of play. Protecting the king is paramount, as every move and strategy is designed to ensure its safety. This central role mirrors that of business strategy within an organization.

Business strategy is the foundation upon which the entire organization is built. It defines the organization's long-term vision, mission, and objectives. Just as the king's safety dictates the flow of the chess game, the business strategy shapes and directs all organizational efforts and decisions.

A well-crafted business strategy articulates the organization's core goals and the path to achieving them. It involves comprehensive market analysis, setting strategic priorities, and identifying competitive advantages. This strategy provides a clear roadmap, guiding the allocation of resources, shaping product offerings, and influencing market positioning. Every department, from marketing and sales to operations and finance to product and engineering, aligns its efforts with this central strategy to ensure coherence and focus.

Much like the king's role in chess, the business strategy is crucial for the organization's survival and success. It requires constant vigilance and adjustment, adapting to changes in the market environment, emerging trends, and shifts in competitive dynamics. Just as a chess player must be strategic in protecting the king while making tactical moves, an organization must navigate its competitive landscape while staying true to its business strategy.

In summary, the business strategy is the linchpin of organizational success, guiding all other strategies and ensuring that every initiative is in harmony with the overarching goals. The safety and success of the organization depend on how effectively this strategy is implemented and protected, much like the king's safety determines the outcome of a chess game.

Queen: Product Strategy

The queen is the most versatile and powerful piece in chess, capable of moving in any direction and influencing the entire board. This adaptability and far-reaching impact make the queen a fitting metaphor for product strategy in an organization.

Product strategy is vital for driving an organization's success in the marketplace. It defines how products will address customer needs, differentiate from competitors, and contribute to growth. Like the queen's expansive movements, a well-crafted product strategy covers a broad range of considerations, including market trends, customer insights, and technological advancements.

A robust product strategy sets a clear vision for the product, including its development, features, and positioning. It involves creating a detailed roadmap that aligns with the business strategy, ensuring the product meets market demands and maintains a competitive edge. The strategy also requires adaptability, allowing the product to evolve in response to changing conditions and emerging opportunities.

Just as the queen's strategic flexibility enables both offensive and defensive maneuvers on the chessboard, a strong product strategy empowers an organization to navigate market complexities and seize growth opportunities. It transforms the business vision into market success by making organizational goals a reality and maintaining a competitive advantage.

Knight: Engineering Strategy

The knight is distinguished by its unique L-shaped movement, which allows it to bypass obstacles and approach challenges from unconventional angles. This distinctive capability makes the knight a powerful symbol for engineering strategy.

Engineering strategy is fundamental for translating a product vision into a functional, high-quality reality. It involves selecting the right technologies, methodologies, and processes to overcome technical challenges and deliver solutions effectively. Just as the knight's movement enables it to maneuver around barriers and reach strategic positions, a well-defined engineering strategy allows teams to navigate complex problems, innovate, and adapt to changing requirements.

A strong engineering strategy prioritizes agility and creativity, enabling teams to approach obstacles with novel solutions and adapt to evolving technological landscapes. It encompasses practices such as iterative development, robust testing, and continuous improvement to ensure that engineering efforts align with the product strategy and overall business goals.

Much like the knight's ability to make unexpected moves that can turn the tide of a chess game, an effective engineering strategy enables an organization to address technical issues, seize new opportunities, and drive progress. By fostering a problem-solving mindset and encouraging innovative approaches, the engineering strategy supports the successful execution of the product vision and contributes significantly to the organization's success.

Good Engineering Strategy

A good engineering strategy is useful.

- *Clarity and Focus*: A good strategy provides clear direction, helping engineering teams focus on critical issues rather than spreading efforts thin. This ensures that the most pressing problems are addressed effectively.

- *Diagnosis of Critical Issues*: Identifying and addressing fundamental technical problems, rather than just treating symptoms.

- *Coherent Action Plan*: Effective strategies include a well-organized action plan. For engineering, this means outlining specific actions, resource needs, and timelines to address key challenges and achieve objectives.

- *Flexibility and Adaptability*: It is adaptable to changing conditions. In engineering, this means being able to adjust the strategy based on new information or emerging technologies.

- *Alignment and Coordination*: Effective strategies ensure alignment with overall goals. A good engineering strategy coordinates efforts across teams, ensuring everyone works toward common objectives.

- *Execution and Focused Effort*: It's all about execution. A good engineering strategy translates plans into actionable tasks and maintains focus, ensuring that efforts are aligned with strategic goals.

Bad Engineering Strategy

Obviously, a bad engineering strategy is the opposite of a good one. But hang on, there's more to it.

- *Fluff*: Uses vague and grandiose language without practical details. For instance, an engineering team might receive a strategy that talks about "revolutionizing user experience through advanced paradigms" without specifying which technologies or methods will be used. This creates confusion and leaves engineers without a clear understanding of what needs to be done.

- *Desire*: Confuses broad aspirations with actionable strategy. An example is stating, "Our goal is to become the leader in AI innovation" without outlining the specific research areas, development milestones, or investment needed. This leaves teams with high-level ambitions but no clear roadmap to achieve them.

- *Avoidance*: Fails to address pressing technical challenges. For example, a strategy might focus on developing new features for a product without first resolving critical bugs or scalability issues in the existing system. This avoids the immediate challenges that need addressing, leading to ongoing problems and customer dissatisfaction.

- *Impractical*: Sets objectives that are not feasible given current constraints. For instance, an engineering strategy might aim to "launch a completely new product line in three months" without considering the team's workload, available resources, or technological readiness. Such objectives are unrealistic and likely to lead to missed deadlines and subpar results.

In summary, a bad engineering strategy is ineffective and fails to provide clear, actionable guidance.

Technology Principles

In any organization, technology principles serve as the bedrock for making informed decisions that align with business goals. These principles are not just technical guidelines; they are the guiding elements that ensure every technology choice, from software architecture to tooling, drives the business forward effectively.

Why Technology Principles Matter

Before diving into specific technologies or architectural practices, you have to establish clear technology principles. These principles act as a compass, guiding your team's decisions and ensuring that the technology choices you make are aligned with the organization's long-term strategy. For instance, when considering a new tool or technology, the question isn't just "Why aren't we choosing X technology?" but rather, "Does Technology X align with our technology principles?"

If a particular technology doesn't fit within these principles, it's a sign that either the principles need reevaluation or that the technology should be reconsidered. This approach prevents the adoption of tools and practices that may seem appealing in the short term but don't support the broader strategic vision of the organization.

Examples of Technology Principles

Here are some common technology principles that might guide your decision-making process:

- *Cloud-First Development*: Prioritizing cloud-native solutions to ensure scalability, flexibility, and efficiency.

- *Convention over Configuration*: Reducing complexity by favoring established conventions over custom configurations, making systems easier to manage and maintain.

- *Design for Scale, Flexibility, and Speed*: Ensuring that every system and process is built with growth in mind, capable of adapting to changing demands without compromising performance.

- *Simplifying Technology Architecture and Process*: Striving for simplicity to reduce the risk of errors, lower maintenance costs, and increase the agility of the development process.

- *Adopting Conway's Law (or its Inverse)*: Designing systems that mirror the organizational structure, or vice versa, to enhance communication and reduce friction in development.

- *Clean Code*: Writing code that is easy to understand, maintain, and extend, reducing technical debt and enhancing the long-term viability of the software.

- *Automation*: Automating repetitive tasks to improve efficiency, reduce human error, and free up valuable resources for more strategic activities.

- *Domain-Driven Design*: Aligning the software design closely with business domains to ensure that the technology directly supports the business objectives.

How Technology Principles Drive Prioritization

For engineering managers, one of the most challenging aspects of the job is prioritizing work in a way that aligns with both technical needs and business goals. This is where technology principles become instrumental. By having a clear set of guiding principles, you can more effectively evaluate which projects, technologies, and tasks should take precedence.

Consider a scenario where your team is faced with multiple requests—from implementing a new feature to addressing technical debt. Without a clear framework, prioritization can become a guessing game, often influenced by the loudest voice in the room. However, when you have established technology principles, they act as a filter for decision-making.

For example, if one of your core principles is "Design for Scale, Flexibility, and Speed," then projects that enhance system scalability or reduce bottlenecks should be prioritized over others that don't directly contribute to these goals. Similarly, if "Clean Code" is a principle, then addressing technical debt might take precedence over adding new features, because clean code directly impacts the long-term maintainability and quality of the software.

In essence, the best technical decisions are those that clearly support the organization's strategy. When your team understands and embraces this, it's easier to make prioritization decisions that are both technically sound and strategically valuable. This alignment not only advances the organization's goals but also fosters a sense of purpose within the team, as they see how their work directly contributes to the broader mission.

Implementing Technology Principles to Guide Prioritization

As an engineering manager, your role involves not only understanding these principles but also using them to guide your team's prioritization. When new projects or tasks arise, evaluate them against your established principles:

- *Alignment with Business Goals*: Does the project directly support the strategic objectives of the organization? If not, should it be deprioritized?

- *Impact on Technical Debt*: Will prioritizing this work help reduce or increase technical debt? How does this align with your principle of maintaining Clean Code?

- *Scalability and Flexibility*: Does the initiative improve the system's ability to scale or adapt to new demands? If Design for Scale, Flexibility, and Speed is a core principle, this should weigh heavily in your prioritization decisions.

- *Simplicity and Maintainability*: Does this task simplify or complicate the current architecture? Simplifying Technology Architecture is a key principle that can help you choose between competing priorities.

By consistently applying these principles, you ensure that your team's work not only meets immediate needs but also contributes to the long-term health and success of the organization. This approach not only helps in making tough decisions but also ensures that your team is always working on what matters most.

Technology Radar

Tech Radar, developed by ThoughtWorks, is a framework for organizations to navigate the ever-evolving technology landscape (Figure 10-5). It provides a structured approach to evaluating and adopting emerging technologies, tools, and practices. By categorizing these technologies into different stages, Tech Radar helps teams make informed decisions about what to prioritize in their technology strategy.

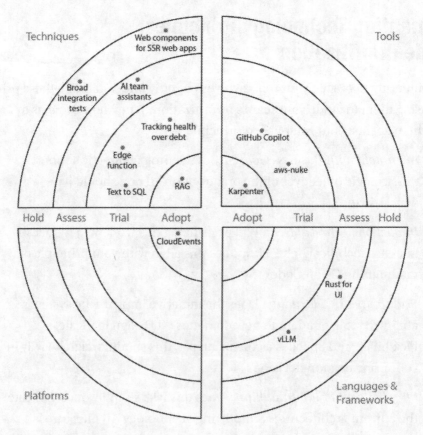

Figure 10-5. *Tech Radar*

At the heart of Tech Radar is its ability to categorize technologies into four distinct quadrants:

- *Adopt*: Technologies recommended for immediate integration and use within the organization

- *Trial*: Technologies that are worth experimenting with and assessing their potential impact

- *Assess*: Technologies that are interesting but require further evaluation before considering adoption

- *Hold*: Technologies that should be avoided or used with caution due to potential risks or misalignment with current goals

This categorization provides a clear framework for prioritizing technology adoption. Teams can quickly understand which technologies are most relevant and beneficial to their strategic objectives. For instance, a technology placed in the Adopt quadrant is seen as a key component to integrate into current projects, whereas one in the Hold quadrant may require reevaluation or be avoided altogether.

Tech Radar's structured approach ensures that technology choices are aligned with the organization's broader goals. It helps teams avoid the pitfalls of adopting trendy but irrelevant technologies and focuses their efforts on tools and practices that will drive significant value. Furthermore, Tech Radar evolves with time, reflecting the latest trends and insights, which supports continuous learning and adaptation.

Build Your Own Radar: Customizing Technology Prioritization

Building on the principles of Tech Radar, Build Your Own Radar (BYOR) offers a more personalized approach to technology evaluation. Developed by ThoughtWorks, BYOR allows organizations to create a customized radar that reflects their unique technological landscape and strategic priorities.

BYOR emphasizes the importance of tailoring the radar to fit the specific needs and context of an organization. Unlike a generic radar, which may not fully address an organization's unique challenges, BYOR enables teams to select and prioritize technologies that are most relevant to their projects and goals.

This customization process involves selecting technologies, tools, and practices that align closely with the organization's current and future needs. By involving various stakeholders in the radar-building process, including developers, architects, and business leaders, BYOR ensures that the radar reflects a wide range of perspectives and needs. This engagement fosters a deeper understanding and alignment around technology priorities.

One of the key advantages of BYOR is its flexibility. As technology trends and organizational goals evolve, the custom radar can be adjusted to remain relevant. This adaptability ensures that the radar continues to serve as a valuable tool for decision-making and prioritization over time.

In essence, BYOR enhances the process of technology prioritization by allowing organizations to build a radar that is directly aligned with their specific context. It empowers teams to make strategic technology choices that are tailored to their needs and objectives, fostering a more effective and responsive approach to technology management.

Engineering Manager's Role

As an engineering manager, your role in Tech Radar management is pivotal to ensuring that technology decisions align with both immediate project needs and long-term strategic goals. Here's a detailed overview of how you can effectively contribute to Tech Radar management:

- *Championing Tech Radar*: Advocate for Tech Radar within your team, integrating it into decision-making processes to ensure technology choices are informed and aligned with best practices.

- *Participating in Evaluation*: Actively contribute to evaluating and categorizing technologies. Your input helps determine which tools and practices are most relevant to your projects.

- *Prioritizing Technologies*: Use Tech Radar to guide decisions on which technologies to adopt, trial, or hold off on. Your understanding of team needs and project goals informs these priorities.

- *Aligning with Strategic Goals*: Ensure that technology choices support the organization's strategic objectives. Your role involves bridging technical needs with broader business goals.

- *Facilitating Collaboration*: Promote collaboration among stakeholders, including developers and business leaders, to ensure diverse perspectives are considered in technology decisions.

- *Managing Adoption*: Oversee the introduction and integration of new technologies, ensuring your team is prepared and systems are adapted as needed.

- *Monitoring and Reviewing*: Regularly review and update Tech Radar to keep it relevant, incorporating team feedback and adapting to technological changes.

- *Driving Improvement*: Foster continuous improvement by staying updated on industry trends and using Tech Radar insights to refine technology strategies.

Your leadership ensures that technology decisions are well-informed, strategically aligned, and effectively implemented, ultimately supporting the success of your projects and the organization's objectives.

Objectives and Key Results in Action

Imagine stepping into a new quarter at a tech company, where you're not just managing a team but driving toward clear, impactful outcomes. You've got a strategic vision from the top—enhancing user engagement with a new feature, but it's up to you and your team to turn this vision into reality. This is where objectives and key results (OKRs) will become your guiding framework.

You along with your product manager gather your team for a kickoff meeting. The room is filled with a mix of anticipation and focused energy as you lay out the plan. The overarching goal is to successfully launch a new user analytics feature by the end of the quarter—an initiative intended to provide deeper insights into user behavior, but to make it actionable, you need to break it down.

The first step is defining your OKRs. You and your product manager brainstorm to refine the high-level objective into something concrete. The objective becomes clear: "Successfully launch the new user analytics feature by the end of the quarter." This objective is specific and actionable, setting a clear target for your team.

Next, you need key results that will measure success. These are not just arbitrary numbers; they need to reflect real progress and impact. You decide on three Key Results:

- Achieve a recommendation score of 8 or higher from at least 80% of beta users.

- Ensure that 40% of monthly active users (MAU) engage with the new feature within the first month after launch.

- Increase the sign-up-to-conversion rate from 15% to 25% by the end of the quarter.

These key results are more than metrics; they are milestones that indicate whether the new feature is making a significant impact. A high recommendation score shows user satisfaction, while the engagement and conversion rates reflect how well the feature is resonating with your user base.

With OKRs set, your focus shifts to execution. During weekly OKR alignment meetings, you and your team discuss progress and tackle any issues that arise. If, for instance, the initial user feedback is less positive than expected, you use these meetings to troubleshoot and adapt your strategy.

In the middle of the quarter, you hold a review session to assess whether the team is on track. This is where real insights come into play. If the engagement rate is lagging, you might need to enhance user training or adjust marketing strategies. Regular reviews ensure that you stay aligned with your Key Results and can pivot when necessary.

To push your team further, you introduce a stretch goal. You aim to increase the recommendation score from 8 to 9, challenging your team to exceed expectations. While this goal is ambitious, it drives innovation and higher performance. Even if you don't fully achieve this stretch goal, the process of striving for it leads to significant improvements.

By the end of the quarter, you and your team review the outcomes. The data tells the story—did you achieve the recommendation score? Did the user engagement meet expectations? Did the conversion rate improve? These results not only provide a clear picture of your performance but also offer insights into what worked and what didn't.

OKR Pitfalls

Setting OKRs can significantly boost your team's alignment and focus, but several common pitfalls can undermine their effectiveness. By recognizing and addressing these pitfalls, you leverage OKRs to drive meaningful progress and avoid potential setbacks.

Outcome vs. Output

One of the primary pitfalls is focusing solely on outputs rather than outcomes. Imagine setting a Key Result like "Complete 15 feature updates by the end of the quarter." While completing features sounds productive, it doesn't necessarily reflect the impact on user experience or business goals. If these updates don't address key user needs or contribute to broader objectives, their value may be minimal. To avoid this, shift your focus from outputs to outcomes. For instance, instead of merely counting feature updates, aim for "Reduce user complaints by 30% through targeted feature improvements." This ensures that your efforts are aligned with achieving tangible results that matter.

Quantity Over Quality

Another common issue is prioritizing quantity over quality. It's tempting to set numerous Key Results in an attempt to cover all bases. For example, setting OKRs like "Increase website traffic by 50%," "Launch 5 new features," and "Reduce customer support tickets by 20%" can overwhelm the team. While each goal might be valuable, focusing on too many objectives can dilute efforts and lead to mediocre results across the board. To address this, concentrate on a few high-impact Key Results. Prioritize quality by selecting goals that drive significant impact, such as "Improve user satisfaction scores by 15%," which can encompass both feature enhancements and support improvements.

Ongoing Engagement

Teams sometimes set ambitious OKRs at the start of the quarter but then neglect them throughout. This set-and-forget approach can result in missed opportunities and decreased morale. Regular check-ins and reviews are essential to keep OKRs relevant and actionable. Weekly stand-up meetings allow you to discuss progress and tackle any issues, while mid-quarter reviews help reassess and realign strategies based on current performance.

Ambiguous Goals

Ambiguous goals are another pitfall that can lead to confusion and misalignment. For instance, a Key Result like "Improve team productivity" lacks clear definitions and can lead to varied interpretations. To avoid this, ensure your OKRs are specific and clear. Instead of vague goals, use precise metrics such as "Increase the average number of completed tasks per week by 20% through enhanced workflow processes." This provides a shared understanding of what success looks like and ensures that everyone is aligned in their efforts.

Unrealistic Expectations

Setting unrealistic expectations can also be problematic. While stretch goals are intended to drive innovation, overly ambitious OKRs can lead to frustration and burnout. For example, aiming for a "100% increase in user retention" might be unattainable given current resources. Instead, balance ambition with realism. Set goals that are challenging yet achievable, such as a "20% increase in user retention." This approach motivates the team without setting them up for failure.

Lack of Alignment

Lack of alignment with broader organizational goals is another common issue. If your OKRs are disconnected from the company's strategic objectives, efforts may become fragmented. For instance, if the company is focused on market expansion, but your team's OKRs are centered solely on internal processes, there may be a disconnect. Ensure that your OKRs align with the organization's broader goals by collaborating with other departments and leadership. This alignment helps ensure that every effort supports the overarching mission.

Inflexibility

Lastly, inflexibility can be a significant obstacle. The business environment is dynamic, and sticking rigidly to OKRs despite changing circumstances can be detrimental. If market conditions shift or new information emerges, continuing to pursue outdated goals can waste resources and miss opportunities. Maintain flexibility and adaptability with your OKRs. Regularly review and adjust them based on new insights or changes in the market to ensure they remain relevant and effective.

By understanding and addressing these common OKR pitfalls, you can set more effective goals, keep your team focused, and drive meaningful progress toward your organization's objectives.

Top-Down and Bottom-Up

Have you ever faced the challenge of aligning ambitious organizational goals with the day-to-day realities of your team? Have you found yourself wondering how to bridge the gap between grand strategic visions and the practical steps needed to achieve them? These are the real-world challenges that engineering and product managers face daily.

The Top-Down Perspective: From Vision to Reality

Think of senior leadership as the architects of a grand blueprint. They craft a vision that outlines the future, a mission that defines the organization's purpose, and a strategy that details the steps to achieve that vision. This blueprint is comprehensive and ambitious, designed to guide the entire organization toward a common goal.

The top-down approach is about translating this high-level vision into something that resonates at every level of the organization. As engineering managers and product managers, you need to ensure that everyone on your team understands where the organization is headed and how their individual contributions align with that direction. The challenge is to communicate this vision in a way that inspires and unifies the team.

The Bottom-Up Perspective: Insights from the Ground

Now, consider the ground level, where the real action happens. Both engineering and product teams are immersed in developing technology and refining products. You and your teams see firsthand the challenges and opportunities that arise. Your insights are grounded in reality, shaped by hands-on experience and direct interactions with the product and the market.

From this vantage point, you identify new tech initiatives, suggest improvements, and develop detailed plans to bring these ideas to life. The bottom-up approach involves leveraging this on-the-ground knowledge to drive innovation and address practical problems. It's a process of continuously refining and adapting strategies based on real-world feedback and evolving needs.

The Bridge: Your Role in Action

As engineering managers and product managers, you are pivotal in bridging the gap between these two perspectives (Figure 10-6). You translate the strategic vision from senior leadership into actionable plans and projects for your teams. Your role involves breaking down the organization's grand ideas into manageable tasks and achievable goals.

You also serve as the conduit for communication, ensuring that feedback from your teams reaches senior leaders and that strategic adjustments are made based on this feedback. This ongoing dialogue helps refine the organization's strategy and adapt plans to meet practical challenges and opportunities.

But there's a point to remember: If you don't control the flow of priorities—whether leaning too heavily on top-down directives or being overly influenced by bottom-up demands—your prioritization process might falter. Don't become a "frozen middle," caught between conflicting directions. Instead, you need to filter and balance inputs smartly from both sides. Striking this balance ensures that you are neither overwhelmed by top-down expectations nor lost in the myriad of bottom-up ideas.

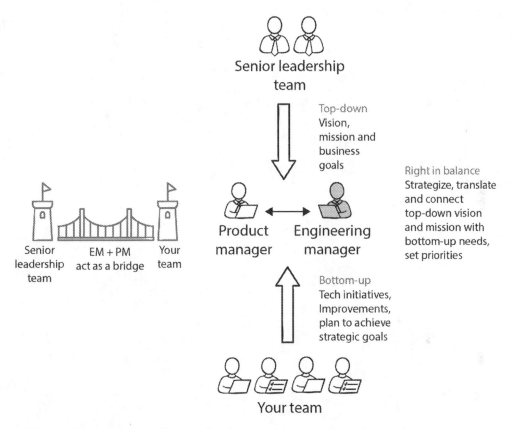

Figure 10-6. *PM-EM acting as a bridge*

In your daily roles, you juggle these demands, ensuring that the strategic vision is actionable and that team insights are effectively incorporated into the organization's plans. You balance strategic ambitions with practical realities, creating a roadmap that is both aspirational and achievable.

Finding the Right Balance

Mastering this balancing act requires a deep understanding of both the strategic vision and the operational realities. As engineering and product managers, you must continuously connect these two worlds, crafting a roadmap that aligns with both aspirational goals and practical execution.

By playing this vital role, you ensure that the organization's vision is not just a distant aspiration but a guiding force that shapes the daily work and innovations of your teams. Through your combined efforts, the grand blueprint becomes a reality, and the organization steadily moves toward its strategic goals.

CHAPTER 11

Pragmatic Approach to Prioritization

"This or that?" It's a question that software engineering teams face almost every single day.

Should we fix this critical bug or push ahead with that new feature? Do we allocate resources to refine our infrastructure, or do we focus on delivering customer-requested enhancements? Should we address the technical debt that's been accumulating or prioritize the upcoming product launch?

These choices are not just frequent; they're constant. Every decision, big or small, shapes the trajectory of your initiatives and ultimately the success of your team. But how do you decide "this" over "that"? How do you ensure that the priorities you set today lead to success tomorrow? The answer lies in *pragmatic prioritization*.

While product managers define the strategic vision and set high-level priorities, your role as an engineering manager is to translate these priorities into actionable plans to deliver impactful outcomes. This approach helps in managing competing priorities, avoiding distractions, and aligning your team efforts with the broader product goals. You must focus on practical, data-informed prioritization rather than relying solely on intuition or external pressures. It involves systematically evaluating initiatives based on their potential impact and the resources required, rather than allowing personal biases or shifting trends to dictate your choices.

Pragmatic prioritization is about doing the right things, within your constraints, to deliver the maximum impact.

In this chapter, we'll deep dive into the following:

- *Prioritization Techniques and Pitfalls:* Explore various techniques to effectively prioritize initiatives, such as the Impact-Effort Matrix, MoSCoW, and Rock, Pebbles, and Sand. Be mindful of the pitfalls, including sticking too rigidly to these methods and being overly dogmatic in their application.

217

© Ananth Ramachandran 2024
A. Ramachandran, *The Complete Engineering Manager*, https://doi.org/10.1007/979-8-8688-0267-6_11

- *Managing Change in Priorities*: Adapting to shifting priorities requires agility and clear communication. Effective management involves realigning team focus with strategic goals, addressing concerns empathetically, and supporting engineers through transitions to maintain productivity and morale.

- *Deprioritization:* Effectively managing deprioritization requires balancing stakeholder demands with strategic goals and resource constraints. Key practices include understanding stakeholder needs, communicating clearly, offering alternatives, and maintaining transparency to manage expectations and preserve positive relationships.

Impact-Effort Matrix

The Impact-Effort Matrix is the foundation of all prioritization frameworks out there. It helps contrast the potential value of initiatives against the effort required, helping you identify projects that offer the greatest returns for the invested effort. This tool simplifies decision-making and resource allocation, ensuring your team focuses on high-impact tasks.

Assessing Impact

Impact refers to the potential positive effect an initiative can have on your product, users, and overall business objectives. It's about understanding the value that completing a specific task will bring. This value can manifest in various forms, such as increased user satisfaction, revenue growth, improved performance, or enhanced competitive advantage.

Your product manager (PM) leads in defining the impact of each initiative. They have to do the following:

- *Understand Business Objectives*: Aligning each initiative with the company's strategic goals, such as revenue growth, user retention, or market expansion. Understanding these objectives ensures that the features prioritized contribute directly to the broader business vision.

- *Engage with Key Stakeholders*: Collaborates with stakeholders across departments—like sales, marketing, and customer support—to gather diverse perspectives on which initiatives will most effectively address cross-functional needs and drive business outcomes.

- *Analyze Customer Feedback and Behavior*: Examines user feedback, reviews, and behavioral data to identify pain points and opportunities. By understanding customer needs and preferences, features that will enhance user satisfaction and engagement will be prioritized.

- *Use Data Analytics*: Leverages analytics tools to assess current feature performance, user drop-off points, and potential growth areas. Data-driven insights help in predicting the impact of new features based on historical trends and user behavior.

- *Assign an Impact Score*: Assigns a relative impact score to each initiative. This score, whether qualitative or quantitative, reflects the expected value of the feature in terms of achieving business objectives and satisfying user needs.

Starting from understanding business objectives to arriving at an impact score, this process often spans weeks or even months, and a product manager (PM) alone can't pull it off. Specialists such as business analysts, user researchers and data analysts provide support throughout. Their expertise ensures comprehensive evaluation and accurate prioritization, enabling the PM to make well-informed decisions that align with strategic goals and deliver significant value.

Your PM starts with impact analysis and discovery several months before planning the upcoming quarter. This early start allows time for comprehensive data collection and stakeholder alignment. Rest assured, this approach ensures the prioritization of initiatives is both informed and strategic, setting the stage for a focused and effective planning cycle.

In this context, you, as an engineering manager, provide technical insights and high-level feasibility assessments. You collaborate with the PM to evaluate how each initiative aligns with technical constraints and opportunities. This includes assessing the potential impact on system performance, scalability, and integration with existing infrastructure.

Taking a proactive approach with a product-driven mindset, your participation in user research and data analysis, driven by curiosity, helps you align closely with the product's goals. Engaging in these activities deepens your understanding of user needs and behaviors, enriching your contributions to feature prioritization and ensuring that engineering efforts align with user expectations and business objectives.

Assessing Effort

Once the impact of the initiatives is defined by the PM, you take over to define the effort involved. You work with your engineering team to provide a high-level estimate of the effort required, typically using T-shirt sizing to classify the complexity and workload of each initiative.

- *Gather the Team*: Organize a meeting with your engineering team to discuss each initiative. As EM, facilitate the discussion, ensuring all perspectives are considered. Engineers provide their technical insights and experience to estimate the effort required.

- *Review Initiatives*: Ensure the team understands the high-level scope and objectives of each initiative based on the information provided by the PM. Examine from a technical perspective, identifying potential challenges and complexities that might influence the effort.

- *Assign High-Level T-Shirt Sizing*: Use T-shirt sizing (XS, S, M, L, XL) to classify the effort required for each initiative. This method provides a high-level estimate of effort and complexity.

- *Acknowledge Uncertainty*: Recognize that these estimates are high-level and come with inherent uncertainty. Incorporate a buffer in the effort estimates to account for unforeseen complexities and unknowns. This approach helps manage expectations and allows for adjustments as more details become available.

- *Communicate with Stakeholders*: Share the preliminary effort scores with the PM and stakeholders, emphasizing that these scores are provisional and subject to change. Provide context on the estimates and outline the need for further refinement.

Plotting Impact-Effort Matrix

Assume that your team is building an e-commerce platform and you've just come out with an impact and effort scores, let's plot the Impact-Effort Matrix (Table 11-1).

Table 11-1. *Impact-Effort Matrix*

Initiative	Impact Score	Effort Score
New Payment Gateway Integration	High (9/10)	XL
Enhanced Search Functionality	Medium (7/10)	L
User Profile Customization	High (8/10)	M
Mobile App Optimization	Medium (6/10)	XS
Advanced Analytics Dashboard	Low (4/10)	L
Improved Checkout Flow	High (9/10)	M
Customer Support Chatbot	Medium (5/10)	S
API Rate Limiting	Low (3/10)	XS
Subscription Management System	High (8/10)	XL
Localization for New Markets	Medium (7/10)	M
Add-to-Cart Button Enhancement	High (8/10)	S
UI Color Scheme Update	Low (5/10)	M

Once the Impact-Effort Matrix (Figure 11-1) is plotted for potential initiatives, you plan the team's roadmap based on capacity, with prioritization as the key focus. This process involves aligning with senior leadership, who provide crucial input on strategic initiatives and help determine what's negotiable and what's not. For instance, prioritizing two XL initiatives might take up most of your resources, leaving little room for other projects. By choosing one XL initiative instead, you can fit in two M-sized initiatives and several smaller tasks.

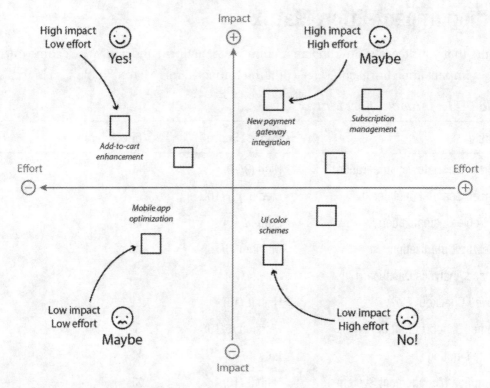

Figure 11-1. *Impact-Effort Matrix*

Stakeholders, who often present medium-sized requests, need to be kept informed about these priorities. It's also wise to leave space for ad hoc requests and operational improvements on both the technical and product sides. This approach ensures that while you meet strategic goals, you also remain flexible and responsive to emerging needs.

MoSCoW

The MoSCoW method is a prioritization framework that helps teams focus on what matters most. It stands for Must Have, Should Have, Could Have, and Won't Have, categorizing tasks or features by priority. This method offers a clear structure for stakeholders to agree on priorities, aiding effective decision-making and resource allocation.

Must Have

Must Have items are critical to the success of an initiative. Without these features or tasks, the product would be incomplete, unusable, or fail to meet essential business needs.

These are characteristics of Must Have items:

- *Essential for launch*: The product cannot function without these features.

- *Legal or compliance requirements*: It is necessary to meet regulatory standards.

- *No workaround available*: There is no alternative solution to fulfill the need.

Example: For an e-commerce platform, a secure payment processing system is a Must Have feature. Without it, customers cannot complete purchases, rendering the platform ineffective.

Should Have

Should Have items are important but not critical. These features significantly enhance the product's functionality and user experience but are not essential for the initial launch or operation.

The following are the characteristics of Should Have items:

- *High value*: Provide substantial benefits to users or the business.

- *Not time-critical*: Can be postponed without major impact.

- *Workaround exists*: Alternative solutions are available, albeit less efficient.

Example: Implementing a wishlist feature on the e-commerce platform is a Should Have. It enhances user engagement but is not essential for basic transactions.

Could Have

Could Have items are desirable but less important. These features can improve the product's appeal and usability but have a minimal impact on overall performance.

The following are the characteristics of Could Have items:

- *Nice to have*: Offer minor improvements or conveniences.

- *Low effort*: Require minimal resources to implement.

- *Low impact*: Their absence does not significantly affect user satisfaction.

Example: Adding multiple language support for non-core markets could be classified as a Could Have for the initial release of the e-commerce platform.

Won't Have

Won't Have items are agreed upon as the lowest priority and are excluded from the current development cycle. These features may be revisited in the future but are not considered necessary at this time.

The following are the characteristics of Won't Have items:

- *Not aligned with current goals*: Do not support immediate business objectives.

- *High effort with low value*: Require substantial resources without corresponding benefits.

- *Deferred to future releases*: Planned for later stages based on resource availability and strategic direction.

Example: Integrating augmented reality features for product visualization might be a Won't Have for the current development phase of the e-commerce platform.

Applying MoSCoW in Prioritization

Applying MoSCoW in prioritization is primarily led by the product manager (PM), supported by you, the EM. The PM defines and categorizes initiatives into Must Have, Should Have, Could Have, And Won't Have, ensuring alignment with business goals. As an EM, you provide technical insights, assess feasibility, and ensure that the team's capacity aligns with the priorities set. This collaboration ensures that both business objectives and technical constraints are considered, leading to a balanced and realistic roadmap.

The MoSCoW method facilitates effective prioritization by categorizing initiatives based on their importance and urgency. Here's how to apply it:

- *Identify and List Requirements*: The PM leads the effort to gather all potential features, tasks, and initiatives from various stakeholders, including the engineering team, clients, and other departments. The EM supports this process by providing insights into technical dependencies and potential challenges.

- *Engage Stakeholders*: The PM organizes workshops or meetings with key stakeholders to discuss the importance of each requirement. The EM participates in these discussions, offering a technical perspective to ensure that all ideas are feasible and aligned with the team's capabilities.

- *Categorize Each Initiative*:

  - *Must Have*: The PM, with input from the EM, identifies features critical for product functionality and compliance. These are non-negotiable and must be delivered.

  - *Should Have*: Together, the PM and EM determine which features are important but not critical for the initial release. These are prioritized next, considering available resources.

  - *Could Have*: The PM and EM list beneficial features that can be considered if time and resources allow but aren't necessary for the current scope.

  - *Won't Have*: The PM, with agreement from the EM and other stakeholders, identifies features that will not be included in this development cycle, ensuring the team focuses on higher-priority tasks.

- *Assess Resources and Timeframes*: The EM evaluates the engineering team's capacity, available resources, and deadlines to ensure that Must Have and Should Have items are achievable within the given timeframe. The PM uses this information to refine the prioritization and adjust expectations.

- *Create the Development Roadmap*: The PM creates a roadmap based on the categorization, scheduling Must Have and Should Have items first. The EM ensures that the roadmap is realistic and that the team is aligned with the plan, preparing to tackle the Could Have items if time permits.

- *Review and Adjust*: Both the PM and EM regularly review the priorities as the project progresses. They remain agile, ready to reclassify items if business needs change, or new information arises, ensuring that the roadmap stays relevant and achievable.

Rock Pebbles and Sand

Heard of Stephen Covey's "Big Rocks" theory from his book *The 7 Habits of Highly Effective People*? He says, "Prioritize big things first; otherwise you run out of time" (Figure 11-2).

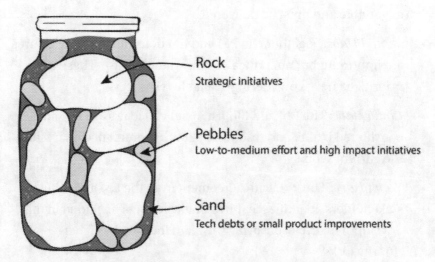

Figure 11-2. Rocks, pebbles, and sand

In the context of building a product or software, this means focusing on strategic initiatives—your "big rocks." These initiatives are not only long-term but also high-impact, typically spanning several months to quarters. They are crucial for advancing your product's vision and achieving significant milestones that drive long-term growth and competitive advantage.

Once you've tackled these big rocks, you shift your attention to the "pebbles." Pebbles are tactical tasks that, while important, don't carry the same weight as the big rocks but still add substantial value. They often involve smaller projects or improvements that can be completed within a few sprints. Pebbles address immediate challenges or provide significant enhancements that align with your strategic goals but require less time and complexity compared to big rocks.

Lastly, there's the "sand," which includes small, quick tasks that need to be done but have minimal impact on the overarching goals. These might involve routine maintenance, minor fixes, or administrative tasks. Sand tasks are typically completed in a short amount of time and don't require extensive planning or resources.

By following this approach, you ensure that your most impactful tasks—your big rocks—are prioritized effectively, while pebbles and sand are managed efficiently. This balanced approach (Table 11-2) helps you stay focused on strategic goals while still addressing necessary smaller tasks that complement your overall priorities.

Table 11-2. *Rocks, Pebbles, and Sand Comparison*

	Rocks	**Pebbles**	**Sand**
Effort	>= 3 months	4 sprints	<= 1 sprint
Maximize	Impact	ROI	Throughput
Scope	Strategic	Tactical	Any
Role of senior leadership	Decider	Observer	None
Role of PM / EM	Driver: PM	Decider: PM	EM: Decider (at times autonomous)
Beware	Insufficient impact	Over-estimating ROI	Over-thinking/Over-planning

Rocks Maximize Impact

Let's imagine a tech company that develops a popular project management product. The company has a vision of becoming the go-to platform for remote teams, and to achieve this, they've identified a rock-sized initiative: developing an integrated video conferencing feature. This initiative is a classic "big rock" in every sense—it's complex, strategic, and expected to take anywhere from six to nine months to complete.

The video conferencing feature isn't just an incremental improvement; it's a transformative addition that could redefine how users interact with the platform. By integrating video conferencing, the tool would allow teams to manage projects and communicate in real time within the same platform, reducing the need to juggle multiple apps and thus creating a more seamless and productive user experience. The impact here is strategic: it positions the company to offer a more complete solution for remote teams, a market segment that's only growing.

However, the company knows that such a project comes with risks. Large projects often overrun their timelines and under-deliver on their promises. To mitigate these risks, the team has set the bar for impact extraordinarily high. They understand that if the feature falls short of expectations, the time and resources spent might not justify the effort. But by aiming for a dramatic impact, even if the project doesn't fully meet its ambitious goals, the results should still be valuable.

As they embark on this initiative, the team employs a deliberative decision-making process. This isn't just about agile sprints or incremental progress; it's about making sure the company is climbing the right mountain in the first place. The decision to focus on video conferencing wasn't made overnight. The product managers (PMs) led the discussion, driving the strategic direction while the executives played a vital role in validating the decision. This approach ensures that everyone is aligned on the importance of the project and the strategic benefits it promises to deliver.

In this example, the rock-sized initiative—the video conferencing feature—illustrates the importance of prioritizing projects that have the potential to deliver the most dramatic and strategic impact. By focusing on these big rocks, the company ensures that its efforts are not just productive but are also aligned with its long-term vision, paving the way for future success.

Pebbles Maximize ROI

Pebbles are distinct from rocks and sand, with their own unique characteristics. While rocks are strategic and long-term, pebbles are tactical initiatives that deliver impact within a few weeks and months. They address immediate challenges or introduce valuable features quickly, making them crucial for near-term success.

Pebbles typically span one to four sprints, requiring more effort than sand but less than rocks. They must have a measurable impact, as dedicating several sprints to a task without tangible results isn't acceptable. The challenge with pebbles is managing their scope; if they start to expand, you have two choices: either reduce the scope to fit the timeframe or reclassify the task as a rock. In doing so, you may find that the impact isn't sufficient, signaling a need to either get more creative or reconsider the idea's priority.

Pebbles are all about maximizing ROI. They deliver the best value in the shortest time, making them an efficient use of the team's resources. However, beware of estimation errors that can drastically reduce ROI. If a task takes longer and delivers less impact than expected, the ROI can drop significantly, rendering the effort far less effective than planned.

Sand Maximizes Throughput

Sand tasks are the small, often overlooked elements of software development that, while individually minor, collectively contribute to the overall quality of a product. These tasks are short-term and typically don't require extensive planning, often taking a few hours to a day to complete. They might include UI tweaks, minor bug fixes, and routine security patches. For example, refactoring a piece of code to improve readability or updating outdated documentation falls into this category. Such tasks, though they may seem insignificant on their own, are vital for maintaining high-quality software. Great user interfaces and robust performance often result from numerous small improvements, such as optimizing a database query or adjusting an API endpoint for better efficiency.

The primary goal with sand tasks is to maximize throughput—how many of these small tasks can be completed per sprint. Measuring the impact of each sand task individually is usually impractical due to their small scale. Instead, the focus should be on efficiently completing as many tasks as possible. This approach enhances overall productivity and helps maintain a high standard of software quality. For instance, fixing several minor bugs or making small performance improvements can significantly enhance user experience, even if each task alone seems trivial.

However, administrative overhead can severely impede the effectiveness of sand tasks. Overly complex prioritization processes or excessive documentation can consume more time than the tasks themselves. To avoid this, streamline how sand tasks are handled. For example, rather than spending time creating detailed user stories for a minor code refactoring, the team should address such tasks directly, minimizing unnecessary bureaucracy.

Prioritizing sand tasks should be driven by intuition and team interests rather than strict metrics. Since the individual value of sand tasks is minimal, focusing on what the team is eager to work on can boost morale and productivity. Allowing teams to manage and schedule these tasks themselves promotes efficiency and prevents micromanagement. This self-management ensures that minor but handy improvements, like optimizing error handling or updating dependencies, are continuously addressed, keeping the software in top shape and maintaining a smooth workflow.

Beware!

Beware of the following issues.

Time-Critical Tasks Take Over

When urgent tasks consistently consume all your time, it indicates a bigger problem that needs immediate attention. If your team is constantly firefighting, it's impossible to make meaningful progress on strategic rocks or even tactical pebbles. This could be due to various factors, such as low productivity, too many responsibilities, architectural issues, or a lack of specialized skills. You must identify the root cause and address it as a priority. Allocate sprint time specifically to solve this issue, or you'll never have the bandwidth to tackle the work that truly drives progress.

Starving the Rock

Allocating only a single story per sprint to your rock leads to excessive context-switching and drags out the project over a long period. This often happens when urgent tasks take precedence over strategic ones, causing the rock to stagnate. The product manager should recognize this pattern and reallocate focus. If necessary, pause pebble work temporarily to allow the team to concentrate on the rock, ensuring that it moves forward meaningfully rather than being starved of attention.

Managing Multiple Pebbles

Trying to work on more than one pebble simultaneously usually backfires due to the added complexity and context-switching. This approach dilutes the team's focus, leading to inefficiencies and lower morale. The only time it makes sense to juggle multiple pebbles is if one is nearing completion or temporarily stalled. Otherwise, it's more effective to complete one pebble before starting another.

Always the Rock, Never the Pebble

If your sprints are consistently dominated by the rock, leaving no room for pebbles, it may actually be a strategic advantage, provided the rock is exceptionally valuable. In some cases, focusing exclusively on the rock for several months can deliver maximum impact. Once the rock reaches a significant milestone or the first complete version is ready, then shift your focus to pebbles, handling smaller updates to the rock as you learn and adapt. This ensures the rock remains central to your strategy while still allowing room for tactical wins.

Neglecting Sand

It's easy to overlook sand tasks since they're small and often seem less critical. However, ignoring these tasks can lead to a bad product and demotivated engineers, as much of the internal maintenance work falls under this category. To prevent this, consider allocating specific sprints to sand tasks or adjusting your sprint planning to ensure they're not neglected. This could involve pausing work on rocks or pebbles temporarily to focus on sand, which can be a refreshing change of pace and boost team morale.

Rushing Into New Work

After completing a rock or pebble, the temptation is to immediately dive into the next big thing. However, this can be a mistake. Often, the completed work needs further refinement, customer feedback integration, or additional small features to maximize its value. Instead of rushing, take the time to solidify the impact of the recent work, ensure it's delivering the expected benefits, and only then move on to new projects. This approach aligns with realistic software development practices and supports a sustainable pace of work.

Trying to Balance Every Sprint

It's not necessary to achieve perfect balance between rocks, pebbles, and sand in every sprint. Instead, focus on balancing work over a more extended period, like several months. This approach helps ensure that nothing critical is neglected, but also allows for sprints that are intentionally imbalanced. Such sprints, focused heavily on one type of work, can lead to greater focus, less context-switching, and higher-quality output. This strategy promotes deep work and ensures that the most critical tasks receive the attention they need at the right time.

Managing a Change in Priorities

Managing a change in priorities is daunting but unavoidable. Take Zoom as an organization, for example. Zoom initially focused on its core videoconferencing features, but as the pandemic continued, user feedback and market dynamics shifted priorities. The company quickly pivoted to enhance features such as breakout rooms, webinar capabilities, and integration with other tools to address the growing demand for comprehensive remote work solutions. This strategic shift allowed Zoom to solidify its position as a leader in remote collaboration tools, meeting the evolving needs of its user base and outperforming competitors.

In the fast-paced world of product development, priorities can shift rapidly, requiring agile responses from both product and engineering teams.

When priorities change, it often means that the work your engineers have been focused on will be paused or even discontinued. This can be challenging as it disrupts their current workflow and requires them to pivot to new initiatives. For instance, if the team has spent months developing a new feature but is suddenly asked to focus on a different, high-priority initiative, the transition can be jarring.

Some team members may find the shift frustrating, especially if they've invested significant effort into the original tasks. Others might see it as an exciting opportunity to work on something more impactful. As an engineering manager, your task is to manage this transition smoothly. This involves not only realigning the team's focus and resources but also addressing the human aspect of change. Communicate clearly and transparently about why the priorities have changed and how the new direction aligns with broader business goals.

Taking the time to listen to your engineers' concerns and providing support during the transition helps in maintaining morale and ensuring a productive shift. It's important to convey that while the current change might disrupt their plans, it's part of a larger strategy to meet evolving market demands or address critical needs. Ultimately, this approach helps keep the team engaged and aligned with the organization's objectives, even as priorities evolve.

Deprioritization

Deprioritization is an essential skill in managing engineering teams and aligning their efforts with strategic objectives. Given time and resource constraints, not every request or feature can be prioritized simultaneously. Effectively managing deprioritization requires balancing stakeholder demands with realistic resource allocation and involves a thoughtful approach.

Managing Stakeholder Requests

Stakeholders often have various demands and expectations, each carrying different levels of urgency and importance. When deprioritizing, the challenge is to manage these requests diplomatically while aligning with the broader strategic goals of the organization.

- *Understand Stakeholder Needs*: Begin by thoroughly understanding each stakeholder's request. Engage in conversations to gather details on their priorities and how their request aligns with business goals. This helps in making informed decisions on what to prioritize or deprioritize.

- *Communicate Clearly and Transparently*: When a request must be deprioritized, communicate this clearly to the stakeholders. Provide a concise explanation of why the request is being moved down the list, focusing on how it fits within the overall strategy and current priorities.

- *Offer Alternatives*: If possible, suggest alternative solutions or compromises. For example, if a stakeholder's request cannot be fulfilled immediately, propose a phased approach or a timeline for when it might be reconsidered.

The Art of Saying "No"

You have to practice saying no to maintain focus and ensure that resources are allocated effectively. It requires tact and diplomacy to balance stakeholder expectations with the reality of limited resources.

- *Frame the Conversation Positively*: When delivering a "no," frame it in a positive manner. Emphasize the value of the current priorities and how they contribute to the organization's strategic goals. For example, "We're currently focusing on feature X, which aligns with our major initiative to enhance user engagement. While we can't address your request immediately, it's something we can revisit in the future."

- *Be Honest and Direct*: Avoid vague responses that can lead to confusion or unrealistic expectations. Be straightforward about why a request cannot be prioritized at the moment. For instance, "Due to the current resource constraints and our commitment to other high-priority projects, we need to delay this request."

- *Provide a Clear Timeline*: If a request is being deprioritized but not rejected outright, provide a clear timeline or conditions under which it might be revisited. This helps manage expectations and shows that their request is valued, even if it's not a priority right now.

- *Empathize and Listen*: Acknowledge the stakeholder's perspective and show empathy. Listening to their concerns can help in crafting a more thoughtful response and maintaining a positive relationship despite the "no."

Balancing Priorities and Managing Expectations

Effective deprioritization involves balancing immediate stakeholder needs with long-term strategic goals. It requires strong communication skills and the ability to navigate complex interpersonal dynamics. By managing requests thoughtfully and handling denials with tact, EMs can maintain stakeholder trust and keep their teams focused on high-impact work.

In summary, mastering the art of saying "no" involves clear communication, empathy, and a strategic approach to prioritization. By understanding stakeholder needs, offering alternatives, and being honest about limitations, EMs can manage deprioritization effectively while fostering positive relationships with stakeholders.

CHAPTER 12

Prioritizing Technical Initiatives

Product development has gotten more ambitious in recent years.

It's gotten ambitious in building and testing out new ideas, expanding into a new market, partner integrations, acquiring new clients, and so on. To stay ahead of the competitors, superior features have to be built with better user experience, all in a short time frame.

As an engineering team building a product or a service from scratch, your main focus for the first few months is to build the high-priority features and get them out of the door to the public. Your team went from choosing a tech stack to running a service or two in production in a short span. In the meantime, you will be sorting out processes in how your team collaborates and produces software.

Now a year has passed. The number of engineers in your team has doubled, the code and technical systems have grown in scope and complexity, and the traffic has gone from thousands of requests per day to half a million. It's a bittersweet experience—you're happy for the ultimate growth of the product and services your team has built but anxious about what's coming up. Parts of your code are being called "legacy," and working with them feels like defusing a bomb. The scariest part is, only the engineer who wrote the code can understand and defuse it.

Time plays a major role in influencing the state of your technical systems. Remember the product feature that your team had to deliver on a short timeline and kept adding code that was already like spaghetti? What about that quick fix you deployed to resolve a P0 technical incident that otherwise would have taken weeks for a proper solution? Adding an inner-join for the umpteenth time to your query that was already quite complex to debug and understand? Congratulations, you've built an empire of technical debt (Figure 12-1).

© Ananth Ramachandran 2024
A. Ramachandran, *The Complete Engineering Manager*, https://doi.org/10.1007/979-8-8688-0267-6_12

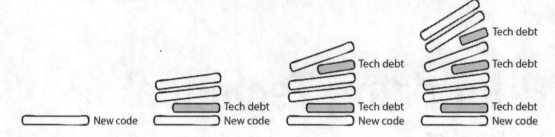

Figure 12-1. *An empire of technical debt*

Technical Debt

From the time Ward Cunningham coined the term *technical debt*, there were multiple attempts to redefine it, but his definition stands the test of time. He says,

> *"With borrowed money, you can do something sooner than you might otherwise, but then until you pay back that money you'll be paying interest. I thought borrowing money was a good idea, I thought that **rushing software out the door** to get some experience with it was a good idea, but that of course, you would eventually go back and as you **learned** things about that software you would repay that loan by **refactoring** the program to reflect your experience as you acquired it".*

They are indeed debts that you incur in your code and systems to prioritize delivery. So there's a natural prioritization happening when building the software. Over time, when you build more features on top of it, you'll start to observe your development slowing down and bugs sneaking in because the code has become complex to understand and debug.

But here's a catch. What if the code is never changed or is thrown away as it is an MVP? What if the premature optimization you did for a specific use case never gets to see the light of day? That's where Cunningham's metaphor (Figure 12-2) proves to be effective.

- *Get the code out of the door*: First and foremost, deliver the code as per the product requirements.

- *Learn*: Learn from real-world usage and feedback, assessing performance and reliability of software under actual conditions.

- *Refactor*: Put the learning back into the software by refactoring and settling back technical debt incurred.

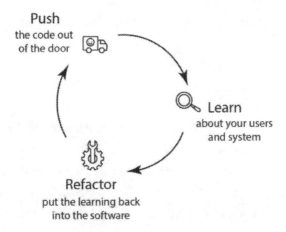

Figure 12-2. *Push-learn-refactor*

Get the Code Out the Door

Getting the code out the door involves delivering functional software quickly to meet business needs, deadlines, or market opportunities. This approach often requires making trade-offs, cutting corners in the technical design, or skipping extensive automated testing to achieve faster time-to-market.

The primary goal is to release a product that provides value to users and stakeholders as soon as possible, allowing an organization to capitalize on immediate opportunities and gain a competitive edge. However, this strategy often results in technical debt, as the hurried development process can introduce inefficiencies, bugs, and architectural compromises that will need to be addressed later.

Remember, if you have written your best code on the first attempt, it's nothing but over-engineering.

Learn

Once the code is out in the wild, the next phase is learning from real-world usage and feedback. This involves gathering data on how users interact with the product, identifying pain points, and assessing the performance and reliability of the software under actual conditions. During this phase, the team can gain valuable insights into what works well and what doesn't, uncovering hidden issues and understanding the true impact of the technical debt incurred during the initial delivery.

Learning from this feedback loop is essential for making informed decisions about future improvements and ensuring that the product evolves in a way that meets user needs and business goals.

Refactor

Refactoring is the act of revisiting the codebase to address the technical debt accumulated during the initial development phase. It involves restructuring the code to improve its readability, maintainability, and performance without changing its behavior. This may include optimizing algorithms, cleaning up redundant or obsolete code, enhancing the architecture to support scalability or simply reorganizing the code to ensure that the software adheres to best practices and standards.

Refactoring is the first step to mitigate the "interest" on technical debt, as it helps prevent the accumulation of further complexity and bugs. By incorporating the lessons learned from user feedback and real-world usage, the team can refine the software to create a more robust, efficient, and sustainable product.

How often do you need to refactor? And how soon? It all depends on how you prioritize settling back technical debts alongside product development.

Anti-patterns to Avoid

More often than not, engineering teams find themselves in one of the following extremes when managing technical debt:

- *Push-Push-Push*: Prioritizing speed over quality in development leads to technical debt, bugs, and burnout. Balancing sprints with time for technical debt reduction, automated testing, and iterative improvements can help manage these issues.

- *Missing Out Learning Opportunities*: Failing to learn from past errors leads to recurring technical debt and inefficiencies. Regular retrospectives, post-mortems, and user feedback are essential for identifying root causes and preventing future debt.

- *Not Coming Back to the Refactor Phase*: Rushing through development without planning for refactoring results in degraded code quality over time. Integrating regular refactoring sessions and thorough code reviews into the development cycle can mitigate this issue.

- *Over-engineering*: Over-engineering involves creating overly complex solutions that exceed current needs, delaying feature releases and reducing flexibility. Focusing on delivering a minimum viable product (MVP) and gathering user feedback can prevent over-engineering.

Push-Push-Push

One common extreme in software development is the "push-push-push" (Figure 12-3) mindset, where the focus is entirely on rapid development and immediate delivery. This approach often prioritizes speed over code quality, comprehensive testing, and proper documentation. The consequences are significant: hastily written code accumulates technical debt, which requires substantial future effort to address; quality issues such as bugs, security vulnerabilities, and performance problems become more prevalent; and team burnout becomes a real risk due to sustained high-pressure environments.

To mitigate these issues, balance sprints by allocating time for technical debt reduction, implementing automated testing through CI/CD pipelines, and adopting iterative development practices that maintain quality while delivering incremental improvements.

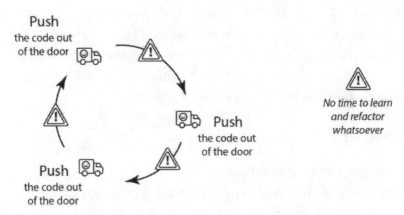

Figure 12-3. *Push-Push-Push: no time to learn and refactor*

Missing Learning Opportunities

Without learning from past experiences, teams are likely to continue making the same errors that contribute to technical debt. For instance, they may repeatedly implement quick fixes that solve immediate issues but introduce long-term complexities and inefficiencies. By not analyzing these patterns, teams miss the opportunity to develop strategies to prevent such debt from accumulating in the future.

Regular retrospectives and post-mortems provide a platform for teams to discuss what went well and what didn't, allowing them to identify the root causes of technical debt. These sessions can reveal systemic issues, such as insufficient planning or inadequate testing practices, that need to be addressed to reduce future debt. User feedback is equally important, as it helps prioritize technical debt that has a direct impact on the user experience, ensuring that the most pressing issues are addressed promptly.

By embedding a culture of continuous learning and improvement, teams can become more adept at managing technical debt. This involves not only recognizing and addressing existing debt but also implementing best practices to prevent its recurrence. Techniques such as code reviews, automated testing, and regular refactoring sessions can be more effectively utilized when informed by the insights gained from reflective practices.

Not Coming Back to the Refactor Phase

Teams rush through the delivery hoping that they can come back and refactor at later stages. But that time never comes for most of them.

Over time, this neglect can severely degrade code quality and stifle innovation. To avoid this extreme, teams should integrate regular refactoring sessions into the development cycle, conduct thorough code reviews to identify areas for improvement, and foster a culture of continuous improvement where refactoring is seen as an integral part of the development process, not an optional afterthought.

Over-engineering

Over-engineering (Figure 12-4) is a common anti-pattern where engineering teams spend excessive time and effort designing and implementing highly complex solutions that go far beyond the current requirements. This approach often stems from a desire to build the "perfect" system, anticipating future needs that may never materialize.

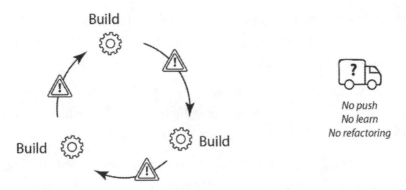

Figure 12-4. *Build-Build-Build: A SIGN OF OVER-ENGINEERING*

Excessive focus on creating a highly sophisticated system can significantly delay the release of valuable features, resulting in missed market opportunities and reduced competitive advantage. Over-engineered systems also often become overly complex and rigid, making them difficult to modify or extend, thus impeding the team's ability to respond quickly to changing requirements or new opportunities.

To avoid the pitfalls of over-engineering, teams should focus on delivering a MVP that meets essential requirements. This approach allows for the quick release of functional software and the gathering of user feedback to inform future development.

(Un)Intentional Debts

There are only two types of technical debts: intentional and unintentional.

Intentional technical debt arises from deliberate decisions made to achieve short-term goals while acknowledging the trade-offs. Think of it as a strategic choice. When your team decides to take shortcuts—perhaps to meet a tight deadline or launch a new feature—they're consciously accruing debt, with a clear plan to pay it back. This type of debt is manageable when communicated transparently and documented well. For example, if you choose to implement a quick solution for user authentication that isn't ideal but allows for a timely launch, you're creating intentional debt. The key is to ensure that this decision is justified and that there's a concrete plan to address it later. For you, understanding and managing intentional debt involves setting realistic timelines and ensuring that the team is committed to refactoring and improving the codebase as planned.

Unintentional technical debt, on the other hand, occurs without conscious decision-making. This debt often results from bad software practices, lack of knowledge, or simply oversight. These are common causes:

- *Poorly Written Code*: When developers don't follow best practices or aren't aware of more efficient coding techniques, the result is often a codebase that's difficult to maintain and prone to bugs.

- *Inadequate Testing*: Skimping with tests or using incomplete testing strategies can leave defects undiscovered, leading to issues that compound over time.

- *Lack of Documentation*: Failure to properly document code or architectural decisions can lead to misunderstandings and mistakes down the line.

- *Legacy Code*: Over time, code that was once considered adequate may no longer meet the needs of the system, particularly as new features are added or requirements change.

Unintentional debt is often more challenging to manage because it's not always immediately visible. It tends to accumulate over time, leading to increased maintenance costs, reduced agility, and potential system failures.

When incurring technical debt isn't a good idea? Let's look at:

- *Structural Issues and Data Modeling Inefficiencies*: Incurring technical debt that affects the underlying architecture or the data models can lead to severe long-term consequences. Structural debt creates foundational problems that can compromise system stability and scalability. For example, poor data modeling can result in data inconsistencies and inefficiencies that are costly to fix and require significant rework. These issues are not just technical but can also impact business operations, leading to increased costs and delays.

- *High-Risk Components*: Technical debt in high-risk areas, such as security or compliance, can expose the organization to vulnerabilities and regulatory penalties. For instance, a quick fix to bypass security measures might save time initially but could lead to potential breaches and legal issues. This type of debt often requires urgent and costly remediation, making it unavoidable to address these components with due diligence from the start.

- *Maintenance Complexity*: Debt that makes code harder to understand or maintain can slow down development and increase the likelihood of bugs. When code becomes convoluted or poorly documented, future developers face a steep learning curve and higher chances of introducing errors. This complexity can stifle innovation and extend development cycles, making the initial shortcuts a costly mistake in the long run.

- *Misalignment with Strategic Goals*: Technical debt that does not align with business priorities can misdirect resources and focus. For instance, if debt is incurred in areas that do not directly contribute to strategic objectives, it can divert attention from key projects and delay important initiatives. Ensuring that technical debt supports or aligns with business goals helps maintain focus and efficiency.

The People Effect

Technical problems in your engineering teams aren't just technical. They definitely have an effect on the people who work with the product: your engineers.

Leaving a broken CI/CD pipeline unfixed, putting out fires more often without addressing them properly, and forcing engineers to work with convoluted codebases without giving them the time to refactor or improve the architecture, all contribute to a stressful and demoralizing work environment. Developer experience (DX) takes a hit, which impacts your team's productivity, morale, and motivation.

Over time, technical systems grow in complexity in all forms—domain, scale, and accidental complexity. And how each of your engineers sees them is different. Some see it as a blocker, whereas for others it's a challenge and an opportunity to learn and thrive.

What are the effects of the growing complexity of your technical systems?

- *Increased Cognitive Load*: The growing complexity of technical systems increases the cognitive load on engineers, requiring more effort to manage intricate interdependencies. This can lead to slower development and decreased productivity as engineers need more time to understand the system.

- *Communication Silos*: Knowledge gets isolated within specialized teams and hinders collaboration. Engineers may struggle to access key technical details from other teams, leading to misaligned goals and inefficiencies. This fragmentation causes delays in decision-making and problem-solving.

- *Low quality deliverable*: The quality of deliverables tends to decline as systems grow in complexity and left unaddressed. Increased pressure to meet deadlines results in more errors and suboptimal solutions. Engineers may feel disheartened by the recurring need to fix bugs, impacting their sense of accomplishment.

- *Frustration and Burnout*: Working with complex systems without prioritizing core technical challenges can leave engineers feeling overwhelmed and undervalued, reducing their job satisfaction and motivation. Persistent stress and a constant sense of falling behind cause emotional exhaustion, leading to higher turnover rates.

You, as an engineering manager, are in a crucial juncture of technical systems and the people managing them. Understanding your engineers' perspectives on the state of your technical systems helps in prioritizing technical initiatives that improve developer experience and overall satisfaction.

- *Reduce Cognitive Load*: Prioritize decoupling systems and modularize into smaller, manageable components, making it easier for engineers to understand and work on specific parts.

- *Advocate for Technical Improvements*: Take actions and help getting buy-in from nontechnical stakeholders to prioritize technical improvements in the midst of active product development.

- *Improving Developer Experience*: Check with your engineers how they feel working with the infrastructure and the challenges that come along with it. What's their debugging experience look like? What are their struggles in deploying changes to production? Investing in tools and best practices to improve developer experience will not only make your engineer's lives easier but let them stay productive.

Prioritized Technical Backlog

Many engineering teams often find themselves frustrated by the lack of prioritization given to technical initiatives, despite months or even years of dedicated work on continuous product development. You might hear engineers lamenting how their key technical projects get sidelined in favor of more visible, user-facing features.

Technical initiatives, no matter how vital, often remain invisible in the broader organizational conversation unless they are clearly documented, articulated, and aligned with the company's strategic goals. A well-structured and maintained technical system is a recipe for long-term success. However, without a tangible and prioritized technical backlog, those technical initiatives risk being perpetually deferred in favor of the next big product feature.

Aligning Technical Work with Product Goals

Imagine a product manager focused on improving the user's search experience on your platform. They're tasked with increasing user engagement, reducing bounce rates, or driving more conversions through better search functionality. Now, if your team proposes a technical initiative to reduce search latency by, say, 20% or to improve the underlying machine learning model that suggests search results, would the product manager dismiss it? Certainly not—if the value of the technical improvement is realized, it makes the conversation easier. When they understand that reducing search latency not only improves the user experience but also contributes to the strategic goals, they're more likely to prioritize it alongside or even ahead of other initiatives.

What to Include in Your Technical Backlog?

To make your technical backlog (Table 12-1) truly effective, it should encompass the following key areas:

- *Technical Debt*: Including technical debts in your backlog ensures they are not overlooked and helps prioritize them alongside new feature development. This approach brings visibility to the areas of your system that, if neglected, could impede progress, allowing you to plan proactive improvements.

- *Maintenance Tasks*: Routine maintenance is the unsung hero of any technical organization. This includes tasks like regular codebase cleaning, performance monitoring, system upgrades, and security patches. While these tasks might not be glamorous, they are essential to the long-term health and efficiency of your systems. Including them in your backlog ensures they're not overlooked.

- *Strategic Technical Initiatives*: These are long-term, forward-looking projects that align directly with business goals and have the potential to drive significant value. For example, optimizing the infrastructure to reduce latency, enhancing machine learning models to improve personalization, or investing in automation to increase development speed. Strategic initiatives should be framed in a way that highlights their impact on key business metrics, making them hard to ignore.

Table 12-1. *Prioritized Technical Backlog*

Priority	Initiative	Description	Value	Objective	Effort
High	Modularize monolith to microservices	Break down the monolithic architecture into smaller, more manageable microservices.	Reduce time-to-market for new features by X%	Increase system scalability by handling X% more concurrent users within Y months	XL
High	Migrate on-premises to cloud	Transition existing on-premises infrastructure to cloud platforms for scalability and flexibility.	Reduce infrastructure costs by X% annually	Improve system reliability with an uptime of at least 99.99%	XL
Medium	Implement end-to-end monitoring	Develop comprehensive monitoring systems to identify and resolve errors in the system promptly.	Decrease mean time to detect (MTTD) and mean time to resolve (MTTR) by X%	Reduce system downtime by X% within Y months	M
Low	Perform maintenance tasks	Regularly update dependencies, apply security patches, and conduct system maintenance activities.	Minimize security breaches and associated costs	Ensure compliance with industry standards and regulations, achieving X% of security audits with no critical vulnerabilities	S

Technical Debt Payback Schemes

Similar to financial debt, technical debt has to be repaid with added interest, represented by effort and complexity. The longer you delay repayment of technical debt, the greater the effort and complexity involved, as you'll find more functionality crowded around code under debt.

You can repay technical debt in the following ways: alongside product development, alongside every sprint or freestyle.

Alongside Product Development

This is a way of addressing technical debt alongside the code of active product development. In other words, focus on the hotspots, or the parts of the code with the highest development activity.

For instance, suppose your engineering team is tasked with developing features to enhance the checkout experience on your e-commerce platform, aiming to increase the conversion rate from 5% to 7%. As this is the third iteration of improving the checkout feature, your team has made significant progress over the past three months since the initial launch.

From the technical debt accumulated during previous iterations of launching the checkout feature, your team identified several key issues:

- Data modeling has become increasingly complex and is no longer scalable.

- The codebase is growing harder to understand and maintain without refactoring.

- Enhancing the checkout experience further could negatively impact system performance.

To address these technical debts alongside active development of the checkout feature, start from understanding the current state of the code. This is where a well-prioritized technical backlog becomes invaluable. When a new product development request comes in, you can refer to this backlog, present it to your product manager, and discuss its significance and priority—ensuring that both ongoing development and technical debt are effectively prioritized.

Alongside Every Sprint

To effectively balance your team's focus between strategic initiatives and technical debt, you might start with an allocation strategy where approximately 80% of your sprint's time is dedicated to high-impact projects and 20% to technical debt settlement. However, the exact percentages can vary based on your team's specific needs and circumstances.

Strategic Initiatives (80%):

- *Developing a New Feature*: Invest substantial resources in building a groundbreaking feature, such as an advanced AI-driven recommendation system.

- *Expanding to New Markets*: Focus on localizing your product for new regions, involving translation, marketing adaptations, and compliance with local regulations.

- *Enhancing User Experience*: Prioritize a major redesign of your app's interface to improve usability and boost user engagement.

Technical Debt Settlement (20%):

- *Refactoring Legacy Code*: Dedicate time to simplifying and improving the maintainability of existing code, facilitating easier future updates.

- *Increasing Test Coverage*: Allocate resources to enhance automated test coverage, reducing the risk of bugs and improving code quality.

- *Updating Dependencies*: Invest time in updating outdated libraries or frameworks to improve performance, security, and compatibility.

The suggested allocation of 80% to strategic initiatives and 20% to technical debt is a starting point. Regularly assess your team's current priorities and challenges. Depending on factors such as the urgency of strategic goals, the amount of technical debt, and overall team capacity, you may need to adjust these percentages to strike the right balance for your specific situation.

Freestyle

Freestyle technical debt settlement is an approach where engineers independently tackle technical debt and make code improvements outside of scheduled sprints or formal initiatives. This approach relies heavily on the initiative and dedication of individual team members. Here's how this can be effectively managed and encouraged:

- *Voluntary Refactoring*: Engineers voluntarily improve and simplify code they encounter during their work. Example: A developer notices an area of the codebase that's overly complex and takes the initiative to refactor it for better readability and maintainability.

- *Code Quality Enhancements*: Team members independently enhance code quality, such as updating documentation or removing deprecated code. Example: An engineer updates outdated comments, eliminates unused code, or adds missing unit tests while working on their tasks.

- *Bug Fixes and Performance Optimizations*: Engineers address minor bugs or performance issues that arise during their regular development work. Example: While fixing a feature, a developer might also optimize a slow-performing query or resolve a small bug they encounter.

- *Process and Tool Improvements*: Engineers independently work on enhancing development tools or processes to benefit the team. Example: An engineer improves internal tooling, streamlines workflows, or suggests better practices for code reviews.

Freestyle technical debt settlement works best in teams that are highly motivated, skilled, and take strong ownership of their work. Motivated teams are more likely to go beyond their assigned tasks to address technical debt and enhance the code on their own initiative. Technical expertise enables engineers to effectively identify and resolve issues within the codebase without needing extra supervision. Teams with a strong sense of ownership are dedicated to maintaining and improving code quality, actively looking for and fixing problems. This approach ensures that voluntary technical debt settlement is both feasible and effective.

Most importantly, this doesn't require extensive prioritization or complex processes; it functions smoothly in high-performing engineering teams, like a well-oiled machine. It just works!

Rock-Sized Technical Initiatives

Rock-sized technical initiatives are strategic in nature, having direct business impact or enhancing the stability and scalability of your technical systems. Let it be building API infrastructure to integrate with partners, modularizing your monolith to microservices, migrating on-prem to cloud or building end-to-end monitoring to resolve system errors quickly, they can take anywhere from months to quarters.

Prioritizing such technical initiatives in the middle of product development is challenging. If you go to your executive and say that your team will not be rolling out any major features for the next few months but invest in rock-sized technical initiatives, they will have all sorts of questions.

Unlike product development, to prioritize technical initiatives, problems have to be felt or at least there should be symptoms. Let's see how a conversation might unfold between an EM and an executive:

> **EM**: "Thanks for taking the time to meet today. I wanted to discuss some strategic technical initiatives that our team believes are essential for our long-term success. I understand we're in the middle of some important product development, but these initiatives will have a significant impact on our ability to scale and innovate moving forward."

> **Exec**: "Of course, I'm all ears. But just to be clear, you're suggesting we might need to pause or slow down on new feature rollouts? That's a tough sell, especially when the market is so competitive right now."

> **EM**: "I totally understand, and I anticipated this would be a challenging conversation. Yes, we're proposing that for the next few months, we prioritize some rock-sized initiatives over new feature development. Specifically, we're looking at modularizing

our monolith into microservices, migrating some of our systems to the cloud, and implementing comprehensive end-to-end monitoring."

Exec: (leaning forward, frowning slightly) "That's a significant shift. Can you walk me through why these are necessary now? I need to be convinced this won't slow us down or hurt our competitive edge."

EM: "Absolutely. Let's start with modularization into microservices. Our current monolithic architecture is becoming a bottleneck. Every time we want to introduce or update a feature, it's like trying to untangle a ball of yarn. It's slowing us down. By breaking it down into microservices, we'll have the flexibility to innovate faster in the future. We can deploy updates independently, which means quicker time-to-market for new features down the line."

Exec: (thoughtful, but still skeptical) "I see the logic, but that sounds like it could take a while. What's the timeline?"

EM: (nodding) "It's not a quick fix, I won't sugarcoat it—it could take several months. But this investment is about enabling speed and flexibility in the long term. Once we've modularized, we'll be able to roll out new features faster and more reliably. It's a foundation for sustained growth."

Exec: "And the other initiatives?"

EM: (more confident now) "Migrating our on-prem systems to the cloud is about scalability. We're nearing the limits of what our current infrastructure can handle. The cloud offers us the ability to scale dynamically with demand, reducing costs and improving reliability. Plus, it opens up opportunities for leveraging cloud-native services that can accelerate our development processes.

Then there's the end-to-end monitoring. This is critical for maintaining the quality and reliability of our service. Right now, our error detection is reactive—we find out about issues when they've already impacted users. With a robust monitoring system, we can catch and resolve issues before they become problems, which directly impacts user satisfaction."

Exec: (leaning back, contemplative) "I get it. It's about laying the groundwork for future growth. But how do we justify the short-term impact—delaying feature rollouts when our competitors might be moving faster?"

EM: "That's the challenge, and I completely understand your concern. But think of it this way: by investing in these initiatives now, we're positioning ourselves to outpace the competition in the long run. We'll be able to deliver more features, more reliably, and with greater agility. It's a short-term trade-off for long-term gain. If we don't address these technical debts now, they'll only grow, and eventually, they'll slow us down more than a temporary pause in feature development ever could."

Exec: (after a long pause, nodding slowly) "You've made a solid case. It's not an easy decision, but I see the strategic importance. We need to ensure the board understands this too—can you prepare a detailed proposal that we can present together?"

EM: (relieved, with a hint of optimism) "Absolutely. I'll get started on that right away. Thank you for hearing me out and considering this. I'm confident that with your support, we can make this transition smoothly and set ourselves up for greater success."

Exec: (smiling, a bit more reassured) "Let's do it. The long-term vision matters, and I trust your judgment. We'll make sure the team understands the importance of this shift."

From the above conversation with the executive, it's clear that prioritizing rock-sized technical initiatives requires a nuanced approach. As an Engineering Manager, your role is pivotal in balancing the immediate demands of product development with the strategic need for foundational improvements. Here's how you can effectively manage and communicate these priorities to ensure long-term success:

- *Clear Communication*: As seen in the conversation, clear and transparent communication is key when advocating for significant technical projects. The engineering team must articulate not only the technical benefits but also the business impact of these initiatives. It's crucial to frame these projects as enablers of future growth rather than mere backend improvements.

- *Aligning with Business Goals*: Ensure that the technical initiatives align with the broader business objectives. For example, if the company's goal is to expand into new markets quickly, modularizing the system into microservices could directly support that by allowing faster, independent deployment of new features tailored to those markets.

- *Risk Management*: Acknowledge and plan for the short-term risks involved, such as potential delays in feature rollouts. This can involve developing contingency plans or identifying parallel work streams that can keep some level of product development active while the technical initiatives are underway.

- *Progress Tracking and Milestones*: Setting clear milestones and regularly tracking progress can help maintain momentum and provide visibility to stakeholders. Demonstrating early wins, like the successful deployment of a first microservice or the first cloud migration, can build confidence in the initiative's value.

- *Stakeholder Engagement*: Engage stakeholders early and often. Keeping executives, product teams, and other key players informed about the progress and expected outcomes of the initiatives helps maintain alignment and support throughout the project's lifecycle.

PART V

Delivering Impactful Projects

Let's be honest—you are hired to deliver. You need to deliver value through impactful projects so the business can survive, thrive, and evolve.

You've been given an entire team to accomplish the mission. The decisions of what processes they use, how you manage dependencies and blockers for delivery, how you report progress to management, and whether you pivot or persevere are on your shoulders.

Careful planning and execution used to be more important than the value itself that was supposed to be delivered. Engineering teams used to spend weeks and months planning for delivering a project and had ceremonies after ceremonies to come to a point where they could actually deliver. Delivering a project of the highest quality was a matter of pride for software engineering teams. Failures were considered dreadful and held them back from delivering solutions swiftly. Changes were accumulated and delivered once in a full moon. Your team had to get it right no matter what.

Times have changed. We're living in a world where ideas turn into products. But does every idea bring value to the organization? Not really. You need to adopt modern delivery practices that enable your team to develop ideas into engineering solutions and to deploy them at a much faster pace to get early feedback and validate your hypothesis. Investing in a big fat solution design up front and working on a project for months without knowing its potential impact is considered a costly undertaking for any software engineering team.

Speed versus quality is still a trending topic in engineering teams. You usually find yourself in contention for quality with nontechnical stakeholders and business people who are on the side of speed. More often than not, a trade-off is made on the engineering side to deliver a project on time. But have you thought about why there's always this split? Is it that they don't want a quality product at the end of the day? Nope. They aren't sure what we mean by quality.

And what about measuring your delivery effectiveness? This is still a mystery for many engineering teams. Measuring productivity through metrics like the number of pull requests merged or story points completed provides only a partial view of your team's effectiveness. While these figures might indicate activity, they don't reflect the actual value delivered to the business. What truly matters is how these efforts contribute to key business outcomes such as customer satisfaction, market speed, and system stability. Over-relying on these metrics can create a misleading sense of progress, as they often don't align with strategic goals or deliver meaningful impact.

To enhance delivery and ensure your team's efforts are impactful, focus on metrics that align with broader business objectives. Reducing work in progress (WIP) helps concentrate efforts on completing projects more efficiently, while metrics like lead time, deployment frequency, change failure rate, and mean time to recovery offer a clearer picture of your team's real-world effectiveness. By measuring and prioritizing what genuinely drives business success, you can better align your team's activities with organizational goals and deliver more significant results.

Last but not the least, project management still exists. You still have to do capacity planning; report progress to management and closely work with your stakeholders; and help your team to raise, eliminate, or avoid blockers when delivering a project. There will be challenging times where a project may not be progressing as expected or you have a hunch that it may not deliver expected value.

In this part, you'll get all the recipes to lead and deliver impactful projects that bring value for your organization.

- ***Modern Delivery Practices***: Risks of big bang launches, How to deliver projects iteratively to learn and adjust your approach through MVP and feasible technical design—Minimum Viable Architecture, Slicing the big fat project, Modular architecture and API-first design, Embracing continuous and progressive delivery.

- ***Measuring Delivery Effectiveness***: A thoughtful conversation with your executive, Limits of Velocity, Measuring what matters through—North Star metrics and the mighty DORA—Lead Time, Deployment Frequency, Change Failure Rate and Mean Time To Recover.

- ***Managing Stakeholders, Progress and Blockers***: Building strong partnerships with your stakeholders, Reporting progress to senior leadership and Managing blockers.

CHAPTER 13

Modern Delivery Practices

It was D-Day. Delivery day for our three-month long project.

Stakeholders were waiting for it, and now, hearing about the launch date has gotten them pretty excited. The launch communication to our users has been set up, the major clients were informed via email directly by our executives, the sister cross-functional teams were notified, and the necessary changes were made on their side to integrate with our part of the system. It feels like a grand ceremony!

On the other hand, we, as an engineering team, are hoping to launch the project smoothly without major hiccups, thanks to the integration testing and all the launch preparation we did nearly for a month. You heard it right—an entire month dedicated solely to preparation. After all, we don't want to deliver faulty software that never works, especially when all eyes are on us. I was on the edge of my seat as we're literally a button click away in releasing this much-awaited project. I know that I am accountable for my team's delivery and the results that we are producing through our work. I was interfacing stakeholders and senior leadership about the progress of the launch so that my team can focus on the execution.

A message pops up in our team's Slack channel: "Feature flag enabled and re-deployed. We'll be live in 10 minutes." This message has received 12 reactions—lots of love from engineers and a fingers-crossed reaction from our product manager. As the countdown ended, the moment we had been working toward for months finally arrived. The feature flag was enabled, and at first, everything seemed to be running smoothly. Our dashboards looked stable, and the team felt a sense of quiet relief as the launch got underway.

However, as days passed, a few issues began to surface. Some users encountered minor glitches, and error logs started appearing more frequently. What initially appeared to be isolated incidents gradually became more widespread. The system began to show signs of strain, with certain features not performing as smoothly as we had anticipated. Our team promptly responded to these issues, but the complexity of launching everything simultaneously made it challenging to stay ahead of the problems.

© Ananth Ramachandran 2024
A. Ramachandran, *The Complete Engineering Manager*, https://doi.org/10.1007/979-8-8688-0267-6_13

By the end of the week, the project was live, but not without some challenges along the way. We managed to keep the system running, but it was clear that the launch hadn't been as smooth as we had anticipated. This experience highlighted the risks inherent in delivering a large, complex project all at once.

As an engineering manager during this phase, I needed to stay vigilant, fully cognizant of the responsibility for the project's success. My priority was closely monitoring system performance, quickly addressing issues alongside my team as they arose, and maintaining clear communication with both my team and key stakeholders. Problem-solving became paramount, demanding quick decisions to stabilize the system while keeping the team motivated and focused. While managing these immediate challenges, I was also mentally preparing for a post-mortem to extract valuable insights and improve our processes for future project delivery.

Risks of Big-Bang Launches

Big-bang launches carry significant risks. Despite thorough preparation, the scale and complexity of deploying everything simultaneously can lead to unforeseen issues that are difficult to manage. While the excitement of a major launch is undeniable, this situation reinforced the value of an iterative approach. Delivering in smaller, more controlled increments might have allowed you to catch and resolve issues earlier, leading to a smoother and more reliable rollout.

What are the risks of a big project?

- *Increased Risk of Failure*: Launching everything simultaneously raises the stakes, where a single issue can cause widespread system failures, leading to significant downtime and business disruption.

- *Limited Feedback and Testing*: The big-bang approach limits iterative testing, making it harder to identify and fix issues early, which often results in costly post-launch fixes.

- *Complex Rollback*: Rolling back changes in a big-bang launch is complicated and risky, especially when multiple components are interdependent, making it difficult to isolate and resolve specific issues.

- *Resource and Team Overload*: The intensity of coordinating a large-scale launch can overwhelm teams and resources, leading to burnout and reduced productivity, with long-lasting effects on future projects.

- *Unpredictable User Impact*: Introducing major changes all at once can lead to unexpected user reactions, causing confusion or dissatisfaction if the new features are not well-received or understood.

- *Missed Iterative Learning*: Big-bang launches forgo the benefits of gradual, iterative improvements, missing opportunities to refine the product and enhance the user experience based on real-time feedback.

Organization and Engineering Mismatch

Given the inherent differences between organizational and engineering perspectives, a natural mismatch often occurs in how these functions approach their work and set priorities. This directly affects software delivery. For instance, a business unit might expect a new feature to be completed within two weeks due to market demands, while engineering teams understand that the feature requires more time due to unforeseen technical challenges and the need to ensure system stability.

Without a mutual understanding, this clash of expectations can spiral into endless debates, causing frustration and delays. This is where your role as an engineering manager becomes pivotal. You act as a bridge between these two worlds, tasked with translating business priorities into actionable engineering tasks and vice versa.

Your challenge is to grasp the essence of business needs and market pressures while explaining the intricacies of technical work in terms that make sense to nontechnical stakeholders. This involves setting realistic expectations by providing clear, evidence-based timelines and articulating the technical constraints that affect development. You must navigate the delicate balance between the urgency of business demands and the practicalities of engineering limitations.

In a healthy working relationship, engineering teams are empowered to excel and deliver successful outcomes, while the organization understands and accommodates the realities of technical work. By bridging the gap between these perspectives, your help ensures that both business and engineering goals are met harmoniously, leading to more effective and successful software delivery.

The ultimate goal is that both the organization and engineering wins.

Iterative Delivery

Delivering value iteratively involves releasing the smallest viable improvements to end users or customers in a continuous cycle. This method allows organizations to quickly observe the impact on user behavior, which can then positively influence business objectives.

For example, enhancing your product's recommendation system to offer more personalized suggestions might lead to increased user engagement and satisfaction. Or, launching a feature such as personalized workout plan in a health and wellness app can directly improve users' lifestyles by addressing their specific needs. Another example could be integrating an AI-powered chatbot to provide instant customer support, thereby enhancing customer experience and retention. In each of these scenarios, the key takeaway is that the value delivered to the end user is what truly counts.

How Iterative?

The iterative approach (Figure 13-1) is about breaking down a project into smaller, manageable pieces and releasing these pieces in short, frequent cycles. Instead of waiting for a perfect, fully formed product to be completed, teams focus on delivering portions of functionality that provide immediate value. The iteration length can vary depending on the team's workflow and the project's nature, but the goal is always to deliver something functional and valuable within each cycle. Over time, these iterations accumulate, leading to a more robust and refined product without the risks associated with a single, large-scale release.

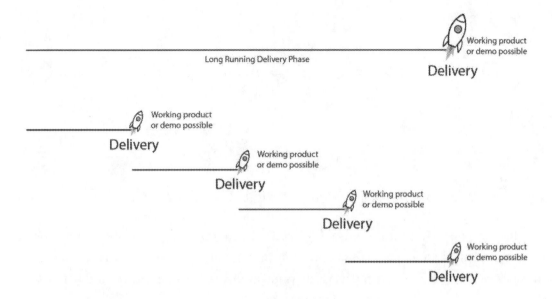

Figure 13-1. *Big-bang delivery vs. iterative delivery*

How Small?

The deliverable should be as small as possible while still providing tangible value to the user. It could be a minor feature improvement, a bug fix, or an enhancement that users can notice and appreciate. The idea is to keep the scope narrow but impactful, allowing the team to focus on quality and speed. The smaller the iteration, the quicker it can be released, tested, and improved upon based on real user feedback.

How Valuable Will It Be?

The value of each iteration is measured by its impact on the end user and, ultimately, on the business. This means every iteration should aim to solve a user problem, enhance user experience, or contribute to the business objectives in some way. While determining the exact value can be challenging, teams should prioritize iterations that align closely with user needs and business goals. This could involve user testing, data analysis, and feedback loops to ensure that each release is not just a ticked-off task but a step toward delivering meaningful outcomes.

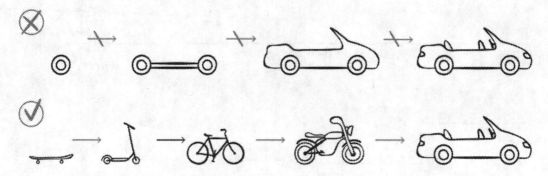

Figure 13-2. *Henrik Kniberg's famous iterative MVP illustration*

By adopting an iterative mindset (Figure 13-2), engineering teams shift from a focus on simply building features to delivering continuous value. This change in approach fosters a culture where every release is an opportunity to learn, improve, and better serve the end user, ultimately leading to a more successful and responsive product.

You, as an engineering manager lead value delivery of your team, such as how to build, who will be involved, when to deliver, and what precisely will be delivered. On the other hand, your product counterpart, the product manager, leads the value definition of "what" and "why" to build. More often than not, you both have to work together in defining the scope of the iterative delivery and the value that will be delivered.

Value Realization

Value definition is a crucial phase in any project. Collaborating closely with your product manager, it's imperative to get this step right. Without a clear and accurate definition of value, it becomes challenging for you and your team to deliver something that truly matters. If the value is not clearly identified or is misunderstood, the end result may not address any real pain points, solve any problems, or seize any opportunities, leading to a lack of meaningful impact.

Value of any delivery can be realized through the following:

- *Value Definition*: This is the foundational step where you work with your product manager to clearly identify and define the value your project aims to deliver. This involves understanding the pain points, problems, and opportunities from the perspective of the end user or customer. It sets the direction for the entire project, ensuring everyone involved is aligned on what success looks like.

- *Value Delivery*: Once value is defined, the next step is to deliver it through projects. This involves translating the defined value into actionable tasks and features that your team can build and release. The focus here is on execution—ensuring that the work being done aligns with the value that was initially defined and making iterative progress toward delivering that value.

- *Value Confirmation*: After delivery, it's essential to confirm that the value has been realized as intended. This step involves measuring outcomes, gathering feedback, and assessing whether the delivered features or solutions are solving the problems, addressing the pain points, or capitalizing on the opportunities that were identified in the value definition phase. It closes the loop, ensuring that the project has indeed delivered the intended value.

In essence, value realization is an ongoing cycle that starts with a clear definition, followed by focused delivery, and ends with confirmation that the intended value has been achieved. This approach ensures that your project remains aligned with its goals and continues to deliver meaningful results.

MVP

A minimum viable product (MVP) is a cornerstone of modern product development, especially when linked to iterative delivery. It's about delivering the smallest, most impactful version of your product to users as quickly as possible. The idea is simple: instead of waiting to release a fully polished product, you deliver a version that's just enough to test your key assumptions and gather feedback. This approach creates a fast feedback loop, where the focus shifts from simply building features to understanding how those features impact the user experience and the business.

In many ways, an MVP embodies the difference between output and outcome. Output is the tangible work your team produces—lines of code, features, designs. But the outcome is what truly matters: how those outputs translate into value for users and the organization. An MVP is designed to deliver outcomes early on. By putting something functional and valuable into users' hands quickly, you can measure whether you're on the right track, using real data rather than assumptions.

The beauty of an MVP lies in its ability to indicate whether to pivot or persevere. Once the MVP is released, the feedback and data you collect will direct your next steps. If the results confirm your assumptions and users find value, you can continue to build on that foundation, adding features and refining the product. If the feedback suggests changes are needed, you can pivot by adjusting your strategy, modifying the product, or exploring new directions. This adaptability helps navigate today's fast-paced environment, where user needs and market conditions can change quickly.

MVPs also allow for a culture of experimentation. By iteratively releasing small versions of your product, you can test different ideas and explore new opportunities without committing to a full-scale build. Each release is an experiment in itself, offering insights into what works and what doesn't. This experimental approach helps uncover problems and opportunities that might not be apparent during initial planning, allowing for continuous learning and adaptation.

Moreover, the MVP approach is inherently tied to the concept of return on investment (ROI). By delivering value in small increments, you start to see returns much earlier in the project lifecycle. This not only reduces the risk of investing heavily in a product that might not succeed but also ensures that resources are focused on what matters most: delivering tangible value to both the business and the users.

Technical Design

The technical design of your software should be planned in a way that supports iterative development and delivery. By collaborating with your product manager and other cross-functional experts in your team, larger projects can be broken down into iterations right from the scoping of requirements. You assist in negotiating the scope, priorities, and feasibility of development with stakeholders. Your technical knowledge helps you advocate effectively for the engineering team's needs and, conversely, challenge your own team on the technical approach and delivery.

Minimum Viable Architecture

In the fast-paced world of software development, a minimum viable architecture (MVA), similar to an MVP, has emerged as a handy strategy for delivering value quickly while maintaining the flexibility to evolve the system. An MVA focuses on establishing just enough architecture to support the current functionality and future growth without over-engineering.

An MVA enables the following:

- *Simplicity*: Starting with the simplest possible architecture that can support the initial requirements. Avoid adding unnecessary complexity.

- *Scalability*: Ensuring that the architecture can scale with increasing load and complexity over time.

- *Flexibility*: Designing the architecture to accommodate changes and extensions without significant rework.

- *Incrementality*: Building the architecture incrementally, adding components and refining the design as new requirements emerge.

Have you heard of the Open/Closed Principle in software development? It suggests adding new functionality with minimal changes to existing code or behavior. Now, consider applying this principle to iterative delivery. When developing a large feature iteratively, guide your team to focus on the initial iteration to avoid over-engineering and maintain a straightforward technical design. Simultaneously, establish key technical foundations like a reusable architecture and data model. This strategy reduces the need for re-architecting in each iteration, keeping your design open for extension but closed for significant modification in future iterations.

Slicing the Big Fat Project

Cut the cake vertically, not horizontally.

Building software vertically (Figure 13-3) involves delivering complete, end-to-end slices of functionality in each iteration, rather than developing isolated components in a sequential manner. This approach ensures that every iteration produces a potentially shippable product increment that provides real user value.

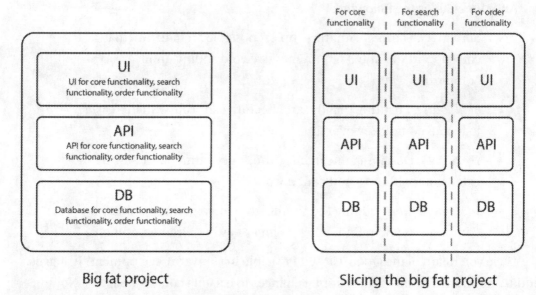

Figure 13-3. *Slicing the big fat project*

In the early days of Spotify, the music streaming giant, the engineering team faced the challenge of delivering a seamless and scalable service while continuously rolling out new features to a growing global audience. Instead of following a traditional horizontal development approach, where teams would focus on isolated components like the backend, frontend, or database separately, Spotify adopted a vertical slicing strategy. This approach, often referred to as "cutting the cake vertically," allowed them to build and deliver complete, end-to-end slices of functionality in each iteration.

By working closely with product managers and cross-functional teams, Spotify's engineers identified vertical slices that encompassed every necessary layer of the application—from the user interface, through the business logic, all the way down to the data storage systems. For example, when building a new playlist feature, the team would develop the entire feature as a single slice, integrating the UI, the logic for managing playlists, and the necessary database structures all at once. This ensured that by the end of each iteration, they had a fully functional, shippable product increment that provided real user value, rather than just a collection of unfinished parts.

This vertical approach not only facilitated continuous delivery but also allowed Spotify to gather immediate feedback from users on fully functional features. As a result, they could make informed adjustments and refinements in subsequent iterations, enhancing the overall user experience. By focusing on delivering complete, integrated features, Spotify was able to maintain agility, quickly respond to user needs, and ensure that all parts of their complex system worked together seamlessly. This strategy played a crucial role in their ability to scale rapidly and consistently deliver a high-quality streaming experience to millions of users worldwide.

As an engineering manager focusing on slicing a large project into vertical slices, your role involves working closely with your product manager to define complete, end-to-end slices that integrate all necessary components, from the user interface to data storage. You ensure that these slices are user-centric and deliver real value in each iteration, making them potentially shippable product increments. By coordinating cross-functional efforts, you ensure that each slice functions cohesively within the overall system. Additionally, you facilitate iterative feedback loops, using insights to refine and adjust subsequent slices, ensuring that the project progresses smoothly and remains aligned with its long-term goals.

Modular Architecture

Amazon is a prime example of an organization that has successfully implemented a modular architecture. Initially, Amazon's e-commerce platform was a monolithic application, which made it difficult to scale and innovate rapidly. To address these challenges, Amazon transitioned to a modular architecture, breaking down the monolithic application into smaller, independent services.

Each service is responsible for a specific business functionality, such as product catalog, payment processing, or user authentication. These services communicate with each other through well-defined APIs, allowing them to operate independently while contributing to the overall functionality of the platform.

The benefits Amazon reaped from this transition are substantial:

- *Scalability*: Individual services can be scaled independently based on demand, optimizing resource utilization.

- *Flexibility*: Teams can deploy updates to specific services without affecting the entire system, facilitating continuous delivery and innovation.

- *Resilience*: The failure of one service does not bring down the entire system, enhancing overall reliability.

For engineering managers, understanding and implementing modular architecture is crucial for the following:

- *Strategic Planning and Execution*: Modular architecture enables better project planning and execution. By breaking down the project into manageable modules, managers can allocate resources more effectively and ensure timely delivery of components.

- *Enhanced Team Collaboration*: Clear module boundaries and well-defined interfaces facilitate better collaboration among teams. Engineering managers can assign modules based on team expertise, improving productivity and quality of output.

- *Risk Mitigation*: By isolating functionality within modules, the impact of potential issues is contained. This modular approach reduces the risk of widespread system failures and simplifies troubleshooting and maintenance.

- *Adaptability and Innovation*: Modular architecture allows for the integration of new technologies and features without extensive rework. Engineering managers can drive innovation and keep the system adaptable to evolving business needs.

Does every engineering team need modular architecture? Well, it depends. While modular architecture offers many advantages, there are scenarios where it may not be necessary or even beneficial. Implementing modular architecture in such cases can lead to unnecessary complexity, overhead, and wasted resources.

Twitter's Journey to Modular Architecture

In the early days of Twitter, when the platform was just a simple idea for sharing short status updates, the engineering team opted for a monolithic architecture. This decision was driven by the need to deliver the product quickly—Twitter was a small startup with a tiny user base, and the primary goal was to get the platform out into the world as fast as possible. A monolithic architecture allowed the team to iterate rapidly, pushing out new features and updates with minimal overhead. The focus was on swift delivery and finding product-market fit, rather than worrying about the long-term complexities of the architecture.

However, as Twitter's popularity surged, the limitations of this approach became painfully clear. The system struggled to scale, leading to frequent outages—so common that the "Fail Whale" became a notorious symbol of the platform's struggles. Every time the team needed to deploy a new feature or fix a bug, they faced the challenge of navigating a massive, interconnected codebase, where changes in one area could cause unexpected issues elsewhere. These challenges slowed down their delivery considerably, turning what was once a streamlined operation into a bottleneck.

Despite these growing pains, Twitter didn't immediately transition to a more modular architecture. The sheer complexity of their monolithic system made the shift daunting, as the team had to balance the risks of disrupting service for millions of users with the potential benefits of a more flexible, scalable architecture. It was only after repeatedly facing these delivery challenges and quality issues that Twitter began the careful, gradual process of breaking down its monolith into modular components, understanding that the architecture that once enabled rapid delivery was now hindering it, and a new approach was needed to sustain a global communication platform.

API-First Design

Adopting an API-first design philosophy can significantly enhance iterative delivery in modern software development. This approach focuses on defining the API as the specification of your system architecture before delving into the implementation details. By prioritizing API design, you lay a solid foundation for structured, flexible, and scalable development cycles.

The core of API-first design is to create a clear, well-documented API specification from the start. This specification acts as a contract between system components and development teams. Establishing how services will interact, the data exchanged, and the functionalities exposed helps align teams and streamline the development process.

The following are the key advantages of API-first design:

- *Parallel Development*: Teams can work on different components, such as front-end and back-end, simultaneously. This parallel work speeds up development and enables quicker iterations.

- *Flexibility and Scalability*: A well-defined API allows for changes and feature additions without disrupting other system parts. For example, enhancing a feature or adding functionality can be done through API updates, ensuring smooth integration.

- *Enhanced Documentation*: Developing comprehensive API documentation alongside the API specification ensures all stakeholders have clear guidance. This reduces miscommunications and accelerates integration efforts.

- *Versioning and Compatibility*: Structured API versioning maintains backward compatibility, ensuring stability and preventing disruptions for existing users when new features are introduced.

In summary, API-first design streamlines development and enhances iterative delivery. It supports parallel work, allows flexible adjustments, and ensures clear communication and documentation. This approach aligns with iterative principles, enabling teams to build and refine products incrementally while maintaining a coherent and scalable architecture.

Continuous and Progressive Delivery

Continuous delivery (CD) has become a standard practice in modern engineering teams, revolutionizing how software is developed and delivered. At its core, CD automates the process of delivering software so that changes can be released swiftly and reliably. By integrating CD into your development pipeline, you ensure that every code change is automatically built, tested, and prepared for release, streamlining the delivery process and reducing the time from development to deployment.

The essence of continuous delivery lies in its automation. Once code changes are committed, a series of automated steps are triggered: the code is built, tested for quality and functionality, and then staged for deployment. This automation reduces manual errors, speeds up the release process, and ensures that your codebase remains in a deployable state at all times. With CD, teams can focus more on writing code and less on managing deployment processes, leading to more frequent and reliable releases.

However, CD can be complemented and enhanced by incorporating progressive delivery practices. Progressive delivery takes the concept of CD a step further by focusing on controlled and incremental releases. This method allows teams to deliver new features or updates to a subset of users before a full-scale rollout.

Here's how progressive delivery can be effectively implemented:

- *Feature Flags*: Feature flags (Figure 13-4) are a powerful tool in progressive delivery. They allow developers to toggle features on or off without deploying new code. By using feature flags, you can release code to production but keep it hidden from users until you're ready. This capability enables you to test new features in a live environment with minimal risk, gathering feedback and making necessary adjustments before a full release.

- *Incremental Launches*: Instead of launching a feature to all users at once, you can release it incrementally. Start by rolling out the feature to a small percentage of your user base or a specific user segment. This gradual rollout allows you to monitor performance, gather user feedback, and identify any issues before expanding the release to a broader audience. Incremental launches reduce the impact of potential problems and provide opportunities for iterative improvements.

- *Technical Setup*: Implementing progressive delivery requires a robust technical setup. This includes a well-structured deployment pipeline, automated testing frameworks, and systems to manage feature flags and incremental rollouts. Your infrastructure should support the ability to control who sees new features and manage the complexities of rolling back or adjusting releases based on real-time feedback.

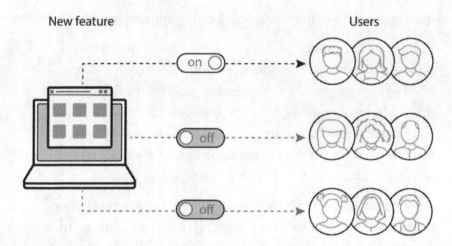

Figure 13-4. *Feature flags*

The integration of progressive delivery with continuous delivery creates a powerful combination for managing releases. While CD ensures that your code is always in a deployable state and ready for release, progressive delivery adds a layer of control and flexibility. This approach minimizes risk by allowing you to test and validate features incrementally, gather user feedback, and make informed decisions about full-scale deployments.

In practice, this means you can release new functionalities more confidently, knowing that you can address issues early and adjust your approach based on actual user experiences. For instance, if a new recommendation engine is introduced, you might start by enabling it for a small group of users to assess its performance and impact on user engagement before making it available to everyone. This careful, data-driven approach helps ensure that each release delivers value and meets user expectations.

In conclusion, continuous delivery lays the groundwork for efficient and reliable software delivery, while progressive delivery enhances this process by introducing controlled and incremental releases. By adopting both practices, engineering teams can achieve a higher level of agility and responsiveness, ensuring that new features and updates are delivered effectively and with minimal risk.

What Could Slow Down Your Team's Delivery?

Are you constantly falling short of delivery goals, project after project? Do productivity concerns frequently come up during one-on-ones with your team members or in retrospectives? Are low scores in developer experience surveys becoming a persistent trend within your teams? Do you and your team often find yourselves heavily reliant on other teams within the organization? These indicators may point to deeper, underlying issues that are impacting your delivery.

To effectively improve your team's delivery, it's essential to first identify the factors causing the slowdown. Let's explore some common industry anti-patterns that can significantly hinder a team's ability to deliver and consider what steps you can take to address them.

Unorganized Teams and Tight Dependency

When teams within your domain are not well-organized in terms of their scope, they often end up stepping on each other's toes, leading to delays and inefficiencies. This issue may stem from how your engineering system is architected or how your team's responsibilities are delineated within the broader organizational context. Perhaps this wasn't a problem when your organization was smaller—when you had just a handful of engineers working together. With fewer people, you had less scope, less communication overhead, and fewer complexities to manage. Back then, delivering changes felt more straightforward and swift.

Fast-forward to today: your domain has expanded, the number of engineers in your organization has multiplied, and you've likely split into multiple teams and services. As the complexity of the system has increased, you may have noticed a dip in productivity. Teams that were once split to facilitate faster value creation might now be experiencing bottlenecks and delays.

This issue often relates to what is known as Inverse Conway's Law: the idea that your system architecture ends up mirroring the communication structure of your organization. If teams are tightly coupled or lack clarity in their scope, the resulting dependencies can slow down the delivery process.

What Can You Do About It?

As your team's scope evolves, gain insight into the system architecture and how teams function within your domain. If you observe friction, consider the following actions:

- *Promote Scalable Architecture and Decoupled Systems*: Encourage a system design that allows teams to work independently of one another, reducing tight dependencies that can slow down progress.

- *Consider Team Re-organization and Re-scoping*: If the current team structure is causing delays, it might be time to reassess and realign teams based on their scopes to minimize overlap and dependencies.

- *Create Useful Documentations*: Develop and maintain comprehensive documentation outlining team responsibilities, system architecture, and integration requirements to prevent misunderstandings and streamline coordination.

- *Implement Clear Communication Channels*: Set up structured communication systems, such as regular sync meetings or collaboration tools, to ensure teams can coordinate effectively and address dependencies promptly.

Legacy Systems and Technical Debt

Have you experienced the frustration of missing deadlines due to outdated systems and accumulated technical debt? Legacy systems and technical debt can create significant roadblocks for engineering teams, causing delays and complications that hinder progress. These issues force teams to navigate old code and manage unforeseen problems, leading to more bugs and increased maintenance work. This can prevent timely delivery of features and slow down overall productivity. Tackling the challenges posed by legacy systems and technical debt is key to maintain an efficient development process. By addressing these issues proactively, teams can enhance their productivity and ensure a smoother path to delivering high-quality solutions.

Effects on Delivery

These are the effects:

Slower Development Cycles: Legacy systems are often built on outdated technologies that the current team no longer supports or fully understands. This results in longer development cycles, as engineers spend more time deciphering old code and finding workarounds for limitations. Additionally, high levels of technical debt mean that new features or updates often require extensive modifications to existing code, slowing down the overall pace of development.

Increased Risk and Fragility: As systems age, they become more fragile. The interdependencies in legacy systems can cause even minor changes to have unforeseen consequences, leading to bugs, crashes, or downtime. Similarly, technical debt, if left unmanaged, can create a brittle codebase where small changes trigger cascading failures, requiring extensive debugging and testing, which delays delivery.

Reduced Flexibility for Innovation: Legacy systems are typically inflexible, making it difficult to adopt new technologies, frameworks, or methodologies. This lack of flexibility stifles innovation, as the team is constrained by the limitations of the old system. High technical debt exacerbates this issue by creating a codebase that is difficult to extend or modify, making it challenging to respond to new business needs or market opportunities.

Lower Team Morale and Productivity: Working with legacy systems and dealing with technical debt can be frustrating for engineers. Constantly battling outdated technology or cleaning up poorly written code can lead to burnout and reduced job satisfaction. This, in turn, affects overall team productivity and can lead to higher turnover rates, further impacting delivery timelines.

What Can You Do About It?

Here's what you can do about it:

- *Gradual Modernization and Refactoring*: To address the challenges of legacy systems, it's essential to prioritize modernization efforts. This can be done incrementally by refactoring parts of the legacy system over time, rather than attempting a complete overhaul all at once. By gradually replacing outdated components with modern alternatives, you can reduce the system's fragility and make it easier to maintain and extend.

- *Active Management of Technical Debt*: Technical debt should be treated as a first-class concern in your development process. Regularly assess and quantify the technical debt in your codebase, and allocate time in your development cycles to address it. This might include refactoring poorly written code, improving documentation, or enhancing test coverage. By actively managing technical debt, you can prevent it from accumulating to a point where it significantly hampers your ability to deliver.

- *Prioritizing High-Impact Areas*: Not all parts of a legacy system or technical debt will have the same impact on delivery. Focus your efforts on high-impact areas—those parts of the system that are most critical to your business operations or most frequently modified. By addressing the most problematic areas first, you can make the most significant improvements in delivery speed and quality.

- *Building a Business Case for Investment*: Modernizing legacy systems and addressing technical debt requires time and resources, which may not always be readily available. As an engineering manager, building a business case for these efforts involves showing how they can lead to faster delivery, reduced risk, and increased innovation. Aligning these technical improvements with business goals helps in securing the necessary investment and support from stakeholders.

- *Leveraging Automation and Tools*: Automation can play a significant role in managing legacy systems and technical debt. Automated testing, continuous integration, and deployment pipelines can help mitigate the risks associated with changing legacy code and ensure that refactoring efforts do not introduce new issues. Additionally, tools for code analysis and technical debt management can provide insights into the most critical areas to address.

By taking a proactive approach to modernizing legacy systems and managing technical debt, you can create a more agile, efficient development environment. This not only improves delivery timelines but also positions your team to better respond to future challenges and opportunities.

Unclear Scope and Outcome

Unclear scope and outcome are pervasive issues that can severely hinder your team's ability to deliver effectively. When the goals of a project are not well-defined or when there is ambiguity in what the team is expected to achieve, progress becomes slow and haphazard. This lack of clarity leads to confusion, misaligned efforts, and frequent changes in direction, which waste valuable time and resources.

In many cases, unclear scope arises from poorly defined requirements or a lack of communication between stakeholders and the development team. If the project's objectives are unclear, teams might assume what needs to be done, resulting in work that misaligns with the project's goals. This misalignment can result in frequent rework, scope creep, and, ultimately, delays in delivery.

Moreover, when the desired outcomes are not well-articulated, it becomes challenging to measure progress or success. Teams might find themselves working on tasks without a clear understanding of how their work contributes to the overall goals of the project. This lack of direction not only affects productivity but also dampens motivation, as developers may feel that their efforts are not making a meaningful impact.

What Can You Do About It?

To address unclear scope and outcome, it's essential to push back against ambiguity right from the start. As an engineering manager, you must work closely with your product manager, stakeholders, and team members to ensure that the project's scope is clearly defined. This involves breaking down high-level goals into specific, actionable tasks that align with the overall objectives. Every team member should have a clear understanding of what success looks like and how their work contributes to the project's goals.

You and your team have to deal with vague requirements too. If the requirements are not clear or if there is uncertainty about the project's direction, don't hesitate to ask questions or seek clarification. It's better to spend time up front ensuring that everyone is on the same page than to dive into development only to discover later that the team was working on the wrong thing.

Establishing clear outcomes is equally important. Define key performance indicators (KPIs) or success metrics that will be used to measure the project's progress and impact. These metrics should be communicated to the team, so everyone understands what they are working toward. This clarity not only helps in aligning efforts but also provides a sense of purpose and direction, motivating the team to deliver their best work.

Finally, maintain regular communication with stakeholders and your team throughout the project. Regular check-ins, updates, and retrospectives can help ensure that the project stays on track and that any emerging ambiguities are addressed promptly. By fostering a culture of transparency and open communication, you can mitigate the risks associated with unclear scope and outcome, leading to more predictable and successful delivery outcomes.

CHAPTER 14

Measuring Delivery Effectiveness

I was working in a 100-member product organization, where it was common to run into executives around the office and have a casual chat. One day, I found myself in the break room, grabbing a coffee when an executive walked in. The atmosphere was relaxed, as it often was in a company of this size.

Executive: "Hey, how's it going? It's been a while since we caught up."

Me: "Pretty good, thanks! Things have been pretty busy on the team, but overall, we're making good progress."

Executive: "That's good to hear. I was just thinking about how the team has been performing. Are you finding that things are running smoothly?"

Me: "Yeah, actually. We've been getting a lot done lately. We had 95 pull requests go through and wrapped up 20 story points this week."

Executive: "Okay, so that's a lot of activity. But I'm curious; what does that mean in terms of real impact? How do those numbers translate into actual value for the business?."

I paused, realizing I needed to think about how to frame my response.

Me: "Well, the pull requests show how much code we've been reviewing and merging, and the story points reflect the amount of work we're completing. So, in a way, it indicates that we're productive and making progress."

Executive: "I see. But how do these metrics help us understand whether we're delivering real value to our customers or achieving our business objectives?."

I started to feel a bit uncertain.

Me: "That's a good question. I mean, we're definitely getting a lot done, but I'm not entirely sure how to connect these metrics directly to the impact on user satisfaction or business goals."

© Ananth Ramachandran 2024
A. Ramachandran, *The Complete Engineering Manager*, https://doi.org/10.1007/979-8-8688-0267-6_14

Executive: "Exactly. It's crucial to link what we're doing with the outcomes we care about. Are there other metrics or ways to measure that might give us a clearer picture of our team's value?."

I looked thoughtful, feeling the weight of the question.

Me: "I suppose we might need to look at other metrics that reflect more on the outcomes rather than just the activity. I'll have to think about what could best show our impact."

Executive: "Definitely. Let's revisit this soon and discuss how we can better align our metrics with what really matters to the business."

Me: "Absolutely. I'll work on figuring that out and get back to you with some ideas. Thanks for bringing this up!."

Executive: "No problem. Enjoy your coffee, and we'll catch up soon."

Does It Really Matter?

Does it really matter how many pull requests your team has merged or how many story points you've completed in a given week or sprint? In the grand scheme of things, not really. While these metrics can give you an idea of your team's productivity, they don't necessarily reflect the true value your team is bringing to the organization.

Number of PRs or story points completed is just one piece of the puzzle. What's far more important is understanding how these efforts translate into real, measurable impact on the business. Are you delivering features that enhance customer satisfaction? Are you reducing the time it takes for your product to reach the market? Are you improving the stability and reliability of your system? These are the kinds of outcomes that genuinely matter to the organization's success.

Focusing solely on activity-based metrics like PRs and story points can lead to a false sense of progress. You might be checking off tasks at a rapid pace, but if those tasks aren't aligned with the company's strategic objectives, you're missing the mark. Instead shift the focus from how much work is getting done to the value that work is delivering.

In the end, it's the business outcomes—such as increased revenue, improved customer retention, or faster time-to-market—that determine whether your team's efforts are truly effective. These are the metrics that resonate with executives and stakeholders because they directly correlate with the success and growth of the business.

So, while it's good to know how productive your team is, it's even more important to ask yourself whether your team is driving the outcomes that matter most to the business. If the answer isn't clear, it might be time to rethink what you're measuring and why.

The Limits of Velocity

Velocity and story points are often seen as target metrics in software development. They're useful tools for understanding how much work a team can handle within a sprint and for planning purposes. However, while these metrics are good for measuring predictability and capacity, they fall short when it comes to assessing the true impact of your team's deliverables.

In fact, velocity is more about ensuring your team is consistently delivering work at a sustainable pace, not about measuring the actual outcomes or value that work is providing to the business. You might be able to predict how much work can be completed in a sprint, but that doesn't necessarily mean the work being done is driving the results that matter.

Your team could be moving at a rapid velocity, cranking out story points at an impressive rate yet still fail to deliver real value at the speed your organization expects. This often happens when the focus is on completing tasks rather than ensuring those tasks are aligned with the right priorities.

As Forsgren, Humble, and Kim point out in *Accelerate*:

> *"First, Velocity is a relative and team-dependent measure, not an absolute one. Teams usually have significantly different contexts which render their velocities incommensurable. Second, when velocity is used as a productivity measure, teams inevitably work to game their velocity. They inflate their estimates and focus on completing as many stories as possible at the expense of collaboration with other teams (which might decrease their velocity and increase the other team's velocity, making them look bad). Not only does this destroy the utility of velocity for its intended purpose, it also inhibits collaboration between teams."*

This quote highlights a viewpoint not to be missed: when velocity is misused as a measure of productivity, it can actually undermine the collaborative spirit that's essential for delivering meaningful value. Teams may inflate estimates or prioritize quantity over quality just to keep their velocity numbers high, which ultimately skews the metric's usefulness and can lead to suboptimal outcomes.

Moreover, if your team is working on the wrong priorities, it doesn't matter how high your velocity is. Speed without direction is meaningless—it won't make any difference to your organization if the work isn't aligned with what the business truly needs.

In essence, while velocity is a helpful metric for planning and maintaining consistency, it's not the definitive measure of success. The real question is not only how fast your team is moving (Figure 14-1), but whether they're moving in the right direction and delivering work that creates genuine value for the business.

Figure 14-1. *Speed is important; direction too!*

Reduce WIP

One of the most effective ways to enhance your team's impact is by reducing the amount of work in progress (Figure 14-2). If your team is juggling too many different projects or tasks at once, it can significantly delay the delivery of meaningful outcomes. When attention is spread thin across multiple initiatives, the time and energy required to complete any single project increases, which in turn delays the overall impact your team can deliver.

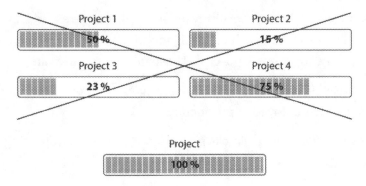

Figure 14-2. *Reduce WIP*

Instead of trying to make incremental progress on various projects simultaneously, it's often more productive to have your team focus on completing one project at a time. By concentrating resources and effort on finishing a single initiative, your team can deliver tangible value more quickly, before moving on to the next priority. This approach not only accelerates the time-to-impact but also ensures that the work being done is thorough and of high quality.

There are, of course, exceptions to this strategy. In some cases, it may not be efficient to involve too many engineers in the same project, especially if the work can't be easily divided or if too many hands on deck would lead to diminishing returns. In such scenarios, it might make sense to have a few parallel efforts, but even then, it's wise to keep the number of active projects manageable to avoid spreading the team too thin.

The key is balance. By reducing WIP and focusing your team's efforts, you can ensure that projects are completed more efficiently and with greater impact, ultimately driving better results for the organization.

Measure What Matters

When assessing your team's delivery effectiveness, it's essential to focus on metrics that truly reflect the impact of your work. While traditional metrics like velocity and work in progress offer insights into team productivity and predictability, they don't necessarily measure the actual value being delivered to the business.

To ensure your team is driving real value, you need to align your delivery metrics with the broader business or product outcomes—often referred to as North Star metrics. These metrics should guide your team's efforts, ensuring that delivery is always focused on improving what matters most to the business.

In the book *Accelerate*, the authors introduced the DevOps research and assessment (DORA) metrics (Figure 14-3), which are designed to measure the efficiency and reliability of your software delivery process. These four key metrics are:

- *Lead Time*: Measures how quickly your team can move from code committed to deployed to production

- *Deployment Frequency*: Tracks how often your team is deploying code to production

- *Change Failure Rate*: Indicates the percentage of deployments that result in failures requiring remediation

- *Mean Time to Recovery (MTTR)*: Captures how quickly your team can recover from a production failure

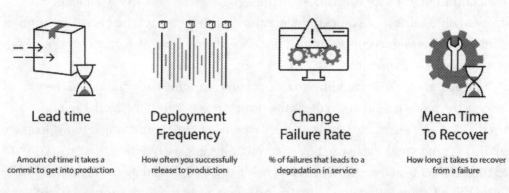

Lead time	Deployment Frequency	Change Failure Rate	Mean Time To Recover
Amount of time it takes a commit to get into production	How often you successfully release to production	% of failures that leads to a degradation in service	How long it takes to recover from a failure

Figure 14-3. *The DORA metrics*

Lead Time

Lead Time measures the duration between when a code commit is made and when that code is live and accessible to end-users in production. This metric offers a clear view of how efficiently a development team can turn ideas into operational features or fixes. It reflects the effectiveness and agility of your development and deployment processes.

Consider a scenario where your team has just completed coding a new feature. Lead Time begins at the moment the code is committed to the repository and ends when that feature is fully deployed to production and available to users. This period includes various stages such as code review, testing, and deployment.

Lead Time is valuable because it reveals how quickly your team can implement changes and deliver value. A short Lead Time typically indicates that your team has an efficient process with minimal delays, allowing for quicker delivery of new features, updates, or bug fixes. For example, if your team consistently deploys changes within a few hours of committing code, it demonstrates a high level of operational efficiency and responsiveness.

Conversely, a long Lead Time can highlight potential issues within the development pipeline. It may suggest inefficiencies such as slow code reviews, manual testing processes, or cumbersome release procedures. For instance, if a feature takes several weeks to move from code commit to deployment, it's a sign that there are stages in the process that could be optimized. It not only reflects the speed of deployment but also provides insight into how well your team manages and executes workflows. Extended Lead Times can lead to delays in delivering new functionalities or critical fixes, which may cause frustration among stakeholders and customers. By focusing on reducing Lead Time, your team can better respond to market demands, address issues promptly, and consistently deliver improvements.

In summary, Lead Time serves as a barometer for your development team's operational efficiency. By understanding and optimizing Lead Time, you can ensure that your team delivers new features and updates quickly and effectively, aligning with the fast-paced demands of the software industry.

Measuring Lead Time

Lead Time is the duration between when a developer commits code and when that code is fully deployed in production. It provides insight into how efficiently your team can move from development to delivery. Here's how you can measure Lead Time:

- *Define the Start Point*: Lead Time begins when a developer commits code to the version control system (e.g., Git). This marks the start of the journey from development to production.

- *Define the End Point*: Lead Time ends when the code is deployed and lives in the production environment, accessible to users. This could be tracked through deployment logs or CI/CD pipelines.

- *Use Development Tools*: Tools like Jira or Git can help automate the tracking of Lead Time. For example, you can log when a Jira ticket is moved to the "In Progress" column and when it's marked as "Done" or "Deployed." Similarly, Git logs can be used to track the time between commits and the corresponding deployment.

- *Calculate the Duration*: Subtract the start time (commit) from the end time (deployment) to get the Lead Time for each task. This can be done manually for individual tasks or automatically aggregated through project management and CI/CD tools.

- *Analyze Patterns*: Over time, you can analyze the average Lead Time to identify trends, bottlenecks, or areas for improvement. If certain stages consistently slow down the process (e.g., code review or testing), you can focus efforts on optimizing those areas.

Introducing Value Lead Time

Lead Time tells you how quickly your team can move a code commit into production, but does it really measure value delivery? Not entirely. Speed is important, but the real question is: How fast are you delivering value to your customers?

Value Lead Time captures the entire journey from when work begins to when customers actually start benefiting from the changes. While Lead Time focuses on the technical process—getting a single commit from development to production—Value Lead Time looks at the bigger picture: how quickly your team delivers features that make a difference to users.

For example, a feature might require several commits and iterations before it's fully functional for customers. Even if code is deployed quickly, the true value isn't realized until users can actually use and benefit from it.

The Difference That Matters

Lead Time measures the speed of your pipeline, highlighting bottlenecks in code review, testing, or deployment, whereas Value Lead Time measures how quickly those changes translate into real, usable features for customers. By focusing on Value Lead Time, you ensure that your team isn't just fast, but also effective in delivering meaningful outcomes to customers. It's about aligning speed with impact, making sure that what you deliver truly makes a difference.

Measuring Value Lead Time

Value Lead Time measures the duration from when your team starts working on a task to when the customer starts experiencing its benefits. Unlike simple Lead Time, which ends when code is deployed, Value Lead Time continues until the feature or change delivers real, usable value to the end-user. Here's how you can measure it:

- *Define Clear Milestones*: Start by breaking down your project into clear, customer-focused milestones. These milestones should represent tangible points where value is delivered, such as a feature going live and being used by customers.

- *Track Start and End Dates*: Record the date when work begins on a project or feature and when it reaches each milestone. The final milestone should be when customers begin using the feature or when its impact becomes visible.

- *Use Task Management Tools*: Tools like Jira can help track these milestones by logging the start and closure dates of tasks or epics. To measure Value Lead Time, you'll need to monitor when a task starts, when it's deployed, and when it actually delivers value.

- *Consider Multiple Deployments*: For complex features, value might not be delivered with a single deployment. In such cases, measure the time from the start of work to when the last deployment required to deliver value is completed and the feature is fully usable by customers.

- *Customer Feedback and Adoption Metrics*: To confirm that value has been delivered, track customer feedback, usage data, or other relevant metrics. This can be tied back to the final milestone in your Value Lead Time measurement.

Deployment Frequency

Deployment Frequency is the measure of how often your team releases code to production. It's a key indicator of how quickly and consistently your team can deliver new features, fixes, and updates to users.

Here's how you can measure Deployment Frequency:

- *Define a Deployment*: Start by clearly defining what counts as a deployment. Typically, this refers to every time code is pushed to production, but it can also include staging environments if that's part of your process.

- *Track Deployment Events*: Use your CI/CD pipeline or deployment tools to track each time code is pushed to production. Most deployment tools automatically log these events, making it easy to measure.

- *Measure the Frequency*: Calculate how often these deployments occur over a specific period—daily, weekly, or monthly. For example, if your team deploys code three times a day, your Deployment Frequency metric equals three deployments/day.

- *Analyze Trends*: Look at the data over time to identify trends. Are deployments becoming more frequent as the team becomes more efficient, or are they slowing down due to bottlenecks? This analysis can help pinpoint areas that need attention.

- *Set Targets*: Based on your team's goals and the needs of your product, set targets for Deployment Frequency. High-performing teams often deploy multiple times a day, but the right frequency depends on your specific context.

What Can Slow Down a Team's Deployment Frequency?

Deployment Frequency, the measure of how often your team pushes code to production, is an indicator of your team's ability to deliver updates swiftly and consistently. However, several factors can slow down this process.

One common issue is tackling large, complex changes—often referred to as "big-bang" changes—that take days or even weeks to develop. These massive updates can create bottlenecks in your deployment process, as they require extensive testing, reviews, and debugging before they can be released. The more time your team spends on these big changes, the less frequently they can deploy.

Another factor that can drag down deployment frequency is delayed code reviews. Imagine a scenario where a pull request sits in the queue for days, waiting for someone to review it. This not only stalls the current deployment but can also create a backlog, slowing down the entire pipeline.

Deployment pipelines themselves can be a source of delays. If your team frequently encounters blockers in the pipeline or, worse, relies on manual processes due to a lack of automation, deployment becomes slow and cumbersome. Manual interventions are not only time-consuming but also increase the risk of human error, further hampering deployment speed.

Should You Really Be Concerned About Deployment Frequency?

While maintaining a healthy deployment frequency is important—without becoming overly fixated on it. The reality is that deployment frequency should be viewed in context. If your team isn't working on projects that require frequent updates, a lower deployment rate is completely acceptable. Not every phase of development demands daily or even weekly deployments, and that's okay.

Instead of treating deployment frequency as a rigid goal, use it as a diagnostic tool. It's an indicator that can help you spot potential inefficiencies or blockers in your development process. If your team's deployment frequency dips unexpectedly, it's worth investigating—but it's more about understanding why than meeting a specific target.

Sometimes, the best way to get to the bottom of deployment issues is to ask your team directly. Engineers often have valuable insights into the challenges they face when deploying code. Are there specific stages of the process that slow them down? Do they encounter frequent issues with the tools or the pipeline? Engaging your team in this discussion can reveal areas where you might need to make improvements.

Does Your Team Have "Friday Blues"?

A common scenario in many development teams is the reluctance to deploy on Fridays. The fear of introducing a bug or issue just before the weekend, which could lead to working overtime, often leads teams to avoid Friday deployments altogether. While this is understandable, it can contribute to a mindset that hinders your team's confidence and willingness to deploy regularly.

As an engineering manager, it's important to address this fear and foster an environment where your team feels secure in deploying code any day of the week, including Fridays. Start by understanding the root of their hesitation. Is it due to a lack of automated testing, a cumbersome release process, or simply a lack of confidence in the stability of the code? Once you identify the cause, you can work with your team to improve the process.

Enhancing automation, streamlining the release process, and building a culture of trust can help alleviate the fear of Friday deployments. When your team feels confident that they can push code safely and efficiently, regardless of the day, your deployment frequency and overall productivity will benefit.

Change Failure Rate

The Change Failure Rate metric captures the percentage of changes deployed to production that result in failures or incidents. This could include anything from bugs and performance issues to full-blown outages. Change Failure Rate indicates the stability and quality of your delivery process.

Imagine your team has just released a new feature, and everything seems to be running smoothly until users start reporting unexpected behavior or outages. As incidents pile up, you might find yourself questioning the effectiveness of your release process. This is where Change Failure Rate comes into play.

A high Change Failure Rate value signals that a significant portion of your changes are causing problems, which can lead to a cascade of issues. Frequent failures can erode user trust, disrupt business operations, and even lead to costly emergency fixes. Understanding and managing this rate helps you identify how well your release process is functioning and whether the changes you're deploying are reliable.

Several factors contribute to a high Change Failure Rate value:

- *Inadequate Testing*: If the testing phase doesn't cover all potential scenarios or is not thorough enough, issues that were not anticipated may make their way into production. This lack of coverage can result in more frequent failures after deployment.

- *Complex Code Changes*: Large or complex changes are more likely to introduce problems. When changes are not broken down into manageable pieces, the risk of unforeseen issues increases.

- *Lack of Code Quality Practices*: Poor coding practices or a lack of adherence to coding standards can lead to unstable releases. Ensuring that your code is well-written and reviewed can help mitigate these issues.

- *Inconsistent Deployment Processes*: If your deployment process lacks consistency or is prone to manual errors, it can increase the likelihood of failures. Automation and standardized procedures can help reduce this risk.

Monitoring your Change Failure Rate helps you to:

- *Identify Weaknesses in Your Process*: A high Change Failure Rate can point to specific areas in your deployment process that need improvement. Whether it's testing practices, code quality, or deployment procedures, understanding where things go wrong can guide you in making necessary adjustments.

- *Improve Overall Stability*: By addressing the factors that contribute to a high Change Failure Rate, you can enhance the stability and reliability of your releases. This leads to fewer disruptions and a more predictable delivery process.

- *Boost Team Confidence*: Reducing the rate of failed changes can improve your team's confidence in deploying code. Knowing that changes are less likely to cause issues can encourage more frequent and less hesitant deployments.

Ultimately, while the Change Failure Rate doesn't measure the speed of your deliveries, it provides valuable insight into the stability and reliability of what you're delivering. By focusing on reducing the Change Failure Rate, you ensure that your releases are robust and less prone to causing problems, which supports a more stable and trustworthy delivery process.

Mean Time to Recover

Mean Time to Recover (MTTR) measures the average time it takes to restore service after a production incident. It is a vital metric for evaluating how quickly your team can respond to and recover from disruptions, which is crucial for maintaining overall system stability and reliability.

In terms of delivery, MTTR is relevant for several reasons:

- *System Stability and Confidence*: A lower MTTR reflects a team's ability to recover swiftly from issues, which enhances system stability and reliability. This stability allows for more frequent and confident deployments, knowing that if something goes wrong, the team can address it promptly. Therefore, MTTR directly impacts the confidence with which your team approaches deployment schedules.

- *Impact on Delivery Timelines*: Extended recovery times can delay subsequent deliveries. If a critical issue arises and takes too long to resolve, it can push back the timelines for new features or fixes. A team with a high MTTR may struggle to maintain consistent delivery schedules, affecting the overall rhythm of releases.

- *Feedback Loop for Continuous Improvement*: Monitoring MTTR provides insights into the efficiency of your incident response and recovery processes. High MTTR can indicate that certain aspects of your delivery pipeline need improvement, such as better monitoring tools, clearer incident response protocols, or more robust testing practices. Addressing these issues can enhance the speed and reliability of future deliveries.

Several factors can influence MTTR:

- *Complex Systems*: Complex systems with numerous dependencies and interconnected components can make diagnosing and resolving issues more challenging. The more layers involved, the harder it becomes to pinpoint and fix problems quickly, which can extend recovery times and affect delivery schedules.

- *Ineffective Monitoring and Alerting*: Without robust monitoring and timely alerts, issues might go unnoticed until they escalate. Delays in recognizing and addressing problems can extend recovery times, impacting how soon your team can resume normal operations and proceed with planned deliveries.

- *Unclear Incident Response Processes*: Recovery can be hindered if there's no clear incident response plan. Lack of defined roles and communication channels can lead to a disorganized and slow recovery process, which in turn can disrupt delivery timelines and project schedules.

- *Inadequate Testing*: Insufficient testing can result in problems making their way into production, which then takes longer to resolve. Issues that weren't anticipated or tested for can delay recovery and push back delivery schedules if they require extensive fixes.

- *Technical Debt*: Accumulated technical debt—outdated or poorly maintained code—can complicate recovery efforts. A cluttered codebase can make diagnosing and fixing issues more difficult, leading to longer recovery times and potentially impacting the delivery of new features or updates.

To improve MTTR and, consequently, delivery effectiveness, focus on enhancing your monitoring and alerting systems. Invest in real-time monitoring tools that provide actionable insights and timely alerts to quickly detect and resolve issues. Streamline your incident response processes with a clear and regularly updated plan, defining roles and communication channels to ensure efficient recovery.

Simplify your system architecture and maintain thorough documentation to facilitate quicker understanding and resolution of issues. Automate testing and deployment processes with CI/CD pipelines to catch problems before they reach production and enable swift rollbacks if necessary. Regularly address technical debt to keep your codebase manageable and reduce recovery times.

While MTTR assesses recovery efficiency and system stability, it does not measure the direct value delivered to customers. It is essential for maintaining a reliable delivery process but doesn't reflect the quality or impact of the features being released.

Balancing Speed and Stability in Your Delivery

Lead time and deployment frequency are key indicators of your team's speed in delivering features, updates, and fixes to production. These metrics show how quickly and efficiently your team can move from code creation to deployment, reflecting your team's ability to deliver value to users at a rapid pace.

On the other hand, the Mean Time to Recover and Change Failure Rate metrics are indicators of your team's stability in delivery and the overall reliability of your systems. These metrics focus on how resilient your team is when issues arise, and how often changes lead to problems in production. Together, MTTR and Change Failure Rate give you insight into the quality of your delivery processes and your team's ability to maintain a stable, reliable production environment.

By balancing speed (lead time and deployment frequency) with stability (MTTR and change failure rate), your team can ensure that it not only delivers quickly but also maintains a high standard of quality and reliability in production. This balance is crucial for achieving sustainable, long-term success in software delivery.

North Star Metric

While DORA metrics help you to understand the speed and stability of your delivery process, they don't directly measure the business outcomes or customer value that your work delivers. Instead, they help ensure that your team is operating efficiently and reliably, which is foundational to achieving those broader business goals.

To truly measure what matters, you should combine these delivery metrics with North Star metrics that capture the real impact of your work on the business—such as customer satisfaction, revenue growth, and feature adoption rates. By doing so, you can ensure that your team's efforts are not only efficient but also aligned with and contributing to the organization's most important objectives.

North Star metrics are essential for connecting the dots between your team's development efforts and the broader goals of your business. They serve as a guiding light, ensuring that every feature and improvement directly contributes to what matters most for your organization.

Example: Enhancing Customer Retention with a North Star Metric

Consider a company that provides a subscription-based video streaming service. Their North Star metric is Customer Retention Rate (CRR), which tracks the percentage of users who continue their subscription over a year. Initially, the company's CRR stands at 75%, indicating that three-quarters of customers stay subscribed.

To address this, the team focuses on developing a personalized recommendation engine. This new feature is designed to suggest content tailored to individual users' tastes based on their viewing history and preferences. The goal is to increase user engagement by making the platform more relevant and enjoyable for each subscriber.

After months of dedicated work, the recommendation engine is deployed. The feature's impact is soon visible. Users begin to discover new content they genuinely enjoy, leading to a noticeable improvement in their overall satisfaction with the service.

Within the next quarter, the CRR rises from 75% to 82%. This increase reflects a successful outcome of the recommendation engine. By enhancing the user experience and making content discovery easier, the feature has significantly contributed to retaining more customers.

Relevance to Delivery

This example demonstrates how North Star metrics like CRR guide and measure the effectiveness of development efforts:

- *Alignment with Business Objectives:* The development of the recommendation engine was strategically aligned with the goal of improving CRR. Every aspect of the project was focused on increasing customer retention, which is crucial for the service's long-term success.

- *Customer-Centric Development:* The recommendation engine was designed with the user in mind, aiming to enrich their experience and engagement. This focus on delivering value to users directly contributed to the higher retention rate.

- *Guiding Prioritization*: The success of this feature highlighted the importance of customer-centric innovations. It provided clear evidence that features enhancing user experience should be prioritized in future development cycles.

- *Measuring Success*: The improvement in CRR from 75% to 82% offers a concrete measure of success. It shows that the recommendation engine not only functioned as intended but also made a meaningful difference in customer retention.

By focusing on North Star metrics such as CRR, teams ensure that their efforts are not just about completing tasks but are aimed at achieving significant business outcomes. This approach helps align development work with strategic goals, ensuring that every feature delivered adds real value and contributes to the organization's success.

Now, think about your own team's North Star metric. What single metric truly reflects the success and direction of your business? Is it customer satisfaction, revenue growth, user engagement, or something else?

What steps are you taking to ensure that every project and feature contributes to this metric? Are your development efforts effectively aligned with your North Star goal?

Reflect on how you can focus your team's work towards this metric and drive meaningful results. The success of your North Star metric can transform not just your delivery process but also the overall impact your team has on your organization.

CHAPTER 15

Managing Stakeholders, Progress, and Blockers

Zoom out. 2x more. Perfect, lock it in. That's the possible wide angle shot of your organization (Figure 15-1).

Figure 15-1. *Zooming out for your organizational view*

You can see business teams, product, data, external partners, and many other relevant stakeholders working together to deliver impactful projects. After all, your team can deliver success to your organization by rarely working alone. You, along with your

© Ananth Ramachandran 2024

A. Ramachandran, *The Complete Engineering Manager*, https://doi.org/10.1007/979-8-8688-0267-6_15

product counterpart, play a key role in interfacing with stakeholders and guiding them from the initial scoping of the project all the way through to delivery. They see you as a technical consultant and a bridge between engineering and anything that's not.

With this broad perspective, it's clear that effective communication with both stakeholders and leadership is essential. Your role isn't just about managing delivery—it's about ensuring that progress, challenges, and strategic shifts are communicated clearly and consistently. By providing regular updates and addressing blockers proactively, you keep everyone aligned and informed, enabling smoother project execution and fostering a collaborative environment. This transparency and engagement are key to navigating the complexities of your projects and driving success across the organization.

Managing Stakeholders

Managing stakeholders is hard. It's even harder if you aren't sure who they are, what they do, what their priorities are and what they expect from your team.

Each of them will be chasing their own department goals, whether it is achieving a strategic business partnership, closing a sales deal with a potential big client, or running a marketing campaign with a new communication strategy to improve your product's monthly active users (MAU). In one way or the other, they look to join hands with your team to achieve their goals.

In most of the cross-functional teams, product managers interface with stakeholders to spearhead the discovery of the work and definition of value to be delivered. The degree of engineering manager's involvement in defining the problem space varies from organization to organization. As an experienced engineering manager having considerable domain experience, you'll be able to lead, collaborate, and negotiate with your stakeholders at ease.

What if you're new to the team and have barely said hello to your stakeholders? Where would you start? How do you see your collaboration with them? It's a partnership more than anything and you should look to build it from scratch.

Building Partnerships

When you start seeing collaboration with stakeholders—such as business teams, operations, customer support, and marketing—as a true partnership, it transforms how your team operates. Stakeholders aren't just setting expectations; they become essential partners in developing and delivering your product or service. This shift turns routine interactions into strategic collaborations where everyone is invested in mutual success.

In this partnership, your team works closely with stakeholders to shape solutions, challenge assumptions, and innovate beyond traditional boundaries. Business teams bring market insights, operations ensure scalability, customer support offers user feedback, and marketing drives the go-to-market strategy. Together, you create a product that's not only technically sound but also aligned with business goals, operational needs, and customer expectations.

This approach naturally breaks down silos, ensuring your team is integrated into the broader business strategy. Regular communication and alignment mean everyone moves in the same direction, whether coordinating a product launch, ensuring smooth deployment, or refining user experiences.

Ultimately, treating stakeholders as partners strengthens relationships, fosters a problem-solving mindset, and enhances your ability to deliver products that are both technically robust and strategically aligned. This partnership-driven approach turns everyday interactions into opportunities for innovation and success, positioning your team as a key driver of business value.

- *Trust*: Build trust by demonstrating credibility and reliability. Be seen as a dependable partner who provides accurate information, acts with integrity, and aligns with organizational goals.

- *Commitment*: Show dedication by actively engaging with stakeholders and taking ownership of shared objectives. Your commitment should be evident through proactive involvement and support for the partnership.

- *Alignment*: Ensure that all parties are aligned on goals, priorities, and expectations. Regularly review and adjust these to maintain focus and prevent miscommunication.

- *Delivery*: Consistently meet commitments and deliver high-quality results. Meeting or exceeding expectations reinforces the effectiveness of the partnership and supports continued collaboration.

Trust

Building and maintaining trust is fundamental to successful stakeholder relationships and project management. When there are repeated instances of overpromising and under delivering, it naturally leads to skepticism about future engagements. Stakeholders start to question the reliability of estimates and the accuracy of committed delivery timelines. They might wonder, "Can I trust this estimate?" and Can I confidently promise our clients the stated delivery dates?" and "Will the engineering team be able to deliver all requested features as expected?" These doubts can linger and affect future collaborations, making it important to address and manage trust proactively.

Trusting Each Other's Expertise and Earning Credibility: A core component of trust is mutual respect for each other's expertise. As an engineering manager, you need to demonstrate a deep understanding of the technical aspects and be capable of making realistic and achievable commitments. Stakeholders, in turn, must trust that your technical insights are accurate and that your estimates are grounded in practical experience. You need to have mutual trust in your expertise for effective collaboration and decision-making. Earning credibility involves consistently delivering high-quality work, providing honest assessments, and maintaining a track record of reliability. By doing so, you reinforce your reputation as a trusted partner and ensure that stakeholders have confidence in your capabilities.

Reliability: Reliability is a key pillar of trust. Consistently meeting deadlines and delivering on commitments helps build a strong reputation for dependability. When your team repeatedly follows through on promises and achieves the milestones set, it reassures stakeholders that they can count on you. This consistent performance helps to cement your role as a reliable partner, reducing concerns and fostering a positive working relationship. Conversely, repeated failures to meet commitments can lead to doubts and a lack of confidence in future engagements. Ensuring reliability through disciplined project management and adherence to deadlines is essential for maintaining trust.

Stepping into Stakeholder's Shoes (Shadowing): Understanding the perspectives and challenges of your stakeholders is a powerful way to build trust. By stepping into their shoes – whether through shadowing their roles, engaging in their workflows, or having in-depth discussions about their priorities—you gain valuable insights into their needs and concerns. This empathy allows you to align your technical work more closely with their business objectives and communication requirements. When stakeholders see that you are genuinely interested in understanding their viewpoint and addressing their challenges, it strengthens the trust between you and fosters a more collaborative and effective working relationship.

Commitment

Imagine a typical conversation between you, as the engineering manager, and a stakeholder. They might ask, "When can we expect the new feature to be ready?" There's an urge to respond immediately with a specific deadline to satisfy their request. However, effective commitment management involves a more thoughtful approach.

Consult with Your Team: Before making any promises, take the time to consult with your engineering team. This collaborative discussion helps you understand the technical complexities and constraints, ensuring that any commitment you make is based on a realistic assessment of what can be achieved. Avoid making impulsive commitments, as hasty promises can lead to unrealistic deadlines and potential disappointments.

Avoid Specific Time-Based Commitments: Rather than providing exact timelines, consider using relative terms like "small," "medium," or "large" to describe the effort involved. This approach offers flexibility and helps manage expectations by avoiding rigid deadlines that may not account for unforeseen challenges.

Under-Promise and Over-Deliver: Embrace the principle of under-promising and over-delivering. Set realistic and conservative expectations, and aim to exceed them whenever possible. By delivering more than initially promised, you build a reputation for reliability and create positive surprises, which strengthen relationships with stakeholders and effectively manage risks.

Confirm Commitment After Discovery: Once you have completed a thorough discovery phase, revisit and confirm your commitment based on the refined understanding of the project scope and potential challenges. Discovery provides significant insights that allow you to make informed promises. If a timeline or specific commitment is required, ensure it is realistic and accounts for any potential obstacles, incorporating buffers for unexpected issues.

Manage Expectations: Regularly revisit and adjust commitments as necessary based on ongoing developments and feedback. Clear communication about any changes or adjustments to commitments helps maintain transparency and trust with stakeholders. By managing expectations effectively and delivering on promises, you ensure a successful collaboration and build a strong, dependable partnership.

Alignment

Effectively align with your stakeholders throughout the course of a project to ensure success and avoid misunderstandings. This process involves regularly updating stakeholders on progress, discussing challenges, and making necessary adjustments based on their feedback.

Regular Alignment: Maintaining consistent communication with stakeholders is key. Schedule regular check-ins or status updates to keep them informed about the project's progress. These updates should cover achievements, upcoming milestones, and any issues that may arise. This ongoing dialogue helps ensure that all parties are on the same page and can address concerns promptly, preventing surprises and fostering a collaborative environment.

Pivot or Persevere: As the project evolves, be prepared to pivot or persevere based on the feedback and insights gathered. If stakeholders raise concerns or if new information comes to light, you may need to adjust your approach. This flexibility allows you to refine the project direction and better meet stakeholder expectations. Conversely, if the project is on track and stakeholders are satisfied, you can continue with the current plan while addressing minor issues as they arise.

Show Demos: To ensure alignment and validate progress, regularly present demos or mini minimum viable products (MVPs) to stakeholders. These demonstrations provide tangible evidence of what has been developed so far and allow stakeholders to offer feedback before the final product is completed. This iterative approach helps confirm that the project is on the right track and aligns with their expectations, making it easier to make adjustments early rather than later.

Launch Plan and Communication Strategy: Develop a detailed launch plan and communication strategy to prepare for the final delivery of the product or service. This plan should outline key activities, timelines, and responsibilities for the launch. Ensure that stakeholders are aware of and involved in this plan, as their input can be crucial for a successful launch. Effective communication during this phase includes informing stakeholders about the launch timeline, key milestones, and any necessary actions they need to take.

Over-Communicate: Avoid assuming that stakeholders are fully informed about all aspects of the project. Over-communicate to ensure clarity and alignment. This means providing detailed updates, clarifying any ambiguities, and actively seeking confirmation that stakeholders understand and agree with the current status and direction. Don't rely on assumptions;

instead, proactively share information and confirm that it has
been received and understood. This approach helps prevent
misalignment and ensures that all parties are truly in sync.

By focusing on these elements of alignment, you create a more collaborative and
transparent environment that supports successful project outcomes and strengthens
stakeholder relationships. Regular communication, flexibility, tangible demonstrations,
a clear launch plan, and thorough information sharing are all essential components of
effective stakeholder alignment.

Delivery

Ultimately, Successful stakeholder relationships depend on consistent delivery. Meeting
one deadline isn't enough; delivering high-quality results repeatedly over time builds
trust and fosters ongoing collaboration.

Consistent Delivery: Commit to delivering results not just once,
but consistently throughout the project. This means meeting
deadlines, maintaining quality, and fulfilling promises regularly.
Consistent delivery reinforces your reliability and ensures
that stakeholders can depend on you to meet their needs and
expectations repeatedly.

Get Things Done: Focus on results and avoid unnecessary
complexity. Strive for efficiency and effectiveness in your work
and how you collaborate with them. This approach ensures that
you deliver tangible outcomes without getting bogged down by
extraneous details or processes, thereby maximizing value and
satisfaction for stakeholders.

Post-Delivery Retrospective: After completing a delivery,
conduct a retrospective to evaluate what went well and identify
areas for improvement. This reflection allows you to learn from
each project, make necessary adjustments, and continuously
enhance your processes. By focusing on continuous improvement,
you ensure that each subsequent delivery is more effective and
better aligned with stakeholder needs.

Transparent Progress and Blockers: Maintain transparency about your delivery progress and any blockers that may arise. Regularly update stakeholders on the status of deliverables, and openly communicate any issues or delays. This transparency helps manage expectations, fosters trust, and allows stakeholders to understand the challenges you're facing and work collaboratively to resolve them.

By focusing on these aspects of delivery, you build a strong foundation for a successful and ongoing relationship with your stakeholders. Consistent, effective delivery, combined with transparency and a commitment to continuous improvement, ensures that you not only meet but exceed stakeholder expectations over time.

Reporting Progress to Management

As an engineering manager, you have to understand how and when your stakeholders and senior leadership expect updates, for maintaining effective communication and ensuring project success. You need to be clear about the preferred format and frequency of updates—whether they should be shared in weekly meetings, bi-weekly reports, or through real-time dashboards. It's equally important to know which specific metrics and KPIs matter most to your stakeholders and leadership. Are they focused on velocity, quality metrics, adherence to timelines, or the overall impact on business objectives?

Your role involves not just ensuring successful delivery, but also making sure that progress is transparently communicated to both your management and stakeholders. This means tailoring your updates to meet their expectations, providing the right level of detail, and highlighting key metrics that resonate with their concerns. By proactively addressing these aspects, you set the stage for more effective delivery progress reports, which are essential tools for keeping everyone aligned and informed.

These reports serve as your platform to regularly update leadership and stakeholders on the team's progress, achievements, and any challenges encountered. They are not merely a formality, but a strategic touchpoint that helps manage expectations, foster collaboration, and ensure the project remains on track, with all parties fully engaged and informed.

Delivery progress reports are crucial for keeping senior leadership informed about the team's progress, achievements, learnings, and any blockers. These sessions provide updates on various aspects of the team's work, which may include progress against quarterly OKRs, plans for the upcoming month, adjustments to the team's strategy, or any challenges and insights gained during the project. The content shared during these reviews should be comprehensive and reflective of what the team believes is important for leadership to know.

The following are key elements that can be part of delivery progress reports:

- *Impact on North Star Metrics*: Analysis of how the current work influences key North Star metrics, providing insight into how progress aligns with broader business goals and objectives.

- *Progress and Achievements*: Status updates on quarterly OKRs, highlighting key accomplishments such as completed features, successful releases, or breakthroughs.

- *Upcoming Plans and Strategy Updates*: A preview of the team's plans for the next month or quarter, including any strategic adjustments and the reasoning behind them.

- *Challenges, Blockers, and Risk Management*: Reporting on major challenges the team is facing, such as technical blockers or external dependencies, along with any emerging risks and mitigation strategies.

- *Learnings and Stakeholder Feedback*: Insights gained from recent work, including retrospectives, user feedback, and how it might influence the team's direction or priorities.

- *Release Timeline Adjustments*: Updates on any changes to release timelines, with explanations for these adjustments.

The primary purpose of these reviews is to ensure transparency and keep the leadership team in the loop. By providing these updates, leadership can better inform other stakeholders, offer valuable input, ask pertinent questions, and gain regular insights into the team's performance and direction. Importantly, these reviews are not meant to impose unrealistic deadlines or pressures on the team. Instead, they serve as a platform to communicate any changes in release timelines and explain the reasons behind those adjustments. Building software is inherently complex, and expectations must be managed accordingly, with regular updates based on the team's learnings and challenges.

Typically, the product manager leads these reviews from a discovery and impact perspective, ensuring that the strategic and value-driven aspects of the work are highlighted. You, on the other hand, focus on the delivery standpoint, providing insights into how well the team is executing the plan, the progress made, and any technical obstacles encountered. Along with your PM, you ensure that the leadership team receives a well-rounded view of the project, fostering a supportive environment that values both transparency and adaptability.

A Sample Delivery Progress Report to Management / Senior Leadership

Progress Report: [Initiative Name]

Date: [Insert Date]

Prepared by: [Your Name], Engineering Manager

Overview: This report provides an update on the [Initiative Name] since our last communication. It outlines recent achievements, upcoming plans, challenges faced, and their impact on our key metrics and OKRs. The aim is to keep all stakeholders and senior leadership informed and aligned with the initiative's current status and future direction.

Progress and Achievements:

- *Current Status: Significant milestones have been reached, including [specific milestones or features]. Key accomplishments include [highlight key achievements, such as completed features or successful releases].*

- *Impact on Key Metrics: Recent progress has had a positive effect on our key metrics, such as [mention specific metrics, e.g., user engagement or conversion rates]. For example, [specific achievement] has resulted in a [percentage or quantitative impact] increase in [metric].*

- *Influence on OKRs: This initiative supports OKR [insert specific OKR number or title], which focuses on [brief description of the OKR]. Our achievements align with the objective of [mention how the achievements contribute to the specific OKR].*

Upcoming Plans and Strategy Updates:

- *Next Steps: The team will focus on [outline key activities or features planned for the next month or quarter]. This includes [describe any strategic changes or new priorities].*

- *Strategic Adjustments: Based on recent feedback and performance data, we will implement [any planned changes to strategy or approach]. These adjustments are designed to further enhance our key metrics and support OKR [insert specific OKR number or title] by [describe how the strategy will impact specific metrics and OKRs].*

Challenges, Blockers, and Risk Management:

- *Current Issues: The team is addressing [describe major technical challenges or blockers], which are affecting our development timeline. We are managing these issues with [mention any mitigation strategies].*

- *Emerging Risks: Potential risks related to [mention any emerging risks] have been identified. Strategies are being developed to mitigate their impact, ensuring progress on our key metrics and alignment with OKR [insert specific OKR number or title].*

Learnings and Stakeholder Feedback:

- *Key Insights: Recent retrospectives have yielded [summarize significant learnings or insights]. These insights are informing adjustments to our priorities and approach, expected to enhance performance against key metrics and support OKR [insert specific OKR number or title].*

- *User Feedback: Feedback from users has led to [describe any changes or updates based on feedback], improving alignment with user needs and positively influencing metrics such as [mention specific metrics] and OKR [insert specific OKR number or title].*

Release Timeline Adjustments:

- *Timeline Updates: Adjustments to the release timeline have been made due to [explain reasons for any changes]. The new timeline is [insert new timeline], with detailed explanations provided. These changes are being managed to minimize their impact on our key metrics and ensure alignment with OKR [insert specific OKR number or title].*

Summary: This report captures the ongoing efforts of our team to drive the successful delivery of [Initiative Name]. By detailing progress, challenges, and adjustments, and reflecting on their impact on key metrics and OKRs, we aim to offer a comprehensive view of our status and direction. Please contact me with any questions or requests for further details.

Next Review Meeting: [Insert Date/Time]
Contact Information: [Your Contact Information]

Managing Blockers

Your team is performing well and on track to deliver a project. A week before the final delivery, an unexpected blocker brings progress to a grinding halt. It can come in various forms—whether it's a last-minute failure of an external service, an unforeseen technical debt surfacing at the worst possible time, or a key team member suddenly becoming unavailable.

As an engineering manager, your role becomes key in these moments. The first step is to assess the situation—understanding the blocker, its implications on the delivery timeline, and its potential impact on the broader organization. Gather your team, encourage open communication, and foster an environment where everyone can contribute in overcoming the challenge. While the team works on identifying potential solutions, you maintain clear and transparent communication with stakeholders. Inform them of the situation, the potential risks involved, and the steps being taken to address the blocker. This not only manages expectations but also reinforces trust in your team's ability to navigate unforeseen issues.

Simultaneously, you may need to reprioritize tasks or shift resources to ensure the team remains focused on resolving the blocker. This might involve negotiating with other teams or external partners to get the necessary support. The goal is to clear the path as quickly as possible, allowing the project to get back on track.

Forms of Blockers

Not all blockers are the same, and recognizing their distinct nature is key to addressing them effectively. By understanding the different types of blockers, you and your team can tailor the approach to resolving each one appropriately.

- *Technical Blockers*: Bugs, dependency issues, and infrastructure challenges can create significant obstacles. Technical debt and a lack of experience with specific technologies also contribute to delays and blockers during development and delivery.

- *Process Blockers*: Poorly defined requirements, scope creep, and having too many tasks in progress can disrupt the team's momentum. Delays in code reviews, waiting for approvals, or lengthy decision-making processes can also turn into blockers.

- *Communication Blockers*: Waiting for inputs from product managers or fellow engineers, along with knowledge silos and communication gaps, can slow down the team's progress and create misunderstandings.

Technical Blockers

Technical blockers can test a team's resilience, especially with high-stakes deadlines. I remember a particularly intense situation where we were under immense pressure to deliver a much-awaited feature set just before the Black Friday sales. The feature, providing a new payment option based on user feedback, was essential for driving revenue during the holiday shopping rush. With marketing campaigns and customer engagement strategies aligned around this launch, the timing couldn't have been more precise.

Just days before the launch, a technical blocker emerged that brought our progress to a standstill. We were finalizing the integration of a new payment gateway, and suddenly, a critical issue arose that caused the feature to malfunction. I quickly convened an emergency meeting with my engineering team to tackle the problem.

"Alright, team, what's the status of the technical blocker?" I asked, doing my best to stay composed despite the mounting pressure.

Sarah, one of our senior developers, responded, "It's related to the payment gateway integration. We didn't catch it during our initial tests."

"Understood," I said. "How long until we can resolve it?"

"It's complex," she acknowledged. "We'll need to delve into the integration code, which could take a few days to identify, fix, test, and re-release.

As if that weren't enough, we faced additional challenges with dependencies. We were relying on an external API for a key component of the feature, and the API provider announced unexpected maintenance. The message read: "Scheduled downtime for maintenance." I quickly updated the team.

"Looks like we're dealing with external constraints," I noted. "We need a workaround or at least a way to mitigate the impact."

John, our DevOps engineer, suggested, "We could mock the API responses to continue our testing."

"Good call", I agreed. "Let's implement that and proceed with testing the rest of the feature."

Infrastructure limitations also added to our woes. Our outdated CI/CD pipeline was struggling to handle the volume of changes, leading to slow deployments. I turned to Tom, our lead engineer, about the sluggish build process.

"Tom, how's the build pipeline holding up?" I asked.

"Not well," he replied, clearly stressed. "The old pipeline is slowing us down significantly."

"Alright, let's prioritize an upgrade to the pipeline," I decided, recognizing that this was essential for meeting our deadline.

Finally, the technical debt from previous quick fixes made the situation more complicated. The shortcuts we had taken had accumulated into a tangled mess of code that was difficult to navigate. I discussed this with Sarah.

"Sarah, I know we're under pressure, but we need to address some of this technical debt. It's becoming a major obstacle."

"I agree," she said. "We'll need to plan some time post-launch to clean this up."

Navigating through these blockers was intense, especially given the importance of the launch for our business. Each issue—technical blockers, dependency problems, infrastructure limitations, and technical debt—intertwined to create a complex web of obstacles. This experience emphasized thorough planning and agile problem-solving. It demonstrated the need to address each blocker effectively to ensure a successful launch and achieve business objectives.

Process Blockers

Process blockers can seriously impact a project's progress. Poorly defined requirements are a common blocker that you need to tackle head-on. When project requirements are vague or incomplete, it leads to confusion and misalignment within the team. This misalignment can cause unnecessary delays as team members spend additional time clarifying and reworking aspects that should have been clearly outlined from the start. Your role involves ensuring that requirements are well-defined and communicated by working with your product manager, setting the stage for a smoother development process.

Scope creep is another issue that you must manage carefully. This occurs when additional features or changes are introduced beyond the original project scope. While these changes might seem beneficial, they can stretch your team's resources and extend timelines. To prevent scope creep, it's essential to establish a clear project scope from the beginning and manage any additional requests through a structured change-management process. Your leadership in enforcing these boundaries helps keep the project on track and within its intended goals.

Having **too many tasks in progress** simultaneously can also hinder your team's momentum. When team members are overloaded with multiple tasks, it often leads to inefficiencies and delays. Overburdening your team can cause bottlenecks, as individuals may have to wait for feedback, approvals, or the completion of other tasks before they can proceed. As an engineering manager, prioritizing tasks effectively and managing workload distribution are key to maintaining project momentum. By focusing on completing high-priority tasks and reducing multitasking, you can help your team stay productive and efficient.

Additionally, delays in code reviews, waiting for approvals, and **lengthy decision-making processes** can also disrupt progress. When code reviews are stalled or approvals are delayed, it prevents your team from advancing as planned. Streamlining these processes and setting clear timelines for reviews and approvals can help mitigate these delays. Your proactive management in expediting these processes ensures that your team can move forward without unnecessary interruptions.

Communication Blockers

Communication blockers are real. It can significantly impede your team's progress and efficiency.

> **Waiting for Inputs from Product Managers or Fellow Engineers**:
> A common communication blocker is waiting for inputs from product managers or fellow engineers. When crucial information or decisions are delayed, it can halt development and lead to missed deadlines. For instance, if your team is working on a feature that requires approval from a product manager, any delay in receiving feedback or finalization can cause work to stagnate. Similarly, waiting for technical input from other engineers can prevent progress on interdependent tasks. As an engineering

manager, ensuring timely and effective communication between team members and stakeholders is essential. This involves setting clear deadlines for feedback, encouraging prompt responses, and fostering an environment where team members can easily seek out and provide necessary information.

Knowledge Silos: Knowledge silos occur when a context is confined to a few individuals within the team. This can result in redundant work, miscommunication, and delays as others struggle to access the information they need. For example, if only one engineer understands a specific piece of legacy code and that engineer is unavailable, the rest of the team may face significant setbacks. To combat knowledge silos, it's vital to promote a culture of knowledge-sharing. Encourage your team to document their work, share insights openly, and collaborate regularly. Implementing tools and practices that facilitate information sharing, such as shared documentation and regular team briefings, can help prevent valuable knowledge from being isolated.

Communication Gaps: Communication gaps arise when there is a lack of clarity or coherence in how information is exchanged within the team. Misunderstandings can occur when team members are not on the same page regarding project goals, requirements, or technical details. For instance, if project goals are communicated unclearly or if updates are not shared consistently, it can lead to confusion and errors. Addressing communication gaps involves establishing clear and regular channels of communication, such as team meetings, project management tools, and status updates. Ensure that all team members are informed about project developments and have a clear understanding of their roles and responsibilities.

Five Whys

Why does the team end up in blockers in the first place? Why did that integration issue show up at the last minute? Why did the project suffer from poorly defined requirements? Why did the knowledge silos occur within your team? Five Why analysis can come in handy to answer these questions.

Five Why analysis is a problem-solving technique used to identify the root cause of an issue or a blocker by repeatedly asking "Why?"—typically five times—until the underlying cause is discovered. Many problems are symptoms of deeper, systemic issues. By delving deeper through successive questions, you can uncover the fundamental cause of a problem rather than just addressing its superficial symptoms.

- *Uncovers Root Causes*: By drilling down to the core issue, Five Why analysis helps in identifying the real cause of a problem rather than just addressing the immediate symptoms. This enables more effective and lasting solutions.

- *Encourages Deep Thinking*: It promotes thorough investigation and critical thinking, which leads to a better understanding of the problem and its context.

- Prevents Recurrence: It addresses the root cause reduces the likelihood of the problem recurring. Fixing the root cause prevents similar issues from arising in the future.

- *Improves Process Efficiency*: By identifying and eliminating underlying issues, organizations can improve processes, reduce inefficiencies, and enhance overall performance.

Let's take a few blockers that your engineering team might encounter and how Five Whys can help resolve them.

Scenario 1: Integration Issue at the Last Minute

1. *Why did the integration issue show up at the last minute?*

   - The integration issue appeared because the new payment gateway API was not fully compatible with our existing system.

2. *Why was the payment gateway API not fully compatible?*

   - The incompatibility arose because the API documentation was outdated and did not reflect recent changes.

3. *Why was the API documentation outdated?*

   • The API provider's updates were not communicated effectively to our development team.

4. *Why were the updates not communicated effectively?*

   • The communication channels between the API provider and our team were not well established or monitored.

5. *Why were the communication channels not well established?*

   • Our project planning did not include a robust process for tracking and integrating third-party changes.

Root Cause: Lack of an effective process for managing and monitoring third-party API changes led to outdated documentation and integration issues that ended up blocking the entire project.

Scenario 2: Knowledge Silos

1. *Why did knowledge silos occur within the team?*

   • Knowledge silos occurred because only a few team members were familiar with certain aspects of the codebase.

2. *Why were only a few team members familiar with those aspects?*

   • The expertise was concentrated due to specific training and previous involvement in those code areas, without broader dissemination of knowledge.

3. *Why was knowledge not more broadly disseminated?*

   • Knowledge dissemination was not prioritized, and there were no formal practices in place for sharing insights across the team.

4. *Why were there no formal practices for knowledge sharing?*

   • The absence of formal practices was due to a lack of emphasis on documentation and team collaboration in the development process.

5. *Why was there a lack of emphasis on documentation and collaboration?*

- There was a focus on meeting deadlines and delivering features quickly, which overshadowed the need for comprehensive documentation and collaboration.

Root Cause: A focus on speed over thoroughness led to inadequate documentation and knowledge sharing practices.

Scenario 3: Delays in Code Reviews

1. *Why were there delays in code reviews?*

- The code reviews were delayed because the review process was overloaded with too many pull requests at once.

2. *Why was the review process overloaded?*

- The review process was overloaded due to a high volume of changes being submitted simultaneously.

3. *Why were there so many changes submitted simultaneously?*

- Many changes were submitted at once because multiple developers worked on interrelated features without coordinating their efforts.

4. *Why did developers work on interrelated features without coordination?*

- There was a lack of synchronization and communication among developers regarding feature development and integration.

5. *Why was there a lack of synchronization and communication?*

- The team did not have a clear process for coordinating development efforts and tracking the status of ongoing work.

Root Cause: Insufficient coordination and communication among developers led to an overloaded review process and delays.

As you can see, Five Why analysis helps your team move beyond surface-level symptoms to address the fundamental issues causing delays. Effective use of this method depends on a mindset that values a structured problem-solving approach. By focusing on root causes rather than symptoms, teams can implement more effective solutions and prevent recurring obstacles.

As an engineering manager, conducting a Five Why analysis in a postmortem setting allows you to systematically identify and address the factors that led to the blockers. This not only helps in resolving the immediate issue but also in refining your processes, improving planning, and setting your team up for smoother future projects. By applying the lessons learned through this method, you can eliminate potential blockers before they arise, ensuring that your team can focus on delivering their best work without unnecessary interruptions.

What Can Your Team Do About Blockers?

Blockers are undeniable. You have to be pragmatic about tackling them but can't run away from them. Identifying, addressing, and resolving blockers efficiently ensures that they don't derail your progress or compromise your goals. Embracing a proactive and solution-oriented approach allows you and your team to overcome obstacles and drive successful project outcomes.

- *Identify/Raise*: Detect and communicate potential blockers early, ensuring they are visible to the entire team and relevant stakeholders.

- *Eliminate*: Resolve blockers quickly by addressing the root cause. Anticipate potential blockers during planning and find workarounds to enable progress and meet the launch deadline.

Identify/Raise

Identifying and raising blockers early is crucial for keeping your project on track. As an engineering manager, it's your responsibility to create an environment where potential obstacles are recognized and communicated before they become full-fledged blockers.

Imagine your team is working on a new feature that requires input from the design team. The best-case scenario is that you've already flagged this dependency during the planning phase. This involves looking at all aspects of the project—from the availability of resources to the readiness of other teams involved. For example, if you know that the design team is already swamped with another high-priority project, you should raise this as a potential blocker before your team starts coding.

During the planning phase, encourage your team to think proactively about what might slow down their progress. Discuss these potential blockers openly and define them as clear dependencies. If, for instance, your team needs finalized UI designs to begin the frontend work, but the design team has communicated that they're behind schedule, don't just assume the designs will arrive in time. Label it as a blocker and make it clear that development on that part of the project cannot proceed until the designs are delivered.

Once development is underway, if a blocker arises, your team should have a clear process for raising it. This means making the blocker visible to everyone involved as soon as it's identified. Use daily stand-ups or group channels to communicate what the blocker is, who or what is causing it, and how it's impacting the delivery timeline. For instance, if your team is ready to start building the UI but the design assets are still incomplete, it's important that the team knows about it immediately so they can adjust their plans accordingly.

Creating a culture where your team feels comfortable saying "I'm blocked," is essential. This openness allows for rapid response and ensures that blockers are resolved quickly. As an engineering manager, it's your job to foster this environment of transparency and to be the first to address any blockers that are raised, ensuring your team can move forward with their work as efficiently as possible.

Eliminate

Imagine your team is working toward a stringent deadline for a feature launch, but you hit a significant blocker. You need a component from another team, but they are swamped with their own tight deadlines and can't assist in time.

To tackle this issue, your team opts for an alternative approach. Instead of waiting for the other team's assistance, you explore and implement a workaround or alternative solution. This could involve adapting existing code, leveraging third-party tools, or modifying the feature's scope to fit within current constraints.

The key steps include:

- *Identify and Analyze*: Quickly identify the blocker and analyze how it affects your timeline. Gather details about the dependency and its impact on the project.

- *Explore Alternatives*: Brainstorm potential workarounds or alternate solutions. This might involve adjusting the feature's requirements or using different technologies to achieve the same goal.

- *Implement and Test*: Develop and integrate the chosen alternative solution. Conduct thorough testing to ensure that it meets the necessary quality standards and does not introduce new issues.

- *Communicate*: Keep your team and stakeholders informed about the new approach and its implications. Share updates on how this alternative resolves the blocker and the adjusted timeline for the project.

By swiftly finding an alternative, your team effectively navigates around the blocker, ensuring that the project remains on track and that the feature is delivered as planned. This proactive problem-solving approach helps maintain momentum and demonstrates the team's ability to adapt to challenges efficiently.

Are You the Blocker?

What if you are the blocker for your team's delivery progress? It's a question that can be hard to face, but it's essential for the success of your team and projects. If you find yourself in this situation, reflect on what led to this and understand the impact it's having on your team's ability to deliver. Recognizing that you might be the one slowing things down is the first step toward making meaningful changes. As a leader, your role is to facilitate progress, not hinder it. By understanding how you might be inadvertently creating roadblocks, you can take action to empower your team, streamline processes, and ultimately enhance productivity.

Over-Reliance on Your Approvals

If your team is frequently waiting for your approval before making progress, you might have unintentionally created a culture of dependency. Perhaps you've been too involved in day-to-day decisions, making your team hesitant to act without your input. This could stem from not fully trusting their abilities or being overly cautious about managing risks.

What can you do instead?

Shift your role from gatekeeper to coach. Start by clearly defining decision-making boundaries within your team. Encourage team members to make decisions independently within these boundaries, and only step in for critical or high-risk decisions. Establish regular check-ins where the team can discuss their decisions and get feedback, but avoid micromanaging. Over time, this will build trust and confidence in their ability to operate autonomously.

Insufficient Delegation

If you're holding onto too many tasks or decisions, you could be slowing down the team's progress. This might happen because you haven't empowered your team enough or because you're not confident in their skills to delegate effectively.

What can do you instead?

Begin by identifying tasks that can be delegated to your team members. Assign these tasks based on their strengths and areas where they need to grow. Provide clear expectations and outcomes but allow them the freedom to approach the task in their own way. Support them through the process by being available for guidance without taking over. This not only speeds up progress but also helps in skill development across the team.

Centralized Communication

If all communication within the team, or between the team and external stakeholders, goes through you, it can create delays. This bottleneck might occur because you haven't set up direct lines of communication for your team, or because you're trying to protect them from certain challenges, which can actually stifle their growth.

What can do you instead?

Empower your team to take ownership of communication. Create direct communication channels between your team and other stakeholders, removing yourself as a middleman. Encourage transparency and openness, ensuring everyone knows who to contact for different types of issues or information. You can also set up guidelines for effective communication to help your team feel confident in managing these interactions.

Lack of Knowledge Sharing

If you're the only one possessing critical knowledge or expertise, your team might struggle to move forward without your input. This situation could have developed if you haven't prioritized sharing knowledge or encouraged continuous learning within the team, leading to gaps in understanding.

What can you do instead?

Cultivate a culture of continuous learning and knowledge sharing within the team. Regularly schedule knowledge-sharing sessions where team members present what they've learned from their work or research. Document key processes, decisions, and technical information in a shared repository accessible to everyone. Additionally, encourage peer learning through pair programming, code reviews, and mentorship programs to ensure that expertise is distributed and not concentrated in one person.

PART VI

Building High-Performing Teams

Rome wasn't built in a day. A high-performing team neither.

You won't be gifted with a high-performing team from day one. You have to build it. It will take months, sometimes even a year or two, depending on where the team currently stands. If you're not sure what makes a team high performing, the chance of becoming one is slim. Is it the individuals in the team that make it a high-performing? Or is it you—the manager? Could a strong vision and mission influence a team's performance? Or is it the act of consistently delivering results to your organization? Perhaps it's the practice of taking extreme ownership particularly in crisis? It's a mix of everything.

A strong engineering culture goes beyond perks like ping-pong tables and fruit baskets. It's defined by the values and practices guiding how a team works, learns, and collaborates, especially in tough times. Key elements include problem-solving, continuous learning, autonomy, collaboration, and adaptability. Building this culture requires consistent effort and alignment with organizational goals, as seen in companies like Google and Netflix, where thoughtful leadership and dedication are crucial for success.

As an engineering manager, your role extends well beyond your immediate team, influencing the broader organization through collaboration with various departments and stakeholders. Your team's performance and the culture you foster impact the organization's reputation and success. To transition from managing daily tasks to leading with a broader influence, you must develop strategic thinking and engage in cross-functional collaboration.

In the final part of the book, we'll delve into building high-performing engineering teams and guiding you an inch closer to becoming an influential organizational leader.

- ***Make Your Team Great Again:*** Discover how to transform your engineering team into a cohesive, high-performing unit, performing like an Orchestra. Learn to identify and address common dysfunctions, Define clear goals, and foster collaboration for exceptional results.

- ***Building a Strong Engineering Culture:*** Establishing five traits of a strong engineering culture, "The Five Fingers"—Problem Solving and Customer Centricity, Continuous Learning and Improvement, Autonomy and Extreme Ownership, Collaboration and Open feedback, and Adaptability, Setting high standards, and Cultural anti-patterns.

- ***Becoming an Organizational Leader:*** Transitioning from an engineering manager to an organizational leader involves expanding your influence beyond technical expertise to include strategic thinking and cross-functional collaboration.

CHAPTER 16

Make Your Team Great Again

Without a team, where would we be? What would we be doing? What impact could we possibly make? It's hard to say. It's hard to imagine the role of an engineering manager without a team. Your team is the main reason for your existence.

Your primary goal as an engineering manager is to build a high-performing team. How you achieve it and what you will change or fix is up to you. Inheriting a team with various dysfunctions, such as lack of accountability, failing to deliver expected outcomes, and poor collaboration is a daunting task. Yet it's the best opportunity for your growth as a leader, offering you challenges and valuable learning experiences.

There's no one-size-fits-all solution for making a team high-performing. Each of the team's dysfunctions requires a different treatment from you. Whether it's coaching individuals to improve their performance that in turn influences the team's, holding individuals accountable for results and letting them take ownership of your domain's scope, demanding clear goals and priorities from your product manager, or proactively addressing conflicts in the domain's scope with sister teams when your team is bad in visualizing dependencies—you need to be willing to take it head-on. If you don't, no one else will.

This chapter will guide you through this journey, focusing on how to set your team up for success and drive them toward high performance. Here's what we'll cover:

- *Know Your Team In and Out*: Understand your team's purpose, roles, and collaboration methods. Define clear goals, success criteria to align efforts, measure progress, and ensure efficient teamwork.

- *What does a high-performing engineering team look like?*: A high-performing engineering team operates like an orchestra, delivering quality work through strong collaboration and accountability. They

© Ananth Ramachandran 2024
A. Ramachandran, *The Complete Engineering Manager*, https://doi.org/10.1007/979-8-8688-0267-6_16

make informed decisions, own their work, and learn from mistakes. As a manager, you guide and synchronize the team to ensure cohesive and effective performance.

- *What will stop your team from becoming high-performing?*: Teams often struggle to become high-performing due to issues like overemphasis on individual performance, over-reliance on key members, inefficient processes, unclear roles, working in silos, and ineffective leadership. Without addressing these concerns, you can't have a high-performing team.

- *Spotting Dysfunctions in Your Team*: Spotting team dysfunctions involves recognizing issues like lack of trust, fear of conflict, and avoidance of accountability. Addressing these dysfunctions is key to improving team effectiveness and achieving high performance.

- *Where does your team stand?*: Assess your team's current performance and determine how to elevate them to a high-performing level.

Know Your Team In and Out

When you start managing an engineering team, it may be newly formed, or you might have inherited it from the previous manager. At the same time, you might be transitioning from an individual contributor to a manager within the same organization or moving to a new organization to take on the role. First, you need to know your team and understand how they work together before embarking on the journey to make them high-performing. Without this insight, you won't know how far you need to go to reach your destination. You must understand the team's purpose, composition, and ways of working together.

- *Purpose, Mission, Goals, and Success Criteria*: Know your why. Establish clear goals and success criteria to guide your team's efforts and measure progress.

- *Roles, People and Structures*: Define roles and responsibilities within your team to ensure clarity and efficiency. Effective collaboration between specializations, such as engineering, product, design, and data, enhances overall team performance.

- *Ways of working together*: Define effective work practices, communication patterns, and decision-making processes. Clear guidelines on task management, communication, and decision-making foster a productive and collaborative team environment.

Purpose and Mission

Your purpose is to understand why your team exists and what problem you are solving for your end customers and the impact created for your business.

A team can hardly achieve its goals and feel motivated without understanding the purpose and mission. Clearly defining these elements provides direction and aligns the team's efforts. The purpose gives the team a sense of why they are working together, helping to foster a shared vision and sense of belonging. The mission outlines the specific objectives and milestones the team strives to achieve, offering a roadmap to measure progress and success.

Let's take the Google Maps team as an example to understand what their team's purpose is and the mission they've set.

Purpose

The purpose of the Google Maps team is to help people navigate and explore the world, providing accurate and real-time geographic information to enhance users' travel and local exploration experiences.

Mission

The mission of the Google Maps team is to build a comprehensive mapping platform offering precise navigation and detailed geographical data. This involves continuously updating maps, improving route optimization, and integrating user feedback. The team leverages AI and machine learning to predict traffic patterns and suggest optimal routes, ensuring the best possible user experience.

How do engineers feel working in such a team with a meaningful purpose and ambitious mission?

- *Sense of Meaning and Fulfillment*: Understanding that their work directly contributes to a significant goal, such as making information universally accessible or helping people navigate the world, gives engineers a sense of meaning and fulfillment. They see their efforts translating into real-world benefits, which can be deeply satisfying.

- *Motivation and Engagement*: An ambitious mission inspires engineers to push their boundaries and strive for excellence. Knowing that their work is part of a larger, innovative vision encourages them to stay engaged, motivated, and committed to their tasks.

- *Pride and Ownership*: Realizing that their contributions are making a substantial impact on millions of users worldwide fosters a sense of pride and ownership. Engineers feel valued and important, knowing that their skills and efforts play a major part in the team's success.

- *Collaboration and Team Spirit*: Clear objectives and well-defined goals promote effective collaboration and teamwork. Engineers understand their roles and how they fit into the bigger picture, leading to a more cohesive and cooperative team environment.

- *Innovation and Creativity*: Ambitious missions often involve complex problems and innovative solutions. Engineers are encouraged to think creatively and come up with novel approaches, which can be intellectually stimulating and rewarding.

- *Professional Growth*: Working toward a challenging mission provides ample opportunities for professional growth and skill development. Engineers can expand their knowledge, learn new technologies, and enhance their problem-solving abilities.

- *Stability and Direction*: A clear purpose and mission provide stability and direction, helping engineers stay focused on their goals. They are less likely to feel lost or uncertain about their tasks, leading to a more productive and efficient workflow.

Goals and Success Criteria

Every team should be crystal clear about the goals they are pursuing and have a well-defined understanding of what success looks like for them. Clear goals and success criteria are essential for any high-performing team to maintain focus and drive. Goals provide direction and ensure that the team's efforts align with the company's strategic objectives, serving as a roadmap toward impactful outcomes and prioritizing tasks that deliver the most value. Success criteria offer specific, quantifiable benchmarks to measure progress, enabling teams to objectively evaluate their performance, make data-driven decisions, and adjust their approach as needed.

When teams understand and align with their goals and success criteria, they gain clarity on what success looks like and how their work contributes to the larger mission. This alignment fosters accountability, drives purpose, and ultimately leads to more efficient and effective product development. While a purpose and mission offer inspiration and a sense of direction, goals and success criteria provide the concrete metrics needed to gauge progress and ensure alignment with the broader vision.

For instance, consider the product and engineering teams behind Google Maps. One of their primary goals could well be to "enhance the accuracy and coverage of global maps." This goal supports Google Maps' mission of providing reliable and comprehensive mapping services. Success criteria for this goal could include achieving 95% accuracy in map data for major cities and expanding Street View coverage to 90% of urban areas in 50 countries by year-end. These criteria provide clear benchmarks, allowing the team to track progress and determine if they are meeting their goal.

While a purpose and mission offer inspiration and a sense of direction, it's the goals and success criteria that provide the concrete metrics needed to gauge whether the team is making progress. The purpose and mission motivate the team by outlining the broader impact of their work, but goals and success criteria ensure that every step they take is aligned with that vision, offering clear indicators that they are on the right path.

What are your team's goals for achieving your mission? How will you measure success? Most importantly, does your team of engineers understand and feel aligned with these objectives?

Roles, People, and Structures

To achieve your goals, you need to have a clear understanding of the roles required within your team. Depending on your team's focus, you might include developers with varied specializations, such as backend, web, and mobile. To ensure high-quality deliverables, consider incorporating QA engineers who handle either manual or automated testing depending on your needs. If you operate within a cross-functional squad, your team may also integrate roles such as product, design, and data and analytics, either as part of the team or as closely collaborating external units. However, bringing roles from engineering, product, design, and analytics together as one team can significantly boost your team's effectiveness.

- *Engineering*: Engineers bring technical expertise and implementation skills, ensuring robust and scalable solutions. You, as an engineering manager, will be considered as part of the engineering team.

- *Product*: Product managers align the team's work with user needs and business goals, providing direction and prioritization.

- *Design*: Designers focus on user experience and interface, making sure the product is intuitive and engaging.

- *Data & Analytics*: Data analysts and scientists provide insights through data, guiding decisions with empirical evidence and identifying trends.

Define clear responsibilities for each specialization to ensure everyone understands their role and contribution to the team's success. Role clarity, especially between you and the product manager, should be the top priority for your team to function frictionless.

Product Manager and You

The product manager (PM) is responsible for the following:

- *Vision and Strategy*: Defining the product vision and strategy. They determine what the product should achieve based on market research, user feedback, and business goals.

- *Prioritization*: Prioritize features and improvements based on customer needs, business value, and resource constraints. They maintain the product backlog, ensuring that the team is focused on the most impactful work.

- *Requirements and Specifications*: The PM translates user needs into detailed requirements and specifications. They create user stories, define acceptance criteria, and work closely with the design team to ensure that product features meet user expectations.

- *Stakeholder Communication*: Manage communication with stakeholders, including customers, executives, and other departments. They ensure that everyone is aligned with the product goals and roadmap.

- *Market and Competitive Analysis*: Conduct market research and competitive analysis to inform product decisions and identify opportunities for differentiation.

As the engineering manager (EM), you are responsible for the following:

- *Technical Execution*: You oversee the technical implementation of the product and ensure that engineering solutions align with the product requirements and are feasible within technical constraints.

- *Team Management and Development*: You are responsible for managing the engineering team, including hiring, mentoring, and performance evaluations. You also foster a positive team culture and support professional growth.

- *Project Planning and Delivery*: You manage the engineering team's workload, including sprint planning, delegation, and ensuring timely delivery of features. You handle technical roadblocks and ensure that engineering tasks are completed on schedule.

- *Quality Assurance*: You ensure that engineering practices maintain high-quality standards. You employ QA experts and collaborate with them to establish testing strategies and address any technical issues that arise.

- *Technical Strategy and Innovation*: You contribute to the technical strategy by evaluating new technologies, improving engineering processes, and ensuring that the team's technical capabilities align with the product's needs.

When it comes to collaboration, you should work closely together with your product manager to ensure alignment and efficiency.

- *Regular Communication*: Align with your PM on product goals, technical constraints, and progress updates. Regular check-ins help ensure that you both are on the same page and that any issues are addressed promptly.

- *Alignment on Priorities*: The PM provides the vision and priorities for the product, while you ensure that the engineering team can meet these priorities with realistic timelines and technical feasibility. Both of you must align on what is achievable within given constraints.

- *Feedback Loop*: You provide feedback on technical challenges and possibilities, which helps the PM make informed decisions about feature prioritization and scope. Conversely, the PM offers insights into user needs and market conditions, which guide you in making technical decisions.

- *Shared Goals*: Both of your roles are ultimately focused on delivering a successful product. You need to work together to balance customer needs, technical capabilities, and business objectives, ensuring that the product not only meets market demands but is also delivered with high quality and efficiency.

By clearly defining and respecting each other's responsibilities, and by maintaining open lines of communication, you can create a harmonious and effective working relationship with your product manager that drives the team toward high performance and successful product delivery.

Your Team of Engineers

One of the key aspects of building and leading a successful engineering team is achieving the right balance of mastery and experience among your engineers. The composition of your team—whether it leans more toward senior engineers with extensive experience or includes a higher number of junior engineers eager to learn—can significantly influence the team's dynamics, productivity, and overall success. This balance is not a one-size-fits-all solution. It depends largely on the complexity of your team's domain and the specific needs of your organization.

Well-Balanced Team

A well-balanced team should ideally include a mix of both senior and junior engineers. Senior engineers bring a wealth of experience, technical expertise, and a deep understanding of industry best practices. Their mastery allows them to tackle complex problems, mentor junior engineers, and make strategic decisions that can shape the direction of the project. However, too many senior engineers can sometimes lead to a lack of diversity in thinking or an imbalance in team dynamics, where mentorship and fresh perspectives might be overlooked.

On the other hand, junior engineers offer fresh ideas, enthusiasm, and a willingness to learn and adapt to new technologies. They bring energy to the team and are often more open to exploring innovative approaches. However, a team with too many junior engineers might struggle with navigating complex challenges due to a lack of experience, potentially leading to slower progress or increased technical debt.

Striking the right balance should be informed by the complexity of the work your team is undertaking. For projects that are technically demanding and require a high level of precision, a greater proportion of senior engineers may be necessary to ensure that the project is executed efficiently and with minimal risk. Conversely, for projects that are more exploratory or involve rapid prototyping, a mix of juniors who can bring fresh perspectives, supported by a few experienced mentors, might be more effective.

Being Product-Minded

Cultivate a product-minded engineering culture within your team. Engineers who are product-minded don't just focus on writing code. They understand and care about the broader context of their work. They think beyond immediate technical challenges to consider how their contributions influence the user experience, support business objectives, and ensure the product's long-term viability. This perspective helps engineers make informed decisions that align with the overall vision and strategy of the product.

Encouraging a product-minded approach involves fostering an environment where engineers are not only aware of but actively engaged with the end goals of the product. This means involving them in discussions about user needs, market trends, and business priorities. When engineers see how their work fits into the larger picture, they are more likely to innovate and make choices that enhance both the functionality and value of the product. By promoting this mindset, you ensure that technical decisions are made with a clear understanding of their impact, leading to solutions that are not only technically sound but also resonate with users and drive the product's success.

Role Adaptability

The ability of engineers to adjust their roles and responsibilities lets you build a resilient and dynamic team. In a fast-evolving technological landscape, flexibility in job functions helps maintain productivity and innovation. This means that engineers should not be confined to their initial job descriptions but should be encouraged to grow and adapt to meet the needs of the team and the organization.

One significant advantage of this flexibility is that it enables the team to quickly respond to shifts in technological requirements. For example, if a new area of expertise becomes necessary, engineers with related skills can be supported in acquiring new capabilities and taking on new tasks. This broadens the team's overall skill set, making it more versatile and better equipped to handle diverse challenges.

Encouraging engineers to explore different aspects of their roles also fosters a culture of continuous learning and growth. When given the opportunity to engage in various areas beyond their primary functions, engineers develop a more comprehensive understanding of the technology and organizational goals. This cross-functional knowledge is invaluable, particularly in complex environments where multiple domains are involved. It also prepares engineers for future leadership positions by exposing them to different facets of the development process.

Furthermore, allowing engineers to shift focus and take on new challenges helps maintain high levels of engagement and motivation. When team members can pursue diverse interests and responsibilities, they are more likely to stay committed and avoid burnout. This dynamic approach to role management not only keeps work interesting but also fosters a sense of ownership and investment in the team's success.

Ways of Working Together

Defining ways of working together to foster a productive and collaborative team. The effectiveness of a team is determined not just by the individual's performance or the leader's capabilities but how they collaborate and work together.

- *Work Definition, Identifying Dependencies and Refinement*: Detailing the scope of work, identifying dependencies, and refining tasks to ensure clarity and alignment. Effective task management and iterative refinement help in adapting to changes and improving the team's efficiency.

- *Communication Patterns and Team Ceremonies*: Set up effective communication practices and team ceremonies to facilitate smooth interactions. Define when to use asynchronous methods (like Slack or emails) versus synchronous methods (like team meetings or 1-1 calls). Establish protocols for one-on-one meetings and team-wide discussions to ensure clarity and timely information sharing.

- *Decision-Making*: Outline the decision-making process, including the potential consequences and communication requirements. Ensure the team understands which decisions are reversible or irreversible and empower them to make informed choices. Ensure that technical decisions are made with adequate input and considerations, incorporating feedback from relevant stakeholders and teams.

You've covered the basics, and your team is ready to go. Now, I know you've been anticipating these questions: what defines a high-performing engineering team, and how do you develop one?

What Does a High-Performing Engineering Team Look Like?

High-performing engineering teams are like an orchestra (Figure 16-1). They deliver high-quality and impactful work consistently by effectively collaborating and operating as "one team."

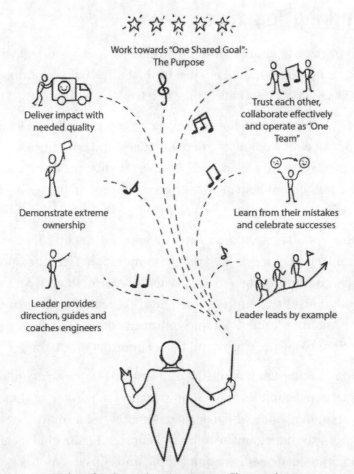

High-performing engineering teams are like an orchestra

Figure 16-1. *High-performing engineering teams are like an orchestra*

They make swift, well-informed decisions and hold themselves accountable for outcomes, demonstrating extreme ownership over their scope, systems, and the environment they work with. They continuously learn from their mistakes through practices like retrospectives and postmortem, which helps them refine their processes and improve. As a result, they earn high credibility and trust across the organization.

Your role is to guide and synchronize the team, ensuring that each member plays their part harmoniously. You provide direction, set the tempo, and facilitate clear communication, allowing the team to collaborate effectively and produce outstanding results. Just as a conductor ensures every musician contributes to a cohesive performance, you align your team's efforts toward shared goals, drive accountability, and foster continuous improvement to achieve a flawless execution of their tasks.

What Will Stop Your Team from Becoming High-Performing?

Let's answer this question.

Individual Performance vs. Team Performance

A common pitfall in developing high-performing teams is an overemphasis on individual performance at the expense of team performance. While recognizing and rewarding individual contributions is important, focusing too much on personal achievements can undermine the team's collective success.

When team members prioritize their own performance metrics, it can lead to fragmented efforts. For example, engineers might concentrate on their personal coding challenges rather than collaborating to solve broader team issues. This can result in a lack of alignment with the team's overall objectives, as personal success takes precedence over shared goals. As a result, the team's productivity and cohesion suffer, preventing the group from achieving integrated and high-quality results.

Additionally, a focus on individual performance can discourage collaboration. Team members might be hesitant to share insights or support colleagues if they believe it could detract from their own success. This reluctance can limit the team's ability to leverage collective knowledge and skills, ultimately impacting overall effectiveness and innovation.

Over-Reliance on One Person

Another significant anti-pattern is over-reliance on a single individual within the team. When too much dependence is placed on one person for critical tasks or knowledge, it can create several challenges.

This dependency can lead to a single point of failure. If the individual responsible for key tasks is unavailable due to illness, vacation, or departure, the entire team's progress can be disrupted. For instance, if a project depends on one developer's expertise, their absence can cause delays and force the team to scramble to find a replacement or bridge the gap.

Over-reliance also creates bottlenecks in the workflow. If one person is overloaded with responsibilities or holds exclusive decision-making power, it can slow down the entire project. For example, if one team member is the sole approver for all the code changes, their backlog of approvals can delay feature releases and impede progress.

Inefficient Processes or Excessive Rigidity

Inefficiencies or excessive rigidity in processes can significantly hinder the team's success. Inefficient processes can lead to wasted time and reduced productivity. For instance, poorly defined workflows or outdated tools can cause confusion and slow down progress. Streamlining processes and adopting effective tools can help eliminate bottlenecks and improve overall efficiency, allowing the team to work more seamlessly and productively. Conversely, excessive rigidity in processes or plans can stifle the team's ability to adapt and respond to changes. If a team rigidly adheres to a predefined plan without accommodating new information or shifting requirements, it can miss opportunities and fail to address emerging issues.

Team Scope, Topology, and Cognitive Load

The clarity of the team's scope, its organizational structure, and the cognitive load placed on its members are important factors that affect performance. Issues in these areas can impede the team's ability to operate effectively.

An unclear team scope can result in confusion and misalignment. When team members do not have a clear understanding of their roles, responsibilities, and objectives, it can lead to inefficiencies and overlap. Defining a clear scope and ensuring that each team member understands their role within that scope is key for maintaining alignment and focus.

The team's organizational structure or topology can also impact performance. A poorly designed structure can create communication barriers and inefficiencies, while an optimal structure facilitates collaboration and effective workflow. Ensuring that the team's organization supports its goals and facilitates smooth interactions is key to maintaining productivity and effectiveness.

Finally, cognitive load is the amount of mental effort required to perform tasks, which can influence a team performance. Overloading team members with too many tasks or complex responsibilities can lead to burnout and decreased productivity. Balancing workload and providing support to manage cognitive load effectively are essential for maintaining a high-performing team.

Working in Silos

When different specializations such as product, engineering, design, and analytics work in isolation from one another, it can hinder the team's ability to achieve its goals. Working in silos prevents the effective integration of diverse perspectives and skills, leading to several issues.

One major issue is a lack of alignment between different functions. When each specialization operates independently, it can result in conflicting priorities and fragmented efforts. For example, if the Product team's goals are not aligned with the Engineering team's capabilities, it can lead to misaligned deliverables and inefficiencies. Another problem is reduced collaboration. When teams work in silos, opportunities for cross-functional collaboration are lost. This lack of interaction can limit innovation and problem-solving, as different perspectives and expertise are not brought together to address challenges.

Lastly, inefficient hand-offs between teams can occur. If specializations do not communicate effectively or share information seamlessly, it can lead to misunderstandings and delays. All specializations should work toward a common goal and collaborate closely to achieve cohesive and high-quality outcomes.

Ineffective Leadership

As an engineering manager, ineffective leadership can manifest in several detrimental ways. One significant issue is a lack of support for your team. When you fail to provide the necessary resources, training, or guidance, you undermine your team's ability to perform effectively and achieve their goals. Support is crucial for empowering your team to overcome challenges and excel in their roles.

Another problem is being a "frozen middle" leader, where you struggle to connect your team's work to the bigger picture. If you cannot align their efforts with broader organizational objectives or communicate how their contributions fit into the overall strategy, it creates a disconnect that can diminish motivation and productivity. You need to bridge this gap by clearly articulating the relevance of your team's work to the organization's goals.

Additionally, ineffective leadership can be marked by poor decision-making or a reluctance to make bold decisions. As a leader, you need to be decisive and willing to take calculated risks. Hesitation or indecision can stall progress and prevent your team from seizing opportunities or addressing challenges effectively. Addressing these issues—providing adequate support, connecting work to organizational goals, making informed, bold decisions—fosters a high-performing team, drives successful outcomes.

Spotting Dysfunctions

Once you understand your team's dynamics and ways of working together, you'll be better positioned to identify dysfunctions (Figure 16-2) that stop your team from becoming high-performing. Patrick Lencioni's framework on team dysfunctions has been a foundational model widely adopted by many organizations over the years.

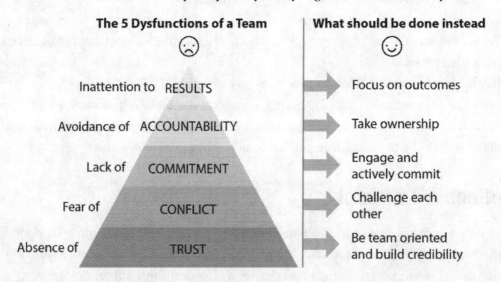

Figure 16-2. *Dysfunctions in an engineering team*

- *Absence of Trust*: Team members avoid admitting mistakes and resist feedback, hurting collaboration. Poor performance and missed deadlines damage the team's credibility across the wider organization.

- *Fear of Conflict*: Avoiding debates leads to superficial harmony and subpar decisions. Critical issues remain unaddressed, causing later complications.

- *Lack of Commitment*: Disengaged team members reduce effort and motivation, creating frustration and imbalanced workloads.

- *Avoidance of Accountability*: Shifting blame and making excuses prevent problem resolution and impact performance, resulting in poor outcomes.

- *Inattention to Results*: Focusing on outputs over outcomes allows missed targets to go unexamined, leading to subpar performance and missed improvement opportunities.

Absence of Trust

The absence of trust in your team manifests in two different ways: internally within your team and externally affecting the credibility of your team within the organization.

Internally, trust issues arise when team members avoid admitting mistakes, resist feedback, and fail to follow through on their commitments. For instance, imagine your team is working together to deliver a feature that is blocking a major release. One engineer, however, consistently fails to coordinate with the rest of the team, missing deadlines and not updating their progress. This has happened before, and each time, the team had to scramble to adjust their plans and cover for this individual. This repeated lack of coordination and failure to meet commitments undermines the team's trust in this engineer. As a result, the team experiences delays, frustration grows, and the overall effectiveness of the group is compromised, making it harder for everyone to rely on this engineer moving forward.

Externally, a lack of trust on your team stems from a poor reputation within the broader organization. If a team has a history of missed deadlines, subpar quality, or unfulfilled promises, they may be viewed with skepticism or doubt by other teams and stakeholders. Also if the team fails to take ownership of their scope, they undermine the trust that other teams have in them.

For example, if your engineering team fails to address technical issues in the services owned by you that leads to critical bugs impacting more customers or frequent downtime, it can lead to widespread problems that impact the entire system. This lack of ownership erodes the trust other teams have in your team's reliability, affecting the overall system's performance and creating friction within the organization. This external distrust further undermines the team's credibility and can hinder their ability to collaborate effectively with other teams, secure necessary resources, or influence organizational decisions.

Fear of Conflict

Fear of conflict in cross-functional teams can impede discussions that need to happen. It creates artificial harmony within a team by discouraging open debates and challenging discussions. This superficial consensus often results in subpar quality of solutions, as critical issues and alternative perspectives are not thoroughly explored. When team members avoid conflict, they may not fully address important problems or think deeply about potential solutions, leading to incomplete or flawed decision-making.

Consider a situation where a team must choose between two architectural approaches for a new platform. One approach is a bold, cutting-edge design that promises significant future benefits but carries some risks. The other is a more traditional, proven method that is safer but less innovative. Some team members have concerns about the risks of the cutting-edge approach, including potential performance and maintenance issues. However, to avoid tension and potential conflict, the team decides to proceed with the riskier approach without a thorough discussion of the concerns.

As development unfolds, the team encounters unforeseen challenges related to the cutting-edge approach—problems with performance, integration difficulties, and increased maintenance overhead. These issues could have been anticipated and mitigated if the team had engaged in a more rigorous examination of the risks and benefits. Instead, the reluctance to confront and debate the technical decision results in avoidable complications, ultimately impacting the project's success and the team's overall efficiency.

Lack of Commitment

Lack of commitment in a team signifies a disconnect between team members and the team's goals, resulting in diminished motivation and engagement. When team members are not fully committed, they often fail to invest the necessary effort and enthusiasm required to drive the project forward. This can manifest as a reluctance to take ownership of tasks, minimal participation in discussions, and a general disinterest in achieving the team's objectives. Their lack of engagement undermines the collective effort needed to meet deadlines and deliver high-quality outcomes.

Moreover, the lack of commitment affects team dynamics and cohesion. When some members are not fully invested, it can create an imbalance whereas more committed individuals feel they are carrying an unfair share of the workload. This imbalance can lead to frustration and decreased morale among the team, further exacerbating the problem.

Avoidance of Accountability

Avoidance of accountability occurs when team members do not take ownership of their responsibilities or the outcomes of their actions, leading to unresolved issues and diminished performance. This avoidance often manifests as shifting blame, making excuses, or failing to address problems directly.

For example, in a software development project, the team is responsible for delivering a new feature by a set deadline. As the deadline approaches, it becomes clear that the feature does not meet the required specifications and is riddled with bugs. Rather than addressing the issues and taking responsibility for the shortcomings, team members might shift the blame to external factors, such as unclear requirements or unrealistic timelines.

This avoidance of accountability results in the feature being delivered late and with poor quality. The lack of ownership over their work means that critical issues are left unaddressed, impacting the project's success and causing frustration among stakeholders who rely on the feature. The cycle of blame and inaction prevents the team from learning from their mistakes and making necessary improvements.

Inattention to Results

Inattention to results occurs when teams fail to prioritize or focus on achieving their collective goals and measuring their impact. This often manifests as a disregard for missed targets and a lack of discussion about performance outcomes. Teams may focus on producing outputs—the tangible deliverables or tasks completed—without considering their alignment with the project's broader objectives.

When teams exhibit inattention to results, they may be more concerned with the volume of work done rather than the actual impact of their efforts. Missed objectives are accepted with little scrutiny or effort to understand why targets were not met. This lack of focus on outcomes—the broader impact and effectiveness of those outputs—results in a culture where subpar performance is tolerated.

Without a clear understanding of how their outputs contribute to desired outcomes, teams risk continuing with ineffective practices and failing to drive meaningful progress. By not addressing the relationship between outputs and outcomes, teams miss opportunities to improve and align their work with strategic goals, ultimately diminishing their overall effectiveness and impact.

Where Does Your Team Stand?

To transform your team into a high-performing unit, you have to know where they currently stand in their development journey. Knowing their stage in Tuckman's model—Forming, Storming, Norming, or Performing—can help you address their specific needs and challenges effectively.

Bruce Tuckman's model of team development outlines the key stages that teams go through as they evolve and work together. The model identifies the four stages shown in Figure 16-3. Each stage represents a phase in the team's development where different challenges and dynamics come into play. Understanding these stages helps leaders guide their teams through the complexities of collaboration, enhance their effectiveness, and ultimately reach high performance.

- *Forming*: Set clear goals and roles, build trust, and foster open communication.

- *Storming*: Mediate conflicts, address challenges, and encourage constructive feedback.

- *Norming*: Establish team norms, promote accountability, and enhance collaboration.

- *Performing*: Empower the team, drive productivity, foster innovation, and sustain high standards.

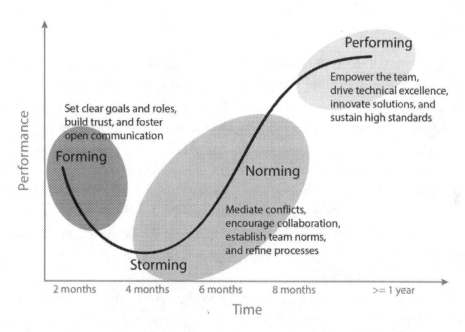

Figure 16-3. *Tuckman's model of team development: Forming, Storming, Norming and Performing*

Forming

In a fast-growing e-commerce company, a new checkout optimization team was formed to enhance the checkout process and drive improvements in user experience. This team, carved out from existing product groups, was tasked with reducing cart abandonment and streamlining the checkout workflow. As you assembled the team, the Forming phase focuses on establishing a clear foundation. You organized kickoff meetings to introduce team members, define their domain, and outline their objectives. With diverse expertise from UX design to customer analytics, you focused on aligning their skills with the team's goals and expected impact.

You then clarified roles and responsibilities, assigning specific areas such as payment integration and interface redesign. You established key processes and workflows to guide their efforts, including sprint reviews and user testing sessions.

Despite the structured approach, challenges arose as team members adjusted to new roles and expectations. You facilitated discussions to resolve conflicts and ensure alignment, setting the stage for a successful transition into the team's core work and maximizing their impact on the checkout experience.

Storming

As your team moved into the Storming phase after a couple of months spent in the Forming phase, the initial excitement began to give way to the complexities of real collaboration. With the team now settled into their roles and the scope of their work clearly defined, the challenges of integrating diverse perspectives and approaches came to the forefront.

During this phase, team members began to confront differing opinions on the best ways to improve the checkout process. Disagreements emerged over priorities, with some advocating for immediate fixes to payment gateway issues, while others pushed for a complete overhaul of the user interface. Conflicts arose as team members struggled to balance quick wins with long-term strategic goals, leading to debates about resource allocation and project timelines.

The Storming phase also highlighted variations in working styles and expectations. While some team members preferred detailed, data-driven approaches, others favored iterative design and rapid prototyping. These differences sometimes led to friction in meetings and slowed progress as the team worked through how to integrate their various methodologies into a cohesive plan.

As you navigated this challenging phase, your role was indispensable in managing conflicts and fostering collaboration. You facilitated open discussions to address disagreements and find common ground, ensuring that every voice was heard while steering the team toward consensus. You also worked to establish clearer processes for decision-making and communication, helping the team to align their efforts and move past initial obstacles. Through these efforts, you aimed to guide the team toward a more unified approach and lay the groundwork for more effective collaboration in the next phases of their development.

Norming

It's been six months since the team was formed and entered the Storming phase, during which they encountered challenges in collaboration, prioritization, and navigating the technical system. Now, the focus shifts to the Norming phase.

As your team transitioned into the Norming phase, there was a notable shift in how the team operated. This phase was marked by increased stability and productivity as the team began to solidify their working relationships and establish effective processes.

During this period, team members started to resolve the conflicts and misunderstandings that had surfaced in the Storming phase. They developed a better understanding of each other's strengths, work styles, and areas of expertise, which fostered a more collaborative environment. Regular meetings became more structured and focused, and there was a noticeable improvement in communication and teamwork.

You played a role in facilitating this transition by reinforcing the team's shared goals and guiding them toward a more cohesive approach. You helped clarify roles and responsibilities, ensuring that each team member knew their specific tasks and how their work contributed to the overall project. This clarity helped reduce confusion and overlap, allowing the team to work more efficiently.

Additionally, you introduced and refined key processes and workflows, such as sprint planning, progress reviews, and integration of user feedback. These structured approaches helped the team maintain focus and make steady progress. As a result, the team began to implement effective solutions to the checkout process, addressing both technical issues and user experience improvements with greater ease.

By the end of the Norming phase, the checkout optimization team had established a more unified and effective way of working together. The improved collaboration and clearer communication set the stage for the team to advance to a higher level of performance, preparing them for the challenges of the Performing phase.

Performing

After a steady Norming phase, your team is entering a much awaited Performing phase. They experienced a significant shift in productivity and effectiveness. With the foundational work of Forming, Storming, and Norming behind them, the team operated in this phase with a high level of cohesion and efficiency.

In this phase, the team was empowered to drive technical excellence and deliver innovative solutions at an increased velocity. Leveraging their combined expertise, they tackled complex challenges and implemented effective improvements to the checkout process. Their work led to notable reductions in cart abandonment rates and enhancements in user satisfaction. The team's ability to collaborate seamlessly and their strong sense of ownership allowed them to address both technical issues and user experience improvements with remarkable speed and quality.

You facilitated high-level planning, ensuring alignment with broader business objectives, and guided the team through regular progress reviews and strategic meetings. This helped maintain focus and adapt quickly to any new challenges or opportunities that arose.

During the Performing phase, the team operated with a high degree of autonomy and self-management. Clear communication channels and well-established workflows contributed to their smooth and accelerated delivery of key milestones. Empowered and driven, the team not only met but often exceeded their performance goals, setting a new standard for excellence in optimizing the checkout experience and significantly impacting the business.

It's a Game of Snakes and Ladders

If your team struggles with various dysfunctions, it may take a year or two to reach a high-performing phase. It's important to understand that high performance is not a permanent state but a dynamic process in the team's development journey. Much like the game of Snakes and Ladders (Figure 16-4), where progress can lead to success or setbacks can cause a slide back, a high-performing team's performance naturally fluctuates over time.

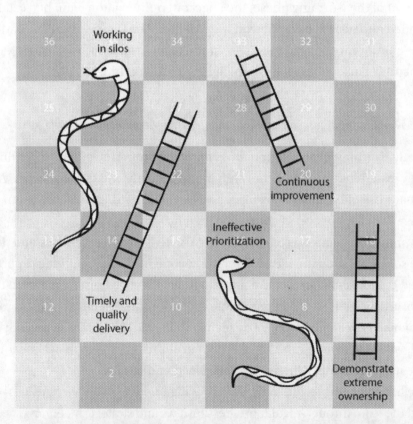

Figure 16-4. *A game of Snakes and Ladders but for an engineering team*

Ladder: Teams climb the ladder when they successfully navigate through the stages of Forming, Storming, and Norming, reaching a state of high performance. This is when they operate with efficiency, deliver innovative solutions, and achieve their goals with increased velocity. The team's cohesion, established workflows, and strong sense of ownership propel them forward, setting new standards of excellence.

Snake: However, external and internal factors can introduce challenges that pull the team back. For instance, a sudden shift in project requirements or an unexpected technical issue can disrupt the team's momentum, causing them to regress to earlier stages. Such setbacks may lead to a temporary return to the Storming phase, where the team must navigate new conflicts and realign their efforts.

Ladder: Despite these setbacks, teams can regain their high-performing status by addressing issues effectively and learning from their experiences. Strategic adjustments, renewed focus, and effective problem-solving can help them climb the ladder again, achieving improved performance and innovative results.

Snake: Another snake might be a key team member leaving unexpectedly, which can disrupt the team's dynamics and progress. This loss may force the team to revisit the Forming or Storming phases as they integrate new members and adjust to the changes. The temporary decline in performance requires careful management to rebuild cohesion and restore effectiveness.

Ladder: With strong leadership and a commitment to continuous improvement, teams can overcome these challenges and ascend the ladder once more. By addressing the root causes of performance issues and implementing effective strategies, they can return to a high-performing state and sustain their success.

Snake: Additionally, prolonged inconsistency in performance or external pressures such as increased workload can act as a snake, pulling the team back. These factors may create friction, leading to a re-evaluation of processes and roles, and a potential fallback to the Storming or even Forming phases as the team recalibrates.

You lead your team through periods of uncertainty, tackling issues as they come up, and steering the team back to peak performance. Offering support, cultivating resilience, and applying strategies to handle setbacks help teams navigate obstacles and advance toward success. A team that consistently performs at a high level over years is considered a sustainable high-performing team. Sustaining high performance is an ongoing challenge that requires vigilance, adaptability, and strong leadership. Are you prepared to guide your team through the inevitable ups and downs to ensure long-term success?

CHAPTER 17

Building a Strong Engineering Culture

"Come and join us. We have the best engineering culture," claims an organization posting a job ad for a senior engineer position. You might ask, is there a standard definition of what makes an engineering culture strong? Not really. Definitely not the ping-pong tables and fruit baskets—there's more to it than that. It's more about what your engineering team believes in and being able to identify themselves in how they work, learn, and collaborate. It influences how decisions are made, how challenges are approached, and how innovation is embraced.

Engineering culture isn't rocket science; it's about consistent practices, especially during tough times—when scope and priorities are uncertain, when failures occur, or even during periods of rapid growth. As an engineering manager, your ability to cultivate and sustain a positive engineering culture will be tested in these moments.

Building a thriving engineering culture takes time and deliberate effort; there are no shortcuts. Companies like Google, Netflix, and Amazon that primarily built their engineering culture on innovation and customer centricity, spent years evolving and adopting the right mindset within their engineering teams. If they had feared failure or ignored customer behavior and feedback, they wouldn't have developed such groundbreaking engineering solutions for the world.

However, mimicking other organizations' cultures won't work. Focus on understanding what drives your engineers and what motivates them to contribute to your team. Equally important is aligning with your organization's goals and embracing core values that promote exceptional engineering, such as solving complex problems, encouraging continuous learning and experimentation, accepting failures as part of growth, and pursuing excellence.

© Ananth Ramachandran 2024
A. Ramachandran, *The Complete Engineering Manager*, https://doi.org/10.1007/979-8-8688-0267-6_17

The Five Fingers

Like the core components of any well-functioning engineering team, these five key traits form the bedrock of a strong engineering culture—what I call the Five Fingers (Figure 17-1).

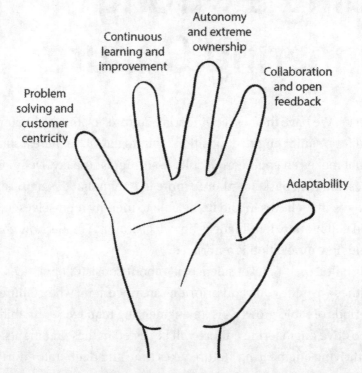

Figure 17-1. *Five Fingers—traits of a strong engineering culture*

The fingers are as follows:

- *Problem-Solving and Customer Centricity*: Solve challenging and complex problems, and deliver value that meets customer needs through innovative, data-driven engineering solutions.

- *Continuous Learning and Improvement*: Embrace learning from failures, foster a no-blame culture, have effective and actionable retrospectives, prioritize knowledge sharing, and cultivate a spirit of experimentation.

- *Autonomy and Extreme Ownership*: Build autonomous teams; take extreme ownership on domain scope, system, and environment; and hold yourself accountable for outcomes.

- *Collaboration and Open feedback*: Promote effective collaboration and teamwork, and maintain openness to share and receive feedback.

- *Adaptability*: Ensure the team is adaptable to changing scopes and priorities, thriving amid uncertainty.

While these principles are straightforward, putting them into practice requires thoughtful leadership and continuous effort. As we explore each one, think about how they relate to your team's current practices and where you might find opportunities to enhance your culture. These principles are not isolated ideas but interconnected elements that, when brought together, build a thriving and cohesive team environment.

Problem-Solving and Customer Centricity

Solving complex and challenging problems is at the heart of what engineers do. Whether it's optimizing a simple algorithm, architecting a large-scale system, or developing a feature that directly addresses a customer's pain point, engineers thrive on the challenge of finding efficient and innovative solutions. But what if your engineers are spending their time and energy on a problem that isn't actually a problem? It's your job to identify and focus on the most important issues that need solving to ensure that the engineering efforts are truly impactful.

You know you have built the right team culture when your team of engineers advocate for user-centricity and prioritize solving real problems for your users, rather than getting sidetracked by shiny new technologies that don't add value. Cultivating this culture means developing engineers who are not only technically skilled but also deeply understand and care about the product and user experience. These product-minded engineers consistently ask questions like "How will this feature enhance the user's experience?" or "Is this the most pressing problem we need to solve?" By embedding this mindset into your team, you ensure that their efforts are aligned with delivering genuine value to your users.

Creating a culture where engineers focus on user-centric problem solving involves a few key strategies.

- Encourage regular interaction with users and stakeholders to gather direct feedback and understand their needs and challenges. This can be achieved through user testing sessions, surveys, and active participation in customer support channels.

- Promote a data-driven approach where decisions are based on user behavior analytics and feedback. By prioritizing problems that have the most significant impact on the user experience, engineers can ensure their efforts are aligned with real needs.

- Recognize and reward engineers who demonstrate a strong commitment to user-centric solutions, reinforcing the importance of this approach within the team. When engineers are motivated by a clear understanding of user needs and the satisfaction of solving meaningful problems, they are more likely to deliver innovative and impactful solutions.

Are you a platform team?

If you are part of a platform team, customer-centricity means embedding a culture that prioritizes the needs of your internal customers—other engineering teams who depend on the platform to build and deploy applications. This requires a deep understanding of their workflows and pain points, achieved through regular communication and feedback sessions. In a customer-centric culture, your team proactively seeks ways to enhance usability, reliability, and performance.

You also prioritize support and documentation, providing comprehensive resources that help internal customers quickly resolve issues and understand the platform's functionalities. This culture emphasizes responsiveness and adaptability, with engineers committed to iterating on their solutions based on feedback. By valuing the input of your internal customers, you foster a collaborative environment where continuous improvement is a shared goal, leading to a robust, user-friendly platform that empowers other teams to succeed.

Continuous Learning and Improvement

Continuous learning and improvement is a cornerstone of a resilient and innovative engineering culture. It's about creating an environment where teams are encouraged to reflect, learn, and grow from their experiences. This principle is embedded in practices such as regular retrospectives, blameless postmortems, and consistent knowledge sharing.

Consider a team that just completed a development sprint. During their retrospective, they might uncover that their deployment process introduced unexpected delays due to manual interventions. This realization prompts a collective decision to automate parts of the deployment pipeline. By focusing on automating repetitive tasks, the team not only reduces deployment time but also minimizes the risk of human error, thus enhancing overall efficiency.

Blameless postmortems are equally important. Imagine a scenario where a critical bug causes a system outage. Instead of focusing on assigning blame, the team conducts a blameless post mortem to understand the failure's root causes. They might find that the issue stemmed from inadequate automated monitoring. In response, they enhance their monitoring systems to detect and address potential issues more proactively, ensuring that similar problems are less likely to recur.

Knowledge sharing strengthens this culture by spreading valuable insights and context. For instance, a team member who attends a workshop might lead a session to share key takeaways, fostering continuous, collaborative learning. Additionally, senior engineers can explain the reasoning behind design choices and system architecture, helping less experienced team members understand both how and why things work, leading to better-informed decisions and more effective contributions.

Autonomy and Extreme Ownership

Autonomy and Extreme Ownership empower engineers and fosters a proactive, accountable work environment. These principles are reflected in how engineers take charge of their tasks and address challenges.

Consider a team tasked with optimizing a critical part of an application. They are given the **autonomy** to determine the best approach to enhance performance. Instead of opting for the latest technology or over-engineering, they choose practical solutions such as refining existing algorithms and improving caching mechanisms. This approach highlights their autonomy in applying their expertise to address core issues effectively.

Extreme ownership involves engineers fully embracing responsibility for their work. For instance, if an engineer identifies a recurring issue in their code, they don't just fix it temporarily. Instead, they take initiative by refactoring the codebase, updating documentation, and implementing preventive measures to avoid similar problems in the future. This proactive stance demonstrates their commitment to improving the system's overall quality and reliability.

Monitoring and automated alerting are integral to an engineer's responsibilities. Engineers who truly embody extreme ownership go beyond traditional task management by proactively incorporating monitoring into their development practices. They understand that maintaining system reliability requires continuous oversight and immediate responsiveness.

For instance, an engineer might set up comprehensive monitoring systems as part of their development work, ensuring that the system's performance is constantly tracked and potential issues are detected early. They are not just passively waiting for problems to arise but actively ensuring that their systems are equipped with robust alerting mechanisms. When an alert is triggered, they take full responsibility for swiftly addressing the issue, investigating the root cause, and implementing improvements to prevent recurrence.

This commitment to monitoring reflects an engineer's sense of ownership over the entire system's health. By integrating these practices into their regular workflow, engineers ensure they are not only reacting to problems but also proactively safeguarding against them. This approach highlights their dedication to maintaining high system standards and their readiness to tackle challenges as they arise.

Collaboration and Open Feedback

Collaboration and Open Feedback are essential for building a high-performing, cohesive engineering team. These elements ensure that team members work effectively together and continuously refine their practices through constructive criticism.

Effective collaboration goes beyond merely working together; it's about achieving shared objectives through collective effort. For example, if a team of front-end and back-end engineers works on integrating a new feature, their close collaboration ensures that the feature is both technically robust and aligned with user experience requirements. By working in tandem, they leverage their combined expertise to deliver a seamless and effective solution.

Open feedback is a cornerstone of this culture. During code reviews, team members provide and receive constructive feedback on each other's work. One engineer might suggest performance optimizations, while another highlights potential security vulnerabilities. This feedback helps improve the quality of the code and fosters an environment where continuous enhancement is prioritized. For example, if a 360-degree review identifies communication issues within the team, they might introduce regular check-ins or new communication tools to address these concerns. This proactive approach to feedback helps build a more collaborative and effective team environment, enhancing overall performance.

Adaptability

Engineering teams need to adapt to thrive in a dynamic environment. It involves the ability to adjust to changing priorities, shifting scopes, and new technologies with flexibility and resilience.

Imagine a development team initially focused on building a new feature. Midway through the project, the company's strategic priorities shift to address an emerging market need. This requires the team to pivot their efforts quickly, reassessing their objectives, updating their project plans, and realigning their workflows to meet the new goals.

When a team faces a change in project scope or strategic focus, they swiftly adapt by acquiring the necessary skills or technologies to meet the new requirements. For example, if the team needs to integrate a new framework or tool that was not part of their original plan, they quickly get up to speed through collective research, training sessions, and collaboration with experts.

This ability to learn and adapt rapidly ensures that the team can efficiently tackle new challenges and continue delivering valuable results aligned with the updated goals. By embracing change and continuously growing, the team maintains productivity and effectively responds to evolving demands.

Setting High Standards

In the role of engineering manager, your primary focus is on cultivating a high-performing engineering team that excels in solving complex problems and delivering impactful solutions. You play a crucial role in embedding the 'Five Fingers' into your team's culture: problem solving and customer centricity, continuous learning and improvement, autonomy and extreme ownership, collaboration and open feedback, and adaptability. These traits are essential for ensuring that your team remains innovative, responsive, and aligned with both user needs and business goals.

A core aspect of your leadership is to set a high bar for performance. By establishing ambitious goals and maintaining rigorous standards, you challenge your team to exceed expectations and drive exceptional results. This approach not only inspires engineers to reach for excellence but also fosters a culture of continuous improvement and innovation. Encouraging your team to strive for higher levels of achievement ensures that they remain motivated and engaged, pushing the boundaries of what's possible.

You also serve as a vital link between strategic objectives and technical execution. Your role involves aligning the team's work with broader business goals, facilitating effective collaboration, and supporting autonomy while holding the team accountable. By championing high standards and fostering a culture of excellence, you guide your team through challenges, adapt to evolving requirements, and achieve sustained success. Your leadership ensures that high performance is embedded in every aspect of the team's work, driving both immediate impact and long-term growth.

Anti-patterns

You have to watch out for following common anti-patterns in your engineering culture and how you can influence them.

Culture That's Broken

A broken culture is characterized by misalignment between values and actions, lack of trust, and widespread dissatisfaction. There used to be a time where perceived culture was adopted and you could sense that in every action and behavior of your team. In a broken culture, your engineers may feel undervalued, misunderstood, and disconnected from the company's goals. Communication is often poor, leading to misunderstandings and frustration. In such a culture, productivity suffers, and innovation stalls.

In a team where the culture of customer centricity is broken, engineers may feel disconnected from the actual needs of the customers. For instance, the team might focus on adding flashy features that look good on paper but do not address the core issues faced by the users. As a result, despite the team's hard work, customer satisfaction remains low. Feedback from customers is often ignored or given little importance, leading to a product that fails to meet user expectations. The disconnect between what users need and what the team delivers creates frustration both for the customers and the engineers.

Culture That Never Exists

In some teams, there is no clear engineering culture at all. This lack of identity can lead to confusion and inconsistency in how the team operates and solves problems. Without a shared vision or common goals, your team may struggle to find direction and purpose.

For instance, in a team where monitoring as a culture never exists, there is no systematic way to track the performance or health of the applications in production. Engineers deploy code and hope for the best, without visibility into how it behaves in the real world. This often leads to situations where critical issues go unnoticed until customers report them, causing disruptions and firefighting. The lack of monitoring means there is no data to drive improvements or quickly identify and resolve issues, leading to a reactive rather than proactive approach.

Culture That's Resistant to Change

A culture resistant to change can stifle innovation and adaptation. New ideas and approaches might be met with skepticism or outright rejection, leaving the team vulnerable to stagnation.

In a team resistant to change, engineers may be comfortable with existing methodologies and technologies, showing reluctance to adopt new approaches. For instance, suppose the organization decides to transition from a traditional development process to an iterative release cycle while also migrating from on-premise servers to a cloud platform like AWS or Azure. The team might resist these changes, preferring to stick with their familiar, long-established processes and on-premise infrastructure.

This resistance could stem from a fear of the unknown, a lack of confidence in their ability to learn new skills, or a belief that the current system is sufficient. As a result, the team struggles to keep up with industry standards, leading to slower development cycles, reduced efficiency, and missed opportunities for innovation and scalability.

Culture of Blame

A culture of blame is characterized by a focus on assigning fault when things go wrong, emphasizing who is responsible for mistakes rather than exploring the underlying issues. This environment often creates a toxic atmosphere where individuals are more concerned with avoiding personal culpability than addressing the root causes of problems.

In such a culture, team members may become hesitant to take risks or propose innovative ideas due to the fear of being blamed. This reluctance can stifle creativity and limit progress. Additionally, a blame-oriented culture erodes trust among team members, reducing collaboration and open communication. Instead of working together to solve problems, individuals may become guarded and less willing to support one another, impacting team morale and cohesion.

Furthermore, focusing on blame often prevents meaningful improvements. By concentrating on individual faults rather than systemic issues, the team may fail to address recurring problems effectively, perpetuating a cycle of mistakes and inefficiencies.

Overall, a culture of blame fosters an environment where fear and defensiveness overshadow constructive problem-solving and teamwork.

Culture of Fear

A culture of fear is one where engineers are afraid to voice their opinions, take risks, or make mistakes. This can lead to stagnation, as individuals are more focused on protecting themselves than on contributing to the organization's success.

For example, if the team lacks a proper testing environment and strategy, engineers might fear the repercussions of pushing code changes that could break the application. This fear can lead to excessive caution, delaying delivery cycles as engineers spend extra time double-checking and avoiding potential risks. The lack of a robust testing strategy exacerbates the issue, as there is no confidence that the application will behave as expected in production.

Penalizing your engineers for failing creates a toxic culture and significantly decreases motivation. Instead, you should hold them accountable and ensure they learn from their failures, fostering a culture of growth and continuous improvement.

What Can You Do?

As an engineering manager, addressing common cultural anti-patterns requires a proactive and strategic approach. To cultivate a strong engineering culture, you should do the following:

- *Foster Open Communication*: Establish clear and open channels for communication across your team. Regularly engage with your team to understand their perspectives, concerns, and feedback. Encourage honest discussions and provide a platform for voicing ideas and issues without fear of retribution.

- *Model and Reinforce Values*: Lead by example. Demonstrate the values and behaviors you expect from your team. Your actions should consistently reflect the culture you aim to build, whether it's fostering a no-blame environment, promoting adaptability, or ensuring alignment with company goals.

- *Align Actions with Culture*: Ensure that the company's values are not just stated but actively reflected in daily practices and decision-making processes. This alignment will help bridge any gaps between perceived and actual culture.

- *Define and Communicate Culture Clearly*: Collaborate with your team to define a clear and cohesive engineering culture. Use team meetings, workshops, and other activities to communicate and reinforce this culture. Make sure everyone understands the shared vision and goals.

- *Encourage Experimentation and Learning*: Create an environment where experimentation is encouraged and mistakes are seen as opportunities for growth. Support continuous learning by providing access to training and resources. Highlight and celebrate successful innovations and learning experiences.

- *Implement and Support Best Practices*: Develop and integrate best practices such as robust monitoring, comprehensive testing strategies, and effective feedback loops. Ensure these practices are part of your team's daily routines to maintain system health, drive improvements, and manage changes effectively.

- *Build Trust and Psychological Safety*: Cultivate a culture of trust where team members feel safe to take risks and express their opinions. Recognize and reward those who demonstrate accountability and courage. Foster psychological safety by addressing issues constructively and supporting team members through challenges.

By taking these actions, you can address and mitigate common anti-patterns, creating a more positive, effective, and resilient engineering culture within your team. Knowingly or unknowingly, your teammates mimic your behavior. Remember, building a strong engineering culture starts with you!

CHAPTER 18

Becoming an Organizational Leader

As an engineering manager, your influence is further reaching than you might think, extending beyond your immediate team to the broader organization.

Your team rarely operates in isolation when striving for highly impactful results. Success often requires collaboration with sister teams, cross-functional experts, senior engineers, leadership, operations, business units, and external partners. Have you thought about how your team's performance reflects on the organization as a whole? You're part of the bigger picture.

Believe it or not, people across the organization are talking about you and your team. Actions, decisions, and the performance of your group are constantly observed and discussed, not just by your immediate superiors but also by other departments and leadership teams. The work you do and the culture you cultivate contribute to the organization's overall reputation and success. You need to recognize that you and your team are integral parts of a larger ecosystem. This interconnectedness means that your efforts, achievements, and even setbacks have a ripple effect that extends beyond your immediate sphere of influence.

As an engineering manager, you've honed your ability to lead technical teams and deliver impactful projects. But how do you take the next step? How do you transition from being a manager focused on day-to-day execution to becoming a leader with broad influence across the entire organization? The journey from engineering manager to organizational leader requires more than just technical prowess—it demands strategic thinking, cross-functional collaboration, and a commitment to personal growth.

In this chapter, we'll explore the key strategies that will help you elevate your role, increase your influence, and position yourself as a leader who shapes the future of your organization. Whether you aspire to lead multiple teams, manage a larger domain, or even become a manager of managers, the path to greater leadership is within your reach.

© Ananth Ramachandran 2024
A. Ramachandran, *The Complete Engineering Manager*, https://doi.org/10.1007/979-8-8688-0267-6_18

Expanding Beyond Technical Expertise

Let's start with the foundation: understanding the business. Imagine you're in a meeting with your company's leadership team. The CFO is discussing the company's financial health, the CMO is talking about the latest marketing campaign, and the head of sales is outlining the challenges in the pipeline. Everyone is looking at you for your input.

John, one of the senior leaders, turns to you and asks, "How is your team's work impacting our bottom line?"

You pause. You know your team is doing great work, but how does that translate into business outcomes? This is the moment you realize that understanding the business isn't just a nice-to-have—it's essential.

To avoid being caught off guard in such moments, take time to learn about how your engineering efforts tie into the company's revenue, customer satisfaction, and long-term goals. Understanding the business allows you to align your team's objectives with the company's strategy, increasing your value and influence.

But don't stop there. Go further by developing cross-functional knowledge. Get to know how other departments like marketing, sales, and finance operate. What challenges do they face? How do they measure success? When you understand the entire ecosystem of the business, you can make more informed decisions and become a more effective advocate for your team. Moreover, this knowledge will help you when you're ready to manage multiple teams or a larger domain.

Stepping into Strategic Thinking

Moving from a tactical to a strategic role is a key part of your evolution as a leader. It's easy to get caught up in the daily grind—making sure projects are on track, solving technical problems, and managing your team's workload. But organizational leaders think in terms of years, not just sprints.

A Conversation on Strategic Thinking: Let's revisit that scenario with John, one of the senior leaders in your organization. Imagine a year later, you're in the same room, but this time, things are different.

John says, "We need to understand how the engineering team can support our goal of increasing market share by 15% next year. What's your plan?"

This time, you come prepared with a strategic vision for your team that aligns with the company's growth objectives. You present your plans for developing a new platform designed to accelerate the time-to-market for new features, enhancing the company's competitive advantage. You also outline your approach to integrating advanced technologies to foster innovation and boost efficiency.

John nods, impressed. "That's exactly the kind of thinking we need," he says.

The following week, you find yourself in a one-on-one conversation with John over lunch.

"John, I've been thinking more about the strategic direction we discussed," you begin, taking a sip of your coffee. "I want to ensure that my team's work doesn't just meet our immediate goals, but that we're setting ourselves up to support the company's long-term vision."

John leans forward, clearly interested. "That's exactly what we need from you. But tell me, how do you plan to balance this with the day-to-day demands? We're still dealing with tight deadlines and operational pressures."

You nod, acknowledging the challenge. "It's about prioritization and delegation. I'm working on empowering my leads to take ownership of the daily operations, giving me more bandwidth to focus on the strategic side. For example, I'm shifting my focus to identifying key innovations that can give us a competitive edge in the market."

John smiles, clearly pleased. "That's the kind of leadership we need as we scale. Keep pushing forward, and don't hesitate to involve me if you need support in making those changes."

This exchange is a pivotal moment in your journey. By engaging in continuous dialogue with senior leaders, you're not only aligning your team's work with the company's broader objectives, but you're also demonstrating your ability to think and act strategically.

Start by setting a long-term vision for your team. Where do you want the team to be in three to five years? How will you get there? Crafting a vision that aligns with the company's goals will help you guide your team through change and growth, rather than just reacting to whatever comes next.

Innovation is another core aspect of strategic thinking. Don't wait for directives from above—proactively seek opportunities to innovate within your team and the broader organization. Whether it's adopting new technologies, optimizing processes, or pioneering new products, leaders who drive change and innovation are seen as forward-thinkers. This not only increases your influence but also positions you as a leader who is shaping the future of the company.

Taking Part in Organizational Restructuring and Transformation

One of the most powerful ways to expand your influence is by taking an active role in organizational restructuring and transformation initiatives. These are moments of significant change within a company, and they offer a unique opportunity for leaders to step up and make a difference.

Consider your company going through a major restructuring. Departments were being reshuffled, roles redefined, and there was a sense of uncertainty in the air. Instead of stepping back, you saw an opportunity.

You approached the CTO and said, "I'd like to lead the initiative to integrate our engineering teams with the product teams. I believe this will streamline our development process and ensure we're more aligned with customer needs."

The CTO was initially reluctant, considering the significant responsibility and the presence of more senior leaders who could assume the role. However, you presented a well-defined plan. You detailed how you would unify cross-functional teams, set up new communication channels, and introduce agile processes to enable faster iterations based on customer feedback.

Impressed by your initiative and detailed approach, the CTO agreed to let you lead the project. Over the next few months, you worked tirelessly to bring your vision to life. You organized workshops, facilitated discussions between different departments, and ensured that every team was aligned with the new structure. The result was a more cohesive organization that could respond more rapidly to market changes.

Your success didn't go unnoticed. Your leadership during the transformation not only solidified your reputation within the company but also positioned you as a key player in future strategic initiatives.

Taking part in such restructuring efforts allows you to demonstrate your leadership abilities in a high-stakes environment. It's a chance to show that you not only can manage change but can drive it. By being proactive and taking ownership of these initiatives, you can significantly expand your influence within the organization.

Growing Into the Next Level

As you develop your brand and broaden your influence, you begin to prepare for advancing to the next level of leadership. This typically involves overseeing multiple teams or taking on a more extensive scope of responsibility.

Transitioning from managing a single team to overseeing multiple teams or even becoming a manager of managers requires a shift in mindset. You'll need to delegate more and trust your direct reports to handle day-to-day operations. Your focus will shift toward setting broader strategies, aligning different teams, and ensuring that all efforts are cohesive and aligned with the company's goals.

Let's take a time where you managed a successful engineering team at a growing startup. You were known for your technical expertise and hands-on leadership style. However, as the company expanded, the CEO asked you to take on a new challenge: overseeing the entire engineering department, which now includes multiple teams.

You knew that you needed to evolve. You started by delegating more responsibility to your team leads, giving them the autonomy to make decisions while you focused on the bigger picture. You spent more time in strategic meetings, understanding the company's direction and ensuring that your department's goals aligned with the overall vision.

One of the most significant changes was how you manage your time. You shifted from being in the weeds of every project to being a mentor and coach for your team leads. You also began focusing on talent development, ensuring that each team had the right mix of skills and leadership to succeed independently. This transition wasn't easy—there were moments of doubt and challenges along the way. But by embracing your new role and focusing on strategic leadership, You successfully grew into your new position, eventually becoming the Head of Engineering.

To succeed at this level, you'll need to develop new skills in areas like talent management, large-scale planning, and resource allocation. Be deliberate about seeking out opportunities that will prepare you for these challenges. For example, if there's an opportunity to take on a larger project that spans multiple teams, jump at it. These experiences will not only prepare you for the next level but also demonstrate your readiness to senior leadership.

Building Your Personal Brand

Let's talk about something that might feel a bit uncomfortable at first: building your personal brand. In today's interconnected world, personal branding is no longer optional—it's essential. As you transition into higher levels of leadership, your reputation and how others perceive you will play a significant role in your success.

Start by identifying what you want to be known for. Is it your ability to drive innovation? Your expertise in scaling teams? Your knack for mentoring future leaders? Whatever it is, make sure your actions consistently reflect these strengths.

Share your knowledge and insights both within and outside your organization.

Whether through internal presentations, company-wide emails, or even external platforms like LinkedIn, showcasing your expertise will help build your brand as a thought leader. Remember, leaders who are seen as experts in their field often have greater influence and are more likely to be sought after for high-impact projects. Develop strong relationships across different departments and levels of the organization. Be proactive in offering help and sharing your insights. The more people trust and respect you, the more influence you'll have when it comes to driving initiatives and making decisions.

Enhancing Leadership and Communication Skills

At the core of leadership lies effective communication. As you transition into a strategic role, conveying complex technical concepts to non-technical stakeholders becomes essential. Your role involves bridging the gap between engineering and the broader organization, translating technical ideas into business impacts that resonate with other leaders.

Work on honing your communication skills by practicing how you present ideas to different audiences. Whether you're talking to executives, peers, or your own team, the ability to convey your message clearly and persuasively is a must-have leadership skill. Building relationships across the organization boosts influence and enables collaboration on impactful initiatives. Spend time getting to know colleagues in other departments, understanding their challenges, and finding ways to work together on shared goals.

Consider seeking out a mentor or coach who can provide guidance as you navigate your leadership journey. Someone who has walked the path before can offer valuable insights, help you avoid common pitfalls, and provide a sounding board for your ideas and concerns.

Driving Collaboration Across Teams

Finally, let's discuss the importance of driving collaboration across teams. As you grow into an organizational leader, you'll need to ensure that different teams within your domain are working together effectively. Collaboration isn't just about getting people to work together—it's about creating an environment where diverse perspectives are valued and the best ideas can emerge.

Start by fostering a culture of open communication and trust. Encourage your teams to share their challenges and successes openly. When people feel comfortable speaking up, they're more likely to contribute valuable insights and solutions.

Leverage your cross-functional knowledge to bring together teams from different parts of the organization. Identify opportunities where collaboration can lead to better outcomes, whether it's through joint projects, shared goals, or regular inter-team meetings.

Let's take a look at Jessica, an engineering manager at a midsize tech company. Jessica noticed that the engineering and marketing teams were often working in silos, which led to misalignment in product launches. Features were being built without a clear understanding of the customer's needs, and marketing campaigns weren't always accurately reflecting the product's capabilities.

Jessica took the initiative to bridge this gap. She organized regular meetings between the engineering and marketing teams, where they could discuss upcoming projects, share customer feedback, and align on goals. She also set up a shared Slack channel for quick communication and collaboration.

Over time, the collaboration between the teams improved dramatically. The marketing team began to provide valuable insights that influenced product development, leading to features that better meet customer needs. In turn, the engineering team was able to deliver products that were easier to market and sell.

By driving this collaboration, Jessica not only improved the product development process but also increased her influence within the company. She was seen as a leader who could break down silos and get teams to work together toward a common goal.

Conclusion: Your Path to Senior Leadership

Becoming an organizational leader is a journey that requires deliberate effort and a willingness to grow beyond your current role. By expanding your business acumen, stepping into strategic thinking, taking part in transformational initiatives, growing into new responsibilities, building your personal brand, enhancing your leadership skills, and driving collaboration, you can increase your influence and position yourself as a leader who makes a lasting impact on your organization.

Remember, leadership isn't just about managing tasks and teams—it's about inspiring others, driving change, and shaping the future of the organization. As you continue on your journey, embrace the challenges and opportunities that come your way. With the right mindset and approach, you can transition from being an engineering manager to a true organizational leader, leaving a legacy that goes far beyond the code you've written or the projects you've delivered.

Index

A

Accountability, 8–10, 327, 345

Adaptability, 8, 17, 27, 153, 270, 336, 356, 359

Adrenaline rush, 40, 41

ADRs, *see* Architecture decision records (ADRs)

Anticipation, 35, 209

Anti-pattern, 238, 275, 339, 360

Architecture decision records (ADRs), 178

Authenticity, 15

B

BHAG, *see* "Big, hairy, audacious goal" (BHAG)

Big-bang launches, 260, 261

Big fat project, 267–269

Big, hairy, audacious goal (BHAG), 191

Blame-oriented culture, 362

Blockers, 311

   communication, 322

   communication blockers, 314, 315

   delegation, 322

   elimination, 319–321

   five why analysis, 316

      code reviews, 318, 319

      integration issue, 316

      knowledge silos, 317

   identify/raise, 319

   knowledge sharing, 322

   over-reliance, approvals, 321

   process blockers, 313, 314

   tasks/shift resources, 311

   team's delivery progress, 321

   technical blockers, 311–313

Build Your Own Radar (BYOR), 207, 208

Business goals, 162, 201, 211, 254, 296

Business strategy, 198, 199

BYOR, *see* Build Your Own Radar (BYOR)

C

Calibration, 93

CD, *see* Continuous delivery (CD)

Chief product officer (CPO), 194

Chief technology officer (CTO), 194

CI/CD pipelines, 239, 243, 295

Clarification, 68, 71, 73

Clear vision, 9–11, 200

Cognitive load, 244, 340

Collaboration, 9, 18, 25, 27, 92, 97, 330, 358, 371

Comfort circle, 45, 47, 48, 55

Comfort zone, 44, 45, 84

Common leadership styles, 12, 13

Communication, 195, 253

   challenges, 111

   channels, 196

   continuous, 124

   patterns, 175

   skills, 370

Conflict, 124, 125, 328

© Ananth Ramachandran 2024
A. Ramachandran, *The Complete Engineering Manager*, https://doi.org/10.1007/979-8-8688-0267-6

S

Printed in the United States
by Baker & Taylor Publisher Services